Selling Shakespeare to Hollywood

The marketing of filmed Shakespeare
adaptations from 1989 into
the new millennium

)

)

Selling Shakespeare to Hollywood

The marketing of filmed Shakespeare adaptations from 1989 into the new millennium

EMMA FRENCH

UNIVERSITY OF HERTFORDSHIRE PRESS

First published in Great Britain in 2006 by
University of Hertfordshire Press
Learning and Information Services
University of Hertfordshire
College Lane
Hatfield
Hertfordshire AL10 9AB
The right of Emma French to be identified as author of this work has been asserted by her in
accordance with the Copyright, Designs and Patents Act 1988.

© Copyright 2006 Emma French

British Library Cataloguing in Publication Data
A catalogue record for this book is available from the British Library

ISBN 1-902806-51-4

Design by Geoff Green Book Design, CB4 5RA
Cover design by John Robertshaw, AL5 2JB
Printed in Great Britain by Antony Rowe Ltd, SN14 6LH

Contents

Acknowledgements

I wish to thank Dr Michael Jardine, Dr Nicholas Rowe and Dr John Peacock for their invaluable help and guidance throughout this project. I am also very grateful to Jane Housham, Kerry Gilliland, Professor Graham Holderness, Professor Russell Jackson, Professor Trevor R. Griffiths, Dr Rowland Wymer, Dr Amanda Holton, Dr Kieron Winn, Dr Jane Kingsley-Smith, Roger, Angela and Adrian French and Jonathan Levi, for their encouragement, comments, feedback and support.

Many thanks are also due to all those film-industry professionals who gave their time and expert opinions in the course of writing this book, in particular to Sara Bird, Jamie Turner, Jeffrey Zeldman, Mick LaSalle, Christopher Dunne, Nigel Cliff, Tony Lee, Colin Kennedy, Emma Cochrane, James Delingpole, Tony Estrada, Ken Green and Sarah Keene.

Preface

Emma French's stimulating and well-researched study of Shakespeare films in the marketplace is especially valuable at a time when 'Shakespeare on Film' figures in so many school, college and university courses, is the object of seminars at international conferences, and has become established as a major element in the study of Shakespeare's plays in and through performance. It is easy to forget that every feature film of Shakespeare, if it is to command the resources for production and distribution to meet sizeable audiences, needs considerable financial support. Typically, the budgets of even the most ambitious Shakespeare films are not in the same league as the 'summer blockbuster'. Nevertheless, before the makers of these films are able to go to work, they need assurances that there will be funds so that production staff and cast will be paid, and that they will be able to meet the considerable expense of post-production (editing, preparing prints, etc.) and getting the film into the cinemas.

Bundles of investment from a variety of sources have to be put together, with all the contributors satisfied that the product will meet their financial or artistic criteria. In the heyday of the studio system, it was possible – indeed sometimes desirable – for studios to produce 'prestige' films in full knowledge that their production costs were unlikely to be fully met, but that the *kudos* earned by enlisting Max Reinhardt to co-direct *A Midsummer Night's Dream* or having Norma Shearer, Leslie Howard and John Barrymore star in a lavish *Romeo and Juliet* would be worth the expenditure. Given that the studios could call on a roster of full-time staff and had production resources standing by for a whole slate of films, with any luck much of the cost might be taken up by other box-office successes. The relative failure of these films did nothing to harm (respectively) Warner Bros. and MGM – although the exhibitors, unhappy at being obliged to do their best with the hand the studios dealt them, were not so happy. After the release of *A Midsummer Night's Dream* one trade journal, *Harrison's Reports*, commented: 'it would be wise if the producers refrained from making pictures out of the plays of Shakespeare' (19 December 1936).

After the wartime success of Laurence Olivier's *Henry V*, and his post-war triumph with *Hamlet* (1948), the actor-director who seemed the great hope for Shakespearean film-making had great difficulty financing his *Richard III*, and failed to find backers for *Macbeth*. The travails (and travels) of Orson Welles in search of backers for his projects has something of a legendary status. The prospect has been improved temporarily by the success of individual films fuelled by the glamour of stars (Burton and Taylor for Zeffirelli's *The Taming of the Shrew*, for example) or eccentrically financed (Polanski's deal with *Playboy* for his *Macbeth*). Convincing the 'money' that a Shakespeare film might be a good investment has become more and more difficult, and the upsurge in optimism occasioned by Kenneth Branagh's *Henry V* and *Much Ado about Nothing* seems to have, well, downsurged. The sources for funding are many and varied, and competition for them is fierce: deals with television companies or with such co-producers as Miramax have their dangers.

By focusing so acutely on the 'selling' of Shakespeare films, Emma French is not diverting attention from their artistic value, but drawing attention to an important component of it. The expectations brought to the films by the audience, to which publicity and promotion contribute significantly, are an important constituent of their effect. By enquiring into the work done by the films, and the way they address the public, this book makes a valuable contribution to the study of what may be a *niche* in film marketing terms, but matters a great deal in the uses we make of 'Shakespeare' and the Shakespeare plays.

Russell Jackson
Birmingham 2005

CHAPTER ONE

Introduction:
Selling Shakespeare to Hollywood

THIS BOOK SEEKS to understand what makes Shakespeare a marketable commodity for the Hollywood film industry and to explain the explosion of interest in filmed Shakespeare adaptations since 1989. It forms the first systematic application of film-marketing analysis to Hollywood filmed Shakespeare adaptations. The late 1990s saw a proliferation of publications on both filmed Shakespeare adaptations and film marketing. The latter category, unfortunately, often focuses on either the marketing and the promotion required for independent films or on the European or global markets, although there are also a number of books focusing on Hollywood film marketing.[1] This book evolved from a desire to fill that gap, and a wish to investigate what the manner in which Hollywood marketed Shakespeare, and Shakespeare was marketed to Hollywood, reveals about high/low hybridity in global consumer culture. The conclusions that I reach about the implications of selling Shakespeare to Hollywood are of significance for those interested in developments across cultural, media, marketing, business and film studies and for the film industry as a whole.

Until now, filmed Shakespeare criticism has largely centred on aesthetic critiques of filmic devices, or on comparisons between the film and the source text. Employing a new angle, I explore the reasons why contemporary filmed Shakespeare prompts cultural anxiety about high-culture adaptation. I argue that a complex hybrid of veneration and irreverence arises out of such anxiety in the marketing of Shakespeare, the balance within which becomes crucial for commercial success. The book seeks to explain an increasingly irreverent approach from the early 1990s to the present day. It tracks the commercial failure of several adaptations marketed as 'faithful', particularly Kenneth Branagh's epic four-hour *Hamlet* and Michael Hoffman's *William Shakespeare's A Midsummer Night's Dream*, and the success of those adaptations that emphasised the hybrid nature of their product, such as *Shakespeare in Love* and *William Shakespeare's Romeo + Juliet*. The two latter adaptations paved the way for an increasingly abstract and postmodern referencing of Shakespeare in marketing material in the new millennium.

There can be no doubt that film marketing provides a valid and productive new angle from which to approach the complex cultural phenomenon that is Shakespeare, enabling a situating of films in the material circumstances of their production and focusing upon the influence of commercial considerations on the type of filmed Shakespeare adaptations that are produced. The marketing of filmed Shakespeare adaptations carefully and self-consciously employed a rhetoric of veneration and irreverence in an effort to secure an effective hybrid balance between these apparently incompatible elements. The maintenance of the hybrid relation between 'high' and 'low' in the marketing of Shakespeare on film has become increasingly sophisticated. An offshoot of the heritage film genre in 1989, today Shakespeare on film has become a genre with recognised sub-genres of its own, including the teen Shakespeare film and the Branagh Shakespeare movie. This shift may be ascribed to the necessity of marketing filmed Shakespeare adaptations as both a discrete entity and, paradoxically, as a medium that transgresses genre, providing the audience with everything from romantic comedy to high tragedy, utilising both American film stars and lesser known British actors. The book concludes that the most successful filmed Shakespeare adaptations are those that effectively blur traditional binaries between high and low, art and commerce, and British heritage and Hollywood popular film in their marketing.

Hollywood films cannot be analysed in isolation from their box-office performance, and there is a gap that must be bridged between the explosion of interest in filmed Shakespeare adaptations and film marketing. For students of film marketing, the book explores a diverse range of recent films from blockbusters to arthouse movies, many of which have not been analysed in this manner before. The book is also of general relevance to any readers interested in Shakespeare's place within modern culture and to those interested in the techniques whereby Hollywood conveys its messages to the masses. It forms a timely, and novel, intervention in the global debate about US cultural imperialism and the 'special relationship' between Britain and the USA.

In this first chapter I provide an accessible theoretical framework for the reader. A chronological process is described in which, as the 1990s progressed, the availability of new marketing tools and dominant postmodernism led to Shakespeare increasingly being sold as an abstract icon, an absence to be filled rather than a fixed figure of literary and historical heritage. The veneration and irreverence master binary explored in this book was blurred in the marketing of filmed Shakespeare adaptations, forming a hybrid that mapped onto the other significant binaries of high/low, art/commerce, British/American and elite/popular. In relation to these binaries, certain theories of literature and culture have been found of particular use: postmodernism, neo-Gramscian hegemony and theories of popular culture. First, therefore, in terms of disciplinary placing, a framework for the eclecticism of the theories being employed is provided. Second, the social, institutional and cultural processes of film marketing that are relevant to this book are investigated. Third, Shakespeare's place in Hollywood and the meaning of Hollywood marketing are explored, before this introductory chapter concludes with brief synopses of each ensuing chapter's contents. This chapter provides a much-needed theoretical model for analysing filmed Shakespeare adaptations in the context of their market.

Theoretical framework: hegemony, postmodernism and theories of popular culture

This book fuses the Gramscian School's focus on the material conditions of cultural production with the heterogeneity of postmodernism. The heterogeneity of the term demands a specific focus in this book on the connotations of postmodernism for filmed Shakespeare adaptations. Fredric Jameson's problematisation of 'postmodernism' indicates that 'the concept is not merely contested, it is also internally conflicted and contradictory', although he goes on to emphasise that 'for good or ill, we cannot *not* use it'.[2] The debate surrounding the massively complex, influential and multivalent term 'postmodernism' provided me with useful guidelines for answering the question of why filmed adaptations of

Shakespeare were such a striking film-marketing phenomenon in the 1990s and early years of the new millennium. 'The 1990s' is a term that I adopt in this book as shorthand for a distinctive generation of films rather than as a strict chronological specific. Thus, for example, I also analyse the 1989 Kenneth Branagh film *Henry V* and a number of filmed Shakespeare adaptations released after 2000 in this book. Jameson suggestively argues that 'with the collapse of the high-modernist ideology of style […] the producers of culture have nowhere to turn but to the past: the imitation of dead styles, speech through all the masks and voices stored up in the imaginary museum of a now global culture'.[3] However, several arguments may be advanced to explain why Shakespeare was appropriated so successfully in box-office terms by film-makers that go beyond the familiar idea of a slavish postmodern recycling and remoulding of canonical texts and the universalising hegemony of the Hollywood film industry in global culture. Having 'nowhere to turn but the past' does not, in my view, adequately account for filmed Shakespeare adaptations of the 1990s and new millennium, some of which, including Julie Taymor's *Titus* and Al Pacino's *Looking for Richard*,[4] seem as preoccupied with the present and the future as the past.

Hollywood film, however, is arguably the quintessential postmodern art form, in large part because it is not possible to dissociate it from its consumer capitalist context of production and dissemination. One commonly criticised feature of postmodernism, its Euro- or Western-centric focus, has enhanced its usefulness in the present context. Postmodernism purports to be a global phenomenon, but in fact focuses on America as its dominant point of reference. The Hollywood film industry's cultural imperialism also rests disproportionately heavily on catering to a North American and European audience, although the significance of other markets must not be understated. The Hollywood film industry and the academic industry of postmodernism both privilege American cultural hegemony while claiming global significance. Alertness to instances of self-conscious postmodernism in the marketing of Shakespeare on film also indicates that postmodernism has contributed to Hollywood's global cultural hegemony.[5]

The variety of manifestations of the postmodern charted in this book counteracts the danger of positing an essentialist postmodern 'condition' or 'norm', a practice of which even such prominent postmodernists as Jean Baudrillard, Jean-François Lyotard and Fredric Jameson have been accused.[6] Considering the shifting relationship between text and audience provides the most relevant means of exploring the complex connections between postmodernism and hegemony. Study of marketing in effect reverses the typical approach to audience studies, as 'reading' marketing materials allows some conclusions to be drawn about the complex relationship between the institution of film and its audiences. Graeme Turner's 'orthodox' balance between text and audience, refusing to grant a 'privileged role for either category in the production of meaning',[7] is adopted in this book. Turner also usefully observes that a flexible, neo-Gramscian theory of hegemony 'has made it possible to examine popular culture without necessarily taking a position for or against its particular manifestations (that is, without being critically elitist or uncritically populist)'.[8] The useful balance posited here between 'elitist' and 'populist' positions is one that I adopt throughout this book.

It must be emphasised, however, that cinema, particularly Hollywood cinema, does not innocently represent 'the people's choice'. My analysis of film-marketing material discourages affiliation with, for example, the Frankfurt School's contention that film audiences are treated as passive by the film industry, easily persuaded to attend films once the corporate film-marketing campaign begins, and unlikely to create their own, subversive readings of the messages conveyed by film-makers and film marketers. It is perhaps also useful to make reference here to a key concept of audience reception derived from advertising, 'partipulation'. Partipulation is a term coined in the 1960s by a prominent American advertising executive, Tony Schwarz, to describe the complicity of consumers in their own manipulation by the forces of advertising, and it is pertinent to considerations of audience manipulation through film marketing. Although willing and active recipients, the understanding of this study is that film audiences have their tastes moulded to a degree by the Hollywood film-marketing industry, even if marketing is a notoriously imprecise art.

Any book exploring high/low cultural interaction must arguably look to Antonio Gramsci. According to Stuart Hall's useful reinterpretation, a Gramscian reading permits replacement of the essentialist notion of a single all-pervasive ideology with a changeable, malleable and provisional hegemonic order. The articulation of power and domination is relevant to the specific cultural struggle and phenomenon of the film marketing of Hollywood Shakespeare adaptations. Although neo-Gramscian hegemony theory came under attack for its limitations in the 1980s (in terms of its alleged determinism), I found it provided the most broadly enabling framework for exploring the relationship between film marketers and film audiences. Hegemony theory is also particularly relevant to the American culture industry with Hollywood at its centre, as Stuart Hall indicates when considering the United States as 'the centre of global cultural production and circulation', which in his view represents 'both a displacement and a hegemonic shift in the *definition* of culture – a movement from high culture to American mainstream popular culture and its mass-cultural, image-mediated, technological forms'.[9] Shakespeare's presence in the Hollywood film industry demonstrably renders Hall's distinction between 'high culture' and 'American mainstream culture' unstable. This book contends that a process of assimilation into rather than effacement of high culture in American mainstream popular culture is taking place in the marketing of filmed Shakespeare adaptations. Emphasis upon Gramscian hegemony's attack upon universalist ideology also provides a point of concord with postmodernism, as both Gramscian hegemony and postmodernism reject totalising narratives in favour of local and contextual specificity. The useful fusion of hegemony and postmodernist theory that I adopt provides a flexible approach to the key issues for the film-marketing industry, such as the degree to which audiences are passive or resistant, how audience resistance can be broken down, and how market segmentation can maximise profit.

Gramsci's relevance to this book is primarily grounded in his fusion of the high and low cultural divide, a fusion replicated in the marketing of filmed Shakespeare adaptations to a mass audience. Although Gramsci makes little mention of cinema, then a new medium, in his writings, in 1916 he did make a prescient comparison between the function and commercial significance of theatre and cinema:

> It [theatre] has become quite simply a business, a shop dealing in cheap junk. It is only by accident that they put on productions that have an eternal universal value. The cinema, which can fulfil this function more easily and more cheaply, is more successful than the theatre and is tending to replace it.[10]

Gramsci's concern at the perceived debasement of theatre must be placed in the context of a widespread early twentieth-century anxiety about the impact of mass culture. This anxiety remains a dominant prejudice in journalistic and academic writing about film adaptations of Shakespeare. Its most prevalent manifestation is in the reactionary concept of 'dumbing down', often deployed in relation to the use of Shakespeare the National Poet in popular-culture contexts.

A neo-Gramscian reading of (popular) culture allows for an active rather than a passive audience, unlike the Frankfurt School and other Marxist theorists, who would, in Swingewood's words, 'refuse any necessary link between the popular and the cultural, and who increasingly divest the people of their autonomy and potential for creative action by transforming them into the passive dupes of a dominant ideology and social system'.[11] A Gramscian reading is relevant to film marketing because the audience for a film can never be assured by means of marketing, nor can marketers control the diverse ways in which film-marketing material may be read. More recent refinements of early cultural-studies theory have also been implemented in order to record receding, although still evident, fears of cultural impoverishment in and by mass media. These refinements may also be juxtaposed, as will be seen, with the 'moral panic' that persists in film reviews and academic debate relating to the adaptation of Shakespeare's work for the cinema. The significant refinement made in this book to neo-Gramscian hegemony theory is to elide still further easy distinctions between high and popular culture, and hence to test almost to destruction any sacred and profane 'master' binary.

Arguably, the medium of film requires a novel set of interpretative criteria and, as Jameson indicates, 'most traditional and modern aesthetic concepts – largely, but not exclusively, designed for literary texts – do not require this simultaneous attention to the multiple dimensions of the material, the social, and the aesthetic'.[12] In other words, the cultural form, meaning and practice of film in particular, as arguably the most commodified of artistic modes, must be denoted in socio-economic as well as aesthetic terms, and studied in terms of both production and consumption. Analysing Hollywood film marketing provides a means of situating the specific cultural phenomenon of 'Shakespeare' in a broader socio-historical context. Straightforward value-laden distinctions between high and low culture are challenged by my study of film marketing. Popular rather than high culture has traditionally been associated with commodification. However, my analysis of the marketing of filmed Shakespeare adaptations indicates that there is also a place for hybrid high and popular culture versions of Shakespeare to be incorporated into global capitalist culture.

One of the key elements of my argument is that the marketing of Shakespeare on film provides a site where the boundaries in the alternate depiction of Shakespeare as high and as popular culture are deliberately liminal and constantly shifting. The collaborative volume *Pulping Fictions* demonstrates why the ideological divide between high and low culture is still a significant one for the marketers of filmed Shakespeare adaptations:

> Despite the fact that the high/lowbrow divide is constantly collapsed in postmodern theory and in contemporary popular cultural practice, there is still a tendency – in both literary and media studies – to privilege the literary or the art-house movie over that which is consumed at a mass level. This cultural elitism is nowhere more apparent than in the adaptation of classic literature into commercial film, where the finished product tends to be judged against the impossible – its closeness to what the writer and/or reader "had in mind".[13]

Fidelity to what Shakespeare 'had in mind' will be treated with as much scepticism in this book as the idea of absolute 'consumer sovereignty', in the sense of the consumer always knowing and getting what s/he wants. This latter concept is, however, a key one for those working in the film-marketing industry, even if it is a necessary belief rather than an accurate view of how much marketing can affect the box office. Skilful marketing of Shakespeare on film has the distinctive goal of reassuring audiences that the market for Shakespeare is ready-made, and that film-makers simply need to convey Shakespeare in new, exciting and comprehensible formats.

Cultural materialism also provides a framework within which the implications of Hollywood's appropriation of a high-culture icon may be analysed, particularly the forms of cultural materialism endorsed by Graham Holderness, Jonathan Dollimore, Alan Sinfield or John Drakakis. In Dollimore and Sinfield's words, '"materialism" is opposed to "idealism": it insists that culture does not (cannot) transcend the material forces and relations of production'. Thus, 'culture is not simply a reflection of the economic and political system, but nor can it be independent of it'.[14] I will scrutinise what Alan Sinfield describes as part of 'the cultural materialist task': 'to assess the modes of cultural construction that (re)produce the patterns of authority and deference in our societies (including the prestigious discourses of high culture) [and] to theorise the scope for dissidence'.[15] Film marketing, by the very nature of its production, resists the dissociation of culture from the realm of the material.

Selling Shakespeare to Hollywood: the tools of the trade

A systematic attempt has been made throughout this book to provide a spectrum of marketing material, selecting elements that seemed particularly worthy of remark in each campaign, rather than, for example, attempting to record every trailer or every press pack for every filmed Shakespeare adaptation that I subject to analysis. After all, the canon of filmed Shakespeare adaptations is itself vigorously contested. Though the methodological problems of obtaining commercially sensitive marketing material are significant, my emphasis is in any case upon material in the public domain, since that is by definition 'marketing' (although, what marketers seek to conceal from the public domain may, of course, be of interest). Other evidence, such as film reviews and interviews with film-industry professionals, is used to substantiate primary material. Film reviews form a telling source of film-industry insights. Colin Kennedy, editor of *Empire* film magazine, indicates that the replication of the marketing priorities of studios in the glossy film magazines such as *Premiere* and *Empire* is not accidental but signifies: 'increasing pressure for our independent editorial to be pulled into an orchestrated marketing campaign and it is the duty of magazines like *Empire* to resist that pull'.[16]

Obtaining first-hand, reliable information on a Hollywood studio's marketing strategy and intentions, or production and advertising budgets, is difficult, but analysis of primary data yields helpful pointers to the strategic objectives. New 1990s technology, for example film web sites and DVD special features, also provides essential sources of primary marketing material. As identifying authorial or directorial intentions in relation to marketing is a difficult enterprise, the inclusion of such devices as Director Commentary on DVD editions of films, and such texts as Michael Almereyda and Kenneth Branagh's introductions to their screenplays, are useful tools. However, they must be viewed as evaluative rather than definitive; valuable exegetical tools, but tools with an agenda. Much important information is contained in published directorial commentary on film-making, but this information is a form of marketing in itself, and cannot be read as impartial. Primary marketing includes film trailers, posters, soundtracks and distributor-created web sites. However, in addition to these extrinsic marketing elements, the product, the film itself, is also part of the marketing of the film, a form of intrinsic or 'auto-marketing'. Film sequels form the most evident example of such auto-marketing, and arguably all Shakespeare films take the form of a sequel, drawing upon an already established brand name, one reason why Shakespeare is an attractive proposition for marketers. My analysis of such a wide variety of film-marketing material provides a significant intervention in the high/low, post-auratic debate.

Louise Levison, a film-marketing expert, has helpfully listed the following distributor's criteria when choosing a film project: uniqueness of storyline, genre, ability of the cast members to attract audiences or buyers on their names alone, past successes of the producers or director, name tie-in from another medium such as a best-selling novel, special audience segment for the type, or genre of film and attached money. Levison concludes that 'being able to sell a film involves a mix of elements, although the story is always the first concern'.[17] These priorities, closely allied with those of the film's target audience, are the cornerstones of what film marketing is taken to be in this book. Levison also observes that:

> The distributor makes decisions regarding the representation of the film in terms of genre, the placement of advertisements in various media, the sales approach for exhibitors and foreign buyers, and the "hype" (word of mouth, promotional events, alliances with special interest groups, and so on) all of which are critical to a film's success. Because marketing is part of the distribution company's area of expertise, it usually is unwilling to give the filmmaker a say in the sales strategy, the poster design, or how the film is portrayed.[18]

Levison usefully emphasises that directors such as Kenneth Branagh and Baz Luhrmann were potentially involved with, but not in charge of, the marketing process. The collective nature of the marketing of their films allows broader conclusions to be drawn about Hollywood's maintenance of cultural hegemony than analysis of only directorial stated intention permits. The distributor is a large collective driven primarily by the need to market its product to as broad an audience as possible, although the intensification of market segmentation must be acknowledged. However, the distributors' commercial drive need not imply a lack of allegiance to concepts of artistic integrity and directorial vision, if those concepts are not antipathetic to profitability.

Film-making and marketing are equally collaborative processes, and any Hollywood film is sold to an extraordinarily diverse range of consumers. Peter Holland indicates that:

> It must be marketable to studio and backers, to stars and directors, to distributors and newspaper feature writers, to chat-show hosts and film reviewers long before it is ever sold directly to the cinema-going public. Thereafter it must be sold on to the video companies, to the film-buyers for television, to the supermarkets who sell the video and the publishers who will produce the book of the film.[19]

Holland here indicates the characteristically twofold nature of the film-marketing process. The market for a film intended for theatrical release comprises those people who will purchase cinema tickets. Marketing also, however, involves selling the concept of the film initially to those who can actually get the film made. For the former marketing target, the cinema audience, market research is conducted by those responsible for the marketing of the film (generally the distributor in the case of Hollywood studio pictures) in order to determine factors such as the age and sex of the core audience for the film. The first stage of the marketing process, in which the production company sells films to global distributors and broadcasters, is not the main focus of this book. It is focusing upon the next stage, in which the distribution companies create and employ marketing strategies that reach their target audience in the most financially effective manner, that indicates how crucial the marketing strategy is, 'perhaps even more important than the film itself', in the opinion of Duncan J. Petrie.[20]

In the context of the role of the distributor, it must be acknowledged that, although analysing Shakespeare's relationship with entertainment marketing in late twentieth-century media is relatively novel, Shakespeare's status as a commercial entity is not a recent cultural development. Precedents may be traced, as they are in *Shakespeare in Love*, to the play-bills of Shakespeare's own time and to Elizabethan and

Jacobean phenomena such as 'sequels' to popular plays and the production of the *First Folio* itself, which marketed Shakespeare to the next generation as an upmarket author. In the *Epistle Dedicatory* to the 1623 *First Folio* John Heminges and Henry Condell marketed the text in a manner familiar from Hollywood marketing, directing the *First Folio*, 'from the most able to him that can but spell: […] it is now public and you will stand for your privileges, we know: to read and censure. Do so, but buy it first'.[21] A flexible model of high/low cultural hybridity is established in this book as the crucial paradigm of the marketing of filmed Shakespeare adaptation. William Shakespeare was himself a shrewd businessman, and he has always been in the marketplace. The art versus commerce debate within Hollywood filmed Shakespeare adaptations has existed since the genre's inception. Colin MacCabe usefully emphasises that 'the attempts to marry elite cultural traditions to vast popular audiences in the search for huge profits make a comparison between early twentieth-century Los Angeles and late sixteenth-century London a genuinely illuminating one'.[22] Late twentieth- and early twenty-first-century Hollywood proved equally illuminating as a comparison point with sixteenth-century conditions of cultural production.

Why Hollywood?

This book contributes to a growing recognition that Shakespeare must be secured in the marketplace in order to survive in not only popular culture but in all cultural forms, a recognition that manifested itself in the 1990s in a far broader range of contexts than Hollywood film alone. The use made by Hollywood film marketers of Shakespeare must furthermore be related to American global imperialism, and the appropriation of Shakespeare must be comprehended as part of that controversial colonising and 'civilising' process. The term 'global' or 'international' functions in the context of Hollywood celebrity and, more broadly, in both the film and cultural studies industries, as a euphemism for targeting the significant, but hardly all-inclusive, American and European audiences. The significance of the broader North American market is evident throughout the film-marketing industry.[23] For example, as Dorothy Viljoen indicates:

The rights to distribute a film in North America are known as "domestic rights"; rights outside North America are collectively "foreign rights". The extent to which a distributor will take rights in a number of different territories will be a matter for negotiation, dependent on the distributor's capacity for releasing the films in the various territories, and the amount being paid in respect of the distribution licence.[24]

North America in the 1990s was thus the focal market for the distribution of commercial films aiming for a theatrical release. The 1998 *Economic Impact Report* produced by the Motion Picture Association of America calculated that the motion picture, television and commercial production industry contributed 27.5 billion dollars to California's economy alone, further demonstrating the economic and cultural significance of Hollywood as the global centre of movie production. According to Louise Levison, 'media and entertainment revenues in the United States grew at more than twice the rate of inflation – 9.8 percent per year – between 1992 and 1998, to $488 billion'.[25] 1990s Hollywood film formed a significant part of this media growth, and extended American global cultural hegemony significantly.

'Hollywood marketing' has therefore been selected as a key term in this book for a number of reasons. Although not all of the films analysed are Hollywood studio pictures, the ethos of how they are marketed is conditioned by Hollywood. Hollywood films are backed by large marketing campaigns, which are the types of campaigns that provide the most useful information on the broad dissemination of Shakespeare. My focus is also on films which received a box-office release, in order to enable comparison of box-office takings, and these films generally have the backing of a large marketing campaign of the type in general only Hollywood can afford. Hollywood signifies a film market in which films may spend years in development and in which there is a considerable financial risk in bringing films to screen. Consequently it is the examples of using Shakespeare in which most was at stake financially from which the most instructive conclusions about the relationship between art and commerce may be drawn. The word 'Hollywood' has many useful connotations, including the centrality of North America in the global film industry, the importance of celebrity and the Oscars as marketing tools and as perhaps *the* representative site of popular-culture production.

Although there is much at stake, Hollywood often adopts a

disingenuous approach to the power of its marketing. Richard Maltby suggests, for example, that Hollywood's mystification of the lack of available material on the film audience is self-conscious:

> Hollywood's apparent ignorance of its audience, indeed, plays a prominent role in the industry's self-mythologisation, which presents multinational corporations as dream factories and helps to disguise the brute determination of the economic in the production of mass entertainment. The history of movie entertainment is consequently often itself presented as a form of entertainment, and the catalogue of surprise hits, unexpected flops and moguls' intuitions constantly reinforces the industry's self-representation that show business is really no business. Central to this perception is the persistent belief that audience tastes and preferences are inherently unpredictable.[26]

Although interrogation of this Hollywood marketing trope is valid, the discourse replicates a censorious attitude to Hollywood's preoccupation with finance that this book vigorously questions. The history of movie entertainment may be interpreted as a valid form of entertainment, evidenced by the high number of consumers of Hollywood trade magazines and the numerous television programmes and publications that claim to look 'inside Hollywood'. It is the suspicion of Hollywood's prioritising of commerce over 'pure' aesthetics that incites such critical objections to the claims made of valid cultural forms within mass entertainment. Although film is treated as a commodity in this book, the aspects of marketing which are unique to film are always acknowledged. As Duncan Petrie argues in the context of this difference, film marketing 'involves the commercial exploitation of an "expectation of a pleasurable experience" […] the culture/commerce divide in film-making is a spurious one. All markets are an inseparable aspect of cultural production and cut right across the high culture/low culture distinction'.[27] The markets are a source of invaluable information on cultural practices and on the role of Shakespeare in popular culture. It is next necessary to examine some of the connotations of the Shakespeare brand name in the context of Hollywood film marketing and the high/low hybrid model, and to assess how those connotations contribute to Shakespeare's marketability.

Shakespeare's place in contemporary Hollywood

Shakespeare functions as a multiple signifier in this book, allowing the broadest possible defining frame of reference and indicating the fact that he alone of Western culture's literary heavyweights exhibits such polysemic celebrity status. Since many different uses are made of the Shakespeare logo, understanding of what is meant by Shakespeare as a national cultural icon is signalled context by context, and that understanding is situated in broader, not purely literary or British cultural, contexts. Shakespeare's particular connotations for a teen audience are examined in the fourth chapter, and the specific characteristics of celebrity Shakespeare are analysed in my study of *Shakespeare in Love*. Critics have discussed in detail how the Shakespeare brand name is subject to constant appropriation and produces elusive, endlessly changing meanings, creating a significant methodological problem for scholars mapping Shakespeare's place in a specific area of popular culture focusing on media celebrity.[28] In the 1999 film *Bowfinger*, Eddie Murphy's character refuses to accept a script being described as 'Shakespeare' because he reads the name as a term of racial abuse: 'Spear-shaker', only thinly disguised. This is a comic expression of a crucial question to address in a marketing context: whether Shakespeare in Hollywood has a different signification than Shakespeare in other contexts, and the extent to which marketers can control meaning through Shakespeare.

The most significant research in the area of the connotations of Shakespeare's work, biography and image for Hollywood film culture is represented by the ground-breaking work of Graham Holderness, Michael Bristol and Gary Taylor. This study establishes the need for this research to be extended in the light of the marketing of filmed Shakespeare adaptations. Anxiety regarding the 'debasement' of Shakespeare through commercialisation, which governs Taylor's statements about the triviality and inconsequentiality of manifestations of Shakespeare in popular culture, is tempered in this book by my focus on marketing, which allows a different method of questioning the setting of boundaries between high and low, elite and popular. Holderness represents a particularly politicised area of cultural analysis, as he is part of a radical group that also includes Jonathan Dollimore and Alan Sinfield, reacting against the dominant formalism of New Criticism.

Although that group's reading of Shakespeare is valid in many ways, Dollimore and Sinfield can arguably be criticised for adhering too strictly to high/low and art/commerce binaries. For example, according to Alan Sinfield, the multiple meanings that the Shakespeare brand name has accrued over centuries, ensuring its survival, depend, 'usually upon an ultimate disavowal of commercial forces; manifest business interest in high-cultural enterprises tends to undermine the status that it aspires to exploit, and hence to undermine one of the convenient legitimisations of the capitalist state'.[29] However, my analysis of film marketing indicates that, although a mystification of commercial objectives is a common trope, the relationship between the commercial and high cultural is not a straightforwardly oppositional one. Analysis of the Shakespeare phenomenon in Hollywood permits the drawing of broader conclusions about Hollywood's commercial practices, the Shakespeare industry, and the debate surrounding Shakespeare's universalism, as perpetuated by figures such as Harold Bloom.

Shakespeare is marketed in Hollywood as both popular and high culture, in contradiction to the uniquely privileged elite status he has occupied in education or the Bloomian vision of Shakespeare as secular cult. As Robert Shaughnessy indicates, if Shakespeare on film is viewed as a broadly popular rather than high-culture phenomenon, a reappraisal of received academic categories and fixed binaries is required, as the Shakespeare brand 'loses its status of distinctive privilege and becomes subject to, and analysable within, the terms of popular film genres, encompassing a seemingly inexhaustible variety of instances of parody, quotation, displacement, translation and travesty'.[30] This is a crucial point in relation to the relevance of postmodernism to the phenomenon of filmed Shakespeare adaptations, particularly the idea of pastiche. However, the marketing of recent filmed Shakespeare adaptations suggests a more hybrid model than the polarised model that Shaughnessy posits, one in which postmodern appropriation does not diminish Shakespeare's 'status of distinctive privilege' even if mocking it.

Michael Bristol has usefully argued throughout his book *Big Time Shakespeare* that the hybridity of Shakespeare as high and low is the key to his popularity. He observes, for example, that 'the market potential for Shakespeare is not limited to the production of quality entertainment for upscale cultural consumers. The cultural capital accumulated in Shakespeare's works can be exploited to generate finance capital in many different ways'.[31] In theory, the use of a figure of such elevated cultural cachet as Shakespeare should have been a marketing disaster for such a high-cost popular medium as film. Why this did not emerge as a correct assumption, and why there has been a shift in Shakespeare's status from film-marketing impediment to film-marketing vehicle is examined in this book. This shift provides a specific instance of the process whereby elite or high-culture artefacts can be translated into popular culture, to the extent that the distinction between high and low becomes untenable. The influence of the Leavisite School of thought in English Studies, and that of the Frankfurt School in Cultural Studies upon the twentieth-century debate on high versus low culture, must be acknowledged as still having a resonance in contemporary discussions of cultural practice, but the study of the marketing of Shakespeare on film further undermines the elitism of the Leavisite position. Peter Holland argues much more convincingly that Shakespeare must be an attractive hedge in terms of commercial viability, vital because of the sheer scale of investment involved in producing a film:

> Repeated and contagious turning towards Shakespeare, the iconic embodiment of elitist high culture, seems founded on a marketing assumption that "Shakespeare" sells. Advertising a film is so costly that the expenditure on a film from the end of principal photography to distribution is now at least as large as the cost of filming itself. But to whom does "Shakespeare" sell its cultural cachet?[32]

The marketing of Shakespeare on film suggests that he was seen as a low-risk banker by film marketers who attempted to ensure that Shakespeare's cultural cachet could be sold to the American mass market and beyond, substantiating Holland's argument.

In a provocative essay published in 1999, Gary Taylor suggests that the popularity of Shakespeare is actually in a slow decline. Here Taylor claims that 'Shakespeareans look for evidence that would confirm the hypothesis of his ubiquitous and expanding cultural mass; they do not look for evidence that would falsify that hypothesis', and continues, in a crucial statement:

> For the corporate accountants of Hollywood, every new Shakespeare film has some of the built-in safety of any other remake, particularly if it is a remake of one of the handful of best-known plays, such as A Midsummer Night's Dream, Much Ado about Nothing, or Romeo and Juliet. Nevertheless,

most of the Shakespeare films released in the 1990s were art films with limited distribution. Trevor Nunn's *Twelfth Night*, for instance, played on only one screen in the entire Boston metropolitan area; Branagh's *Hamlet*, like his early *Henry V*, had to offer theaters willing to show it a monopoly, so that for several weeks they were guaranteed to be the only retailer in a city of more than a million people; *Looking for Richard* is still hard to find, even in video stores. Most Shakespeare films make a profit, not in theatrical release, but in video rentals and sales, particularly in the educational market.[33]

Taylor legitimately emphasises that it is not just the presence of the Shakespeare brand name that makes filmed adaptations of Shakespeare good box office. Virtually all films rely on profits from video release as well as theatrical release, not only Shakespeare films, but I am more interested in looking at why some filmed Shakespeare adaptations did make a profit in theatrical release, while some did not. Gary Taylor's observations do, however, provide a useful alternative perspective on the prevailing idea of Shakespeare's cultural longevity. Teen filmed Shakespeare adaptations and Branagh's films are very carefully marketed to tread the fine line between mass accessibility and cultural impoverishment. The emphasis in the marketing of post-1989 filmed Shakespeare adaptations is on making Shakespeare's language more readily comprehensible and entertaining, in order to guarantee the audience access to his genius. Stephen Brown contends that high art is 'particularly prone to appropriation by advertisers because of its ability [...] to imbue mass market products, and by extension, their consumers, with an indelible aura of taste, refinement and exclusivity'.[34] The Shakespeare cultural phenomenon provides these ready-made qualities for film marketers, who in return promise, in the words of a poster tag line for *Love's Labour's Lost*, to give 'a new spin on the old song and dance'.

It is necessary to identify why Shakespeare was a desirable commodity for Hollywood before examining the different manifestations of that desirability. Clarifying specific reasons for Shakespeare's heightened popularity as a source for adaptation from the early 1990s onwards is a difficult process, and it is legitimate to initially consider some straightforward general reasons. One is the recycling of texts. In marketing terms, as Louise Levison states: 'the commercial tie-in of a book with its ready-made market of readers is important to distributors. It gives them the all-important "hook" for publicizing the film'.[35]

Audiences seek familiarity in subject material as well as originality: as the film critic Mick LaSalle observed, 'ready-made stories with a ready-made audience have always been appealing'.[36] The special features describing the making of films now included on many DVDs have created an example of the phenomenon of media interdependency. Hostile critics of commercial filmed Shakespeare adaptations frequently employ the argument that they are derivative, reductive and hubris-ridden in imagining that their adaptation can measure up against such an original. The celebrated Bloomian position, that Shakespeare is not just any genius; he is the transcendent defining source of our humanity itself, retains significant power, and is on one level perpetuated by film marketers' dependence on Shakespeare's universal appeal. Speaking of the character of Hamlet, Bloom argues that 'Hamlet and Western self-consciousness have been the same for about the last two centuries of romantic sensibility'.[37] Bloom's accounts of Shakespeare's place in Western culture are characterised by their reverential stance, and he consistently rewrites 'cultural' as 'popular culture', replacing 'high culture' with 'myth'. Bloom uses the term 'popular culture' primarily in an aesthetic sense, while I wish to use it as a more neutral term for cultural products that reach a wide audience.

The appropriation of Shakespeare by popular cultural forms exhibits a complex relationship with such reverence, alternately satirising, mimicking and reinforcing it. Shakespeare's limitless openness to appropriation is a myth that must be interrogated, as Shakespeare's universalism is a cultural construct like any other and, as Daniel Fischlin and Mark Fortier argue, 'intercultural adaptations destabilize any reductive notion of Shakespeare's ability to transcend difference'.[38] Fischlin and Fortier refer to the growing influence of post-colonialism, and encourage inclusion of Hollywood film versions of Shakespeare under the umbrella of historically specific 'intercultural adaptations'. Bloom's stance may also be fruitfully contrasted with neo-Gramscian hegemony, which provides a space for irreverence, as the audience is granted the ability by the theory to make its own active reading of a text, which will not necessarily encourage a stance of veneration. Irreverence itself is a form of homage to Shakespeare, as it provides the Shakespeare marketing mill with more material and keeps the brand name 'Shakespeare' visible to the public eye.

In order to represent filmed Shakespeare adaptations as canonical, even the most irreverent adaptations, such as *Prospero's Books*, are often deployed to suggest that Shakespeare is always used in a conservative manner by Hollywood. This study challenges Deborah Cartmell's conclusion that:

> Shakespeare certainly brings in the audiences (Jarman's *Tempest* and Greenaway's *Prospero's Books* are their most commercially successful films), but in order to gain critical and academic acclaim these movies need to preserve a view of Shakespeare's conservatism that is arguably epitomized by Olivier's *Henry V.* In order to be marketed to film audiences and those responsible for teaching Shakespeare, reverence for the text and the author are prerequisites. This may provide us with the vital clue as to why Shakespeare on screen has made it into the canon.[39]

Cartmell fails to fully acknowledge that both Jarman's *Tempest* and Greenaway's *Prospero's Books* extensively and irreverently alter the Shakespeare text they adapt from. This study will indicate that, although a display of veneration was important for the education market, this did not preclude the simultaneous marketing of films such as *William Shakespeare's Romeo + Juliet* and *Shakespeare in Love* as irreverent adaptations. In the above extract, Cartmell is also trying to make both filmed Shakespeare adaptation and the study of it a more respectable pursuit, a laudable intent. However, at times she makes the contradictory point that filmed Shakespeare adaptations are 'inferior' to their source:

> A successful adaptation of Shakespeare must then convey an "anxiety of influence", an awareness that the reproduction is both dependent on and inferior to the original. Yet, while it has been argued that Shakespeare was originally chosen for screen in order to increase the cultural capital of the cinema, Shakespeare on screen from the mid-1940s onwards openly popularizes [:] unashamedly admitting itself to be a desecrator of the original. It seems that to "popularize" necessarily implies a diminishment of the source.[40]

This study seeks to refute Cartmell's equation of 'popularising' with 'desecration', although unashamed admission of 'desecration' is a significant concept that is analysed in relation to Branagh and *Shakespeare in Love.* A far less common occurrence, however, is any reference to the authorship controversy or to Shakespeare's place in a collaborative theatre company. It will be seen that film marketers instead typically affirm Shakespeare's genius and unique achievement. Study of the marketing of filmed Shakespeare adaptations in Hollywood generally indicates a surprisingly low level of engagement with two issues of pressing interest to academia and the media: authorship and collaboration. 'Shakespeare' to film marketers describes both the man and his works simultaneously, and very rarely with any interrogation. The Harold Bloom model of a solitary, god-like genius is thus a potentially misleading representation of a businessman and a collaborator. Shakespeare was branded as a postmodern phenomenon in 1990s film marketing, a product of the impact of advanced consumer capitalism, and film marketing carefully fuses Shakespeare as a popular, commercial artefact with Shakespeare as a historical and literary establishment figure.

Hollywood Shakespeare in this study is, of course, part of a broader dynamic of globalisation, but within the global Shakespeare phenomenon, connections between British and American Shakespeares are the focus of my book. Through engagement with cultural-studies texts concerning post-colonialism, the question of Anglo-American relations has been explored to discover whether or not 'The Empire Writes Back'[41] through Hollywood's adaptations of Shakespeare. Angela Carter usefully explores the phenomenon in her 1992 novel *Wise Children*:

> Think what was at stake. The entire production was at stake. His Hollywood future – that is, his chance to take North America back for England, Shakespeare and St George. That is, to make his father's old dream everybody's dream. And his chance to make an awful lot of money, too. Don't let's forget the money.[42]

This passage, which describes the cultural aspirations of a British Shakespearian actor exporting his art to Hollywood, aptly encapsulates the primary preoccupation of this book, as it blurs traditional binaries between high culture/Britain/art and low culture/America/money. As Shakespeare possesses unique cultural significance amongst writers, consequently Shakespeare may be employed to win America back for Britain. He may be employed by the elite to convey culture to the masses, and he is also a lucrative commodity. In the broadest possible sense, 'writing back' means recognising that America may be viewed in certain circumstances as a post-colonial nation in relation to Britain and Europe. Post-colonialism in the context of the relationship between Hollywood filmed Shakespeare adaptation and Britain is not, however, subversive: it is a conservative appropriation of literary iconicity represented as innovation.

Taxonomy and chapter breakdown

This book presents a cross-section of filmed Shakespeare adaptations, and no claim is made to have achieved the impossible: creating a full taxonomy of filmed Shakespeare adaptations.[43] Methodological problems surround how close a film must be to the 'original' text to qualify as a Shakespeare adaptation and whether cutting or modernising the verse forms an adaptation or a new product. Although aesthetically a film may be judged in its own terms, not as an adaptation of Shakespeare, it is necessary to decide what constitutes a Shakespeare adaptation and what does not. Simple concepts of fidelity of adaptation (as by, for example, counting the number of lines from the 'original') may be undermined in many ways, beginning with an awareness that Shakespeare's own texts were written as working theatre documents, highly open to adaptation and modification themselves. Furthermore, many of the most critically acclaimed filmed Shakespeare adaptations are very free adaptations, notably Akira Kurosawa's *Throne of Blood* and *Ran* and Grigori Kosintsev's *Hamlet*, neither of which retains Shakespeare's language but which present an interpretation of the text generally admired as valid. On the ostensibly opposite end of the scale of adaptation, Branagh's *Hamlet* claims to present a complete text in the right order yet remains an adaptation, as meaning in film is not governed solely by the text used, and that text was, furthermore, a conflation of several versions of the *Hamlet* play text. As Alan Dessen notes, 'there is a large gap between the "good" quarto of *Romeo and Juliet* and *West Side Story*, but, along that spectrum, at what point do production and interpretation turn into rewriting, even translation?'[44] Only films that position themselves as filmed Shakespeare adaptations in their primary or secondary marketing are analysed in this book, because that enables the effects of foregrounding Shakespeare to be explored. Richard Burt alludes to recent criticisms of appropriation:

> What critics implicitly tend to cordon off from legitimate academic study is a field of Shakespeare citations and replays that threatens the coherence of their critical practice. That coherence depends on a firm boundary

being in place between Shakespeare adaptations and citations that can be regarded as dialogical and hermeneutic and those that are postdialogical and posthermeneutic. Whereas the former can be assigned a meaning and hence be read as political or protopolitical, the latter do not.[45]

Marketing ultimately provides a means of creating a workable taxonomy, because the focus is upon Hollywood studio pictures and larger independent films characterised by a relatively large budget, some familiar faces in the cast and a desire to market the Shakespeare brand name to a wide audience, rather than the vast quantity of small independents, films made of staged adaptations and so on.

My second chapter, focusing on posters and trailers, is placed after this introduction because it provides a general introduction to marketing tools and methods. The chapter explores the role of posters and trailers in the marketing of filmed Shakespeare adaptations and the use of the powerful marketing tool of celebrity. Sexual content as a marketing tool is next considered. In further original research, I consider the marketing role of film soundtracks in trailers and carry out a comparative, in-depth study of the quotation of Shakespeare in poster tag lines. Whilst posters, trailers and the deployment of celebrity are often analysed in passing in filmed Shakespeare criticism, the comparative study of a wide range of these marketing tools enables meaningful conclusions to be drawn. Key issues, debates and controversies raised by marketing and the significant increase in the volume of filmed Shakespeare adaptations in the 1990s are addressed, involving placement in a broader social, historical and political context. The chapter's evaluation of why certain poster and trailer campaigns were particularly effective is intended to be helpful for students of film marketing and those in the film-marketing industry.

My third chapter analyses the marketing of Kenneth Branagh's filmed Shakespeare adaptations. Marketing provides a much-needed, and illuminating, new angle on a director who has become a favourite within academic research. Kenneth Branagh's uniquely significant contribution to the enhancement of Shakespeare's cultural currency in 1990s Hollywood necessitates a chapter dedicated to analysing the extent to and manner in which effective film-marketing techniques contributed to and defined this achievement. The chapter argues that the familiar hostile critique of Branagh as opportunistically populist is flawed, and instead moves closer to Alison Light's appraisal that 'Branagh's humanism, combined with the go-getting energy of his fund-raising, can sit comfortably with the more aggressive forms of international capital and nostalgia for something culturally impressive but socially reassuring'.[46] This chapter adopts a meta-critical position; replicating the studied hybridity of Branagh's own approach to high and popular culture. The focus in the chapter is upon reading Branagh as a businessman rather than an *auteur*. Analysis of his success in terms of his marketing skills is a topic of potential interest to any aspiring screenwriters, directors or producers of filmed Shakespeare adaptations.

The fourth chapter analyses a new genre phenomenon: Hollywood teen Shakespeare movies, in particular *William Shakespeare's Romeo + Juliet, 10 Things I Hate About You, O, Never Been Kissed* and *Get Over It*. The relationship between text and audience is considered, and the films are placed in the context of broader trends in Hollywood teen movies. The chapter argues that the teen filmed Shakespeare phenomenon is a recognisably distinct genre from 1996 onwards, the year in which Baz Luhrmann's film *William Shakespeare's Romeo + Juliet* was released, and that the marketing of these films demonstrates the growing postmodern irreverence that characterised the latter half of the decade. These films were aimed at the youth audience, and students will find this chapter of particular relevance as an exploration of how these films were sold specifically to them by Hollywood marketers.

Shakespeare in Love is the most significant single film associated with Shakespeare in the period under study, in terms of its financial performance, Oscar recognition and its impact on the Hollywood studio system and the manner in which filmed Shakespeare adaptations are marketed, and it therefore merits its own chapter. My fifth chapter tackles a range of pressing cultural concerns, including the relationship between Miramax and *Shakespeare in Love*, the Oscars as a marketing tool, marketing and merchandising tie-ins for *Shakespeare in Love* and a conclusion considering *Shakespeare in Love* and post-colonialism. Analysis of the changing politics of representation in late 1990s Hollywood film marketing, with particular reference to postmodernism, indicates that the marketing campaign for *Shakespeare in Love* exemplifies postmodern cultural transactions. This chapter will demonstrate to both film-industry professionals and film-marketing scholars how a joint British/American filmed Shakespeare project achieved such commercial and critical success.

The sixth and final chapter takes the opportunity to draw overall conclusions and to map the latest trends in how Shakespeare is sold to Hollywood. Studying Hollywood filmed Shakespeare adaptations provides an opportunity to test traditional distinctions between 'high' and 'low' cultural forms in late twentieth-century and early twenty-first-century versions of bardolatry. The binary of veneration and irreverence is codependent and symbiotic rather than crudely oppositional. The very fact of this book is an illustration of the phenomenon that it investigates, as it explores differentiation and interrelation between Shakespeare and 'Shakespeare', text and the marketing of the text, high and low and between art and commerce.

CHAPTER TWO

The use of posters and trailers to sell Shakespeare

ANALYSIS OF TWO of the most significant marketing tools, posters and trailers, indicates that a hybrid version of high and low Shakespeare is present in the marketing of filmed Shakespeare adaptations, enabling an expansion of appeal for some films beyond the arthouse to the multiplex through strategic balancing of veneration and irreverence. Richard Burt's belief that Hollywood filmed Shakespeare adaptations represent an infantilised American form of post-colonialism – 'Mel Gibson and Hollywood are the measure of an intelligent Shakespeare',[1] with its implicit suggestion that casting American stars is inauthentic – not only reminds us how difficult the use of the concept of 'authenticity' is as a term in the context of Shakespeare but also points to the danger in implying, albeit playfully, that only a British version of Shakespeare can be 'correct'.

Posters and trailers will be seen to embody the inclusive/exclusive marketing paradox, as, although it is commercially necessary to popularise Shakespeare in order to broaden his appeal, too much modernisation, mockery and parody threaten to damage the aura of the sacred, educationally uplifting quality of the text, which forms one of the most potent components of the Shakespeare brand. It will be seen that marketing texts such as posters and trailers are often deliberately unclassifiable as high or low culture precisely so that they can reach as broad an audience as possible. Although a neglected media for academic analysis, they demand attention as complex cultural artefacts with a range of unstable and variable meanings dependent on context, audience and the historical moment at which they appear. 'Hybridity' is the key to commercial success, as in the present context it refers to the judicious blending of elite and popular elements. Broad appeal marketing can rarely afford to be subtle and, despite protestations by film-makers and marketers that Shakespeare was a hard sell to 1990s Hollywood studios, the Shakespeare brand formed a sales tool powerful enough to create an entire sub-genre of film-making. Although differences between campaigns and the complication of reading posters and trailers as a coherent body of texts are fully acknowledged, significant broader conclusions can be drawn from their analysis.

This chapter demonstrates the importance of posters and trailers in the overall marketing process, and subsequently addresses the question of which corporate entities create and seek to control meaning in posters and trailers. I will examine the role of celebrities and of sexual content as marketing tools in posters and trailers, the relationship that developed in the early to mid-1990s between trailers and music soundtracks, and the significance of tag lines on posters. Analysis of film posters and trailers enables an under-researched area of cultural studies to be mapped, in order to promote a new discursive space outside the confines of the established discourses of film criticism and marketing.[2] Analysis of posters and trailers also demonstrates that the marketing of Shakespeare does have some features that contrast with the marketing of other related products. Posters and trailers communicate much about the marketers' view of the anticipated audience being targeted for filmed Shakespeare adaptations, and the material that is expected to appeal to that audience, and their analysis spans the fields of cultural history, semiotics and textual criticism.

The significance of posters and trailers

Posters and trailers matter, of that there is no doubt. Martin Dale, a film-marketing expert, states: 'the sales companies send out marketing information about their films throughout the year, but they gear their main promotional push for the key markets. The key tools are the poster and the press book'.[3] Fred Goldberg, also a film-marketing authority, claims that 'an effective trailer can play a major role in building awareness for the movie'.[4] Both posters and trailers 'position' a film for its potential audience, in terms of genre, stars, content, tone and music. In cinemas, trailers, unlike posters, have a captive audience. In a sense they represent a capitalist ideal, as they are a form of advertising which purports to be something else: the audience pays to have a product sold to them, in a similar way to product placement within films. Furthermore, posters and trailers are the first marketing tools that reach the cinemas, although they must be complemented by others that reach an audience outside the cinemas, such as television spots and newspaper advertising. Trailers also grew in importance in the 1990s as the possibility of other multimedia applications increased. For example, opportunities increased in America and the UK for them to be screened in retail and leisure venues with video walls as well as in cinemas.

Focus upon posters and trailers as specific marketing tools adds clarity to the film marketers' desire to distil the essence of filmed Shakespeare adaptations, by emphasising their most marketable elements rather than their subtleties. Posters and trailers in particular have a limited space or time frame in which to make their impact, in comparison to, for example, an in-depth review, ensuring that they must foreground their films' attractions succinctly. In support of this imperative, Judith Kahn, who is a significant figure in the history of the marketing of 1970s and 1980s Hollywood studio pictures, advised the film-maker Michael Barlin on how to conduct his film-marketing campaign at the Sundance Film Festival in the following terms:

> She said all I'd need would be a trailer, postcards to hand out and some posters. She didn't like my trailer too much – she thinks in a trailer I should "focus more on Rusty and his grand plans in life that get thwarted forcing him to go down a gangster route" – she thinks showing obstacles he encounters would be funnier too.[5]

Barlin's feedback is useful on two levels, confirming the significance of posters and trailers in all film-marketing campaigns, even his small independent film, and indicating the importance to film marketers of a clear distillation of a film's core narrative in the trailer.

Analysis of posters and trailers invites a cultural materialist approach which posits specific relationships between the adapted Shakespeare text and marketing material, enabling Shakespeare to be situated in a particular cultural and economic milieu. Paul Watson comments that 'Hollywood productions now seem to aspire to be successfully understood and enjoyed without even being seen. The promotional drama itself provides a cultural text that invariably exceeds and outlives the movie it prefigures'. In a crucial statement on the significance of film marketing, he continues, 'likewise, many of the pleasures associated with contemporary cinema lie in the gestalt image of a film in the public image of its promotion'.[6]

Watson's concept of promotion providing pleasure is pertinent to posters and trailers. If well produced, they may succeed as aesthetic objects as well as commercial hooks for their target audience, in the same manner as certain sophisticated television-advertising campaigns that can gain a cult status. Posters and trailers are thus particularly useful resources for breaking down easy binaries between art and commerce. The presentation and archiving of posters as high culture in art galleries and museums forms another instance of a blurring of the distinction between advertising and art.

Wheeler Winston Dixon's observations on the technical and aesthetic proficiency required by modern marketing media emphasise the pressing need for film marketers to convey the most striking and impressive facets of their film in the trailer:

> The E Entertainment channel regularly runs a programme entitled *Coming Attractions*, composed of nothing but the theatrical "trailers" (or "previews") from upcoming feature film releases. The host of the program blandly assures the audience that the show is devoted to "the best part of going to the movies ... the previews", a direct acknowledgement that the previews are often better edited, better produced, and certainly more interesting than the films they profess to announce. The content of contemporary mainstream films is almost incidental to the production/ distribution/exhibition process, since cinema patronage is essentially a non-refundable experience.[7]

The brevity of trailers necessitates skilful editing and high production values if they are to affect their audience, and convey the key messages film marketers wish to promote. The massive marketing campaign in 1999 for *Star Wars: Episode One – The Phantom Menace* was distinguished by the novel trend of cinema patrons attending screenings of other films solely to view the trailers for *Star Wars: Episode One*, and then leaving the cinema before the main feature was screened. It is evident from such information that the 1990s witnessed an increasing acknowledgement amongst film marketers of both the commercial and aesthetic significance of trailers, and trailers interestingly grew to become an end in themselves in terms of entertainment, a stand-alone attraction for film consumers as well as the traditionally inescapable form of advertising which precedes the feature that has drawn them to the cinema. Both posters and trailers have a 'following' amongst certain groups of consumers, from vintage-poster collectors to the *Star Wars* trailer fans.

An important point of emphasis is that Shakespeare film directors and producers do not have total control over trailers, which are produced by a production company, a fact offering a useful insight into how Shakespeare is sold to the public, detached from the artistic concerns of the film-maker. It is necessary to emphasise the collaborative nature of film marketing as it ensures that no single artistic vision dominates in a primarily commercial endeavour. Russell Jackson indicates the place of trailer creation in the film-marketing process, as during its development a film must be marketed to a chain of buyers:

> First to the major distributors, then by them to the distributors in different
> territories, who in turn must sell it to their own clients, the exhibitors. The
> promotional films used for this then give way to trailers for theatrical use,
> which are put together from available footage by editors and directors who
> have no connection with the original work.[8]

Often trailers are made in America and then used internationally. If it is a British film, then the trailer may be made in Britain, but in the case of Hollywood pictures the trailer screened in Britain is generally a version of the trailer screened in North American cinemas. Similarly, with posters, quite often it is the North American campaigns which are then adapted for other markets, as was the case for *Shakespeare in Love* and *Looking for Richard*, signifying that Hollywood marketing extends far beyond the domestic US market. Fred Goldberg emphasises that the makers of trailers, vendors or creative agencies may be subdivided by the film genres they specialise in, such as 'action trailers', 'love stories' or 'specialized (art) movies', and he makes a significant point concerning the chain of command: 'advertising executives at the distribution company generally select the vendor after a quick consultation with the producer'.[9]

In the co-production agreement for a film, as Dorothy Viljoen explains, amongst the necessary decisions to be made regarding promotion and publicity, the number and duration of trailers, and whether the same trailers will be used globally, or different ones for different regions, must be decided. If responsibility devolves regionally, on one producer or on a third-party publicist, they must be approved by all producers and meet requirements in terms of credits, logos and advertising breaks. The director and screenwriter's rights also vary regionally, indicating that although co-producers have considerable control over the content of trailers, there are numerous regional and corporate variants that act as exceptions or constraints to the input they may provide.[10] Hence, whilst the producer is involved, it is uncommon for the director to be directly involved in selecting the vendor, and film genre plays a key role in determining the vendor who will produce the trailer. It is also the distributor who decides which trailers will run at the beginning of both cinema performances of any given film and on videos and DVDs.

The most significant factors determining which trailers run before which films are the certificates of the films whose trailers are being shown (which must be graded the same as, or lower than, the main feature), and previous deals that distributors have made with other distribution companies that determine which of their films they will advertise in trailer form.[11] Problems encountered by the producers of *Natural Born Killers* when they objected to the posters produced for the film by Warners indicate a more complex chain of command in the marketing schema than simple directorial approval:

> We went to Oliver [Stone] (who had approved the horrible thing in the first place, probably in a moment during the final mix when he wasn't paying much attention) and told him we thought it was a disaster. I wrote him another memo [...] attaching posters from *Reservoir Dogs* and *The Crow*, to demonstrate the kind of imagery an audience who would like this film would respond to, and to convince him that this wouldn't happen with the kind of sanitised poster the likes of which Warners had delivered ... I showed him another poster that the Warner Brothers art department had actually come up with. (The art department seemed more sensitive to what the film was about, despite the vetoes that came down from their high bosses in marketing.)[12]

Hamsher indicates a tension between an art department concerned with aesthetics and fidelity to directorial intention, and philistine, distant marketing bureaucrats who are more commercially orientated, replicating the conflict between art and commerce so prevalent in the evidence that this book analyses. Hamsher also demonstrates a desire to match poster imagery to audience, although, of course, what different texts signify to different readers is not necessarily as intended. Two tried and tested means of marrying art and money in successful marketing, enlisting celebrity and sexual content, are analysed next, in order to examine the insights their use provides into how Hollywood sold Shakespeare.

Celebrity as a marketing tool in posters and trailers

Short teaser shots of film stars, particularly in close-up, form an important element of most film trailers, as they are a succinct means of highlighting the presence of those stars and maximising the impact their presence has upon the target audience. Andy Medhurst convincingly argues that 'bankable' authors as well as actors may be used in this manner, using John Grisham, 'the first name on screen in the trailer for *The Gingerbread Man*, in skyscraper-sized font',[13] as an example. In a similar fashion, in the early to mid-1990s Shakespeare's name features prominently in the title, poster art work and trailers for Hollywood filmed Shakespeare adaptations, but in the late 1990s and into the new millennium, Shakespeare's name is summoned less explicitly in these advertising media, and this invites comment. It is possible that referencing Shakespeare evolved into what might be termed 'postmodern homage' rather than an attempt to reverently promote a faithful adaptation of Shakespeare. Shakespeare's image was appropriated in increasingly creative and sophisticated ways in 1990s film marketing, and it is important also to note that, as filmed Shakespeare adaptation gained credibility as a distinct genre, it was as important to situate Shakespeare films in other recognisable film genres such as romantic comedy as it was to foreground the presence of Shakespeare.

The crucial role of both genre and celebrity in the marketing for *William Shakespeare's Romeo + Juliet* is borne out by differences between the theatrical and the video trailers. The full theatrical trailer for the film focuses upon a broad cast of characters, and features all of the principals, including the Friar, Captain Prince, Tybalt, Mercutio and Benvolio at least twice. The increased time span of the full trailer enables the showcasing of the less recognisable but nevertheless marketable celebrities, and also allows the trailer to demonstrate the film's fidelity to Shakespeare's play in a manner that the shorter trailer could not do without diminishing the immediacy and simplicity of its impact. The longer trailer still positions the film powerfully as a love story, but it also introduces other elements such as the gun-toting Tybalt, broadening the target audience by promoting it as an action film and a thriller, whilst maintaining a strong narrative to avoid confusing the audience.

Another reason for inferring fidelity to Shakespeare's play in the poster and trailer for *William Shakespeare's Romeo + Juliet* is shared with the marketing of *Shakespeare in Love*: postmodern, anachronistic juxtaposition of old and new is employed to create a jarring effect. This effect reassures the audience that any stereotypical expectations they might have of a traditional Shakespeare or heritage film adaptation will be subverted. In the theatrical trailer for Luhrmann's film, focus on exposition is unusually intense. The trailer's narrative is carefully crafted to make it easily comprehensible and to ensure that the Shakespearean language is not deployed at the expense of audience understanding. With teenagers as the prime target, the film marketers appear to have considered it particularly important to avoid daunting them with difficult language when selling the film, and the trailer hence emphasises action over words. The trailer tracks Romeo and Juliet from first meeting to death in chronological order and illustrates the most significant plot occurrences in between, through image, voice-over and easily comprehensible textual inserts. One exemplary scene in which Romeo announces to the Friar that 'my heart's dear love is set/ on the fair daughter of rich Capulet' features a startled, anxious reaction shot from the Friar, followed by a black screen on which two revolvers figure with the text 'ancient grudge'. Luhrmann's ironic sight jokes, which pepper the film, are carefully excluded from the trailer, in order to consolidate the film's positioning as a conventional love story.

Emphasis on accessibility is thus a priority in the theatrical trailer: with such a familiar basic plot the film marketers' concern with issuing 'spoilers' to the trailer audience is negated, and assuring the potential audience that the use of Shakespearian language will illuminate rather than obscure their understanding of the plot is paramount. This is one instance of Shakespeare film marketing differing from other forms of marketing, as reassuring the audience that they will understand the language and story of filmed Shakespeare adaptations is more important than creating suspense. In contrast, the shorter video trailer for *William Shakespeare's Romeo + Juliet* has different priorities. The two stars had both gained a much higher celebrity profile after the success of the film in cinemas, and a corollary of that success was the assumption of the distributors of the video that the film was already familiar to much of their new trailer's audience. The trailer particularly focuses upon DiCaprio, who appears alone in close-up six different times. Danes features three times in close-up, and only one other cast member, John Leguizamo, who played Tybalt, makes an appearance, for just one shot. Focus on DiCaprio and Danes performs the narrative purpose of emphasising the film's intense concentration on the central love story, but more emphatically, it makes use of the attractive young leads to sell the film to a teen audience. Video is a different medium to film, commanding a small-scale, more personal aesthetic rather than large-screen spectacle. Emphasising romance as well as spectacle is also an appropriate recognition of the different demands of video, and arguably represents a desire to reach the educational market by focusing on the set-piece love speeches between Romeo and Juliet rather than the action sequences which make such an impact in cinema trailers.[14]

Baz Luhrmann expresses anxiety about the hegemony of celebrity in his eagerness to privilege aesthetic over commercial decisions in the introduction to his film screenplay, remarking of Leonardo DiCaprio's Romeo that 'it's important to reveal these eternal characters anew for every generation and Leonardo is particularly suited for this. He does seem to symbolise his generation',[15] a symbolism generated by Luhrmann, who employs frequent close-ups of DiCaprio's face, creating his iconic status as a teen idol. Film marketers, particularly for a film seeking a teen audience, must ensure that posters and trailers are encoded for maximum accessibility, while taking into account that in certain 'lifestyle' areas their target audience is highly sophisticated and 'knowing'. Celebrity forms a strong feature of that branding and encoding in the campaign for *William Shakespeare's Romeo + Juliet*. DiCaprio has a certain set of connections and meanings that he conveys, allowing him to bring something to Shakespeare, as a teen idol, and also granting him credibility as a young actor who can 'do' Shakespeare. This suggests an effective blend of reverence and irreverence, which can be seen as a hallmark of the film in general.

In the campaign for *William Shakespeare's Romeo + Juliet*, a shot of DiCaprio in his armour is used ten times in the theatrical trailer and five times in the video trailer. This recurring image is supplemented in the video trailer by one shot of Romeo in crumpled black tie and two culminating shots of DiCaprio in a Hawaiian shirt. One of the film's posters juxtaposes the text 'William Shakespeare' in the title with a picture of Leonardo DiCaprio (Romeo) brandishing a hand gun and wearing a Hawaiian shirt. The interplay between the sacred and the profane in filmed Shakespeare adaptations is converted into a pervasive visual motif in the film's poster and trailer. The placing of Shakespeare's name has the effect of foregrounding the 'authenticity' of the production, and hence its educational marketability, as does its use of the original verse and retention of much of the storyline, whilst also ensuring the teen audience's awareness that this is a fashionable and exciting reworking. 'Shakespearian' or 'Elizabethan' words are translated into comprehensible soundbites for a teen audience. The recurring presence of Catholic imagery in the trailer, converted to kitsch in the form of neon crucifixes and rose-lined church pews, references Madonna's incorporation of Catholic imagery into the popular culture image bank, most notably in the promotional music videos for the hit records 'Like a Prayer' and 'La Isla Bonita'. Commercialised and repeated through the film's marketing, the iconic representation of the celebrity protagonists is enhanced by Catholic images as recurring visual motifs, particularly crucifixes, rosaries and the Virgin Mary.

The poster campaign for *William Shakespeare's Romeo + Juliet* indicates that the marketing team for that film were emphasising the film's fusion of 'Old World' costumes with distinctively American clothing such as Hawaiian shirts. A poster used in both American and British campaigns illustrates Romeo and Juliet in the costumes they wear to the ball where they meet: DiCaprio clad in armour, resembling a courtly knight, and Danes dressed as an angel, an ephemeral image anticipating their deaths. On the poster these two images feature at the bottom of six images of Danes and DiCaprio that form the poster image, atop an illustration of a bullet which appears to be tearing through the poster at the base. In the poster, DiCaprio figures in four of the six images, twice in the Hawaiian shirt and twice in armour. Danes appears in three of the images, at all times dressed as an angel. The poster's use of contemporary-looking blue colour for the top two images, natural light for the middle two and sepia-tint for the two pictures at the base visually presents a fusion of modern film styles with heritage film, old and new.

The campaign for Al Pacino's *Looking for Richard*, a film explicitly focused on the high/low cultural divide, displays the same postmodern jarring of old and new, and UK and US, in terms of costuming and

Poster for Baz Luhrmann's *William Shakespeare's Romeo + Juliet* (PHOTOFEST)

setting. Distributed by Fox Searchlight, the film grossed 1.27 million dollars at the US box office.[16] The tag line for the film, which includes enactment of excerpts from Shakespeare's play *Richard III* is 'A four hundred year old work-in-progress', but the American poster chooses to make visual reference to the title, with Al Pacino literally looking for something, rather than the tag line. This has the effect of emphasising the celebrity presence of Al Pacino and minimising the Elizabethan resonance, which, arguably, cuts across the thrust of the film itself, in which Pacino sets out to sell Shakespeare to America rather than himself. Managing and heightening audience expectations is one of the key purposes served by posters. In this case, the film marketers cleverly subvert any easy equation between Manhattan as a site of low cultural production and England as the home of high culture that might offend North American audiences. Manhattan is instead presented belligerently as the natural successor to Britain as a modern Anglophone cultural centre. The British poster differs from the American poster, and depicts Pacino, wearing a baseball cap, in the foreground of a Manhattan street scene, with a bus shelter directly behind him on which a poster advertising him as Richard III in a stage production can be seen. The New York scene emphasises the urban(e) American aspects of the film to a British audience, and the poster makes a postmodern parody of the conventions of both film posters and celebrity marketing. Another UK poster represents Pacino in a baseball cap and a leather jacket smiling in front of a poster advertising 'Al Pacino's Looking for Richard'. In Britain, this has the resonance of an American film star seeking to interpret a British icon.

Looking for Richard narrates Al Pacino's struggle with the obstacles of British high culture and history as a North American celebrity wishing to play Richard III. In a journey from the pseudo-medieval Cloisters of New York to the pseudo-Elizabethan Globe Theatre in London, Shakespeare is exported back to Britain by Americans: Sam Wanamaker at the Globe as well as Al Pacino. The film's posters and trailers explore the nature of American appropriations of Shakespeare and the discourse of celebrity. Pacino's casual clothing and baseball cap visually position him as both quintessentially American and as an American tourist, seeking to understand the relevance of the English icons Shakespeare and Richard III to contemporary America. The binary between American 'trash culture' and Shakespeare as both British and universal classic is also exploited by the posters and trailers for the film.

In the video trailer for *Looking for Richard*, Pacino dominates, and the other actors feature both far less frequently and less clearly, often in rapid-cut shots that obscure their identity. Pacino is visually distinguished from Richard III in the poster and throughout the trailer in a parody of the high/low binary – as Richard he wears a skull cap or full monarchical regalia including a crown, as Pacino he wears a baseball cap, sunglasses and an Armani coat; here the marketers offer a visual encapsulation of the film's main point: unlikely continuity between the cap and the crown, celebrity and king. These variations in clothing also represent a parody of the traditional garb of the English medieval monarch and the modern Hollywood star, two clichéd but powerful significations of sovereignty and celebrity respectively. Simultaneously, the genres of the heritage movie and Hollywood classic cinema and modern celebrity event movies are summoned in the costumes featured in the marketing campaign.

The posters and trailers for *Looking for Richard* extensively exploit the complex binary of the Hollywood and Stratford-upon-Avon celebrity Shakespeares, and the parallel binary of irreverence and veneration in the representation of those Shakespeares. Shakespeare's celebrity in 1990s film-marketing material was employed to enhance the cultural currency of the products that Shakespeare 'sold'. Roger Ebert's review of *Looking for Richard* hence appeals to the educational value and social *kudos* of knowledge of Shakespeare in statements such as 'the point is that the appreciation of Shakespeare is an ongoing project for any literate person', whilst praising the fact that his expectation that the film would be 'some kind of popular vulgarisation' is frustrated. Ebert raises the issue of celebrity in relation to Pacino's Prospero-like approach in the film:

> Pacino conducts the film like a magician or impresario […] He provides a running commentary, he discusses line readings, he does man-on-the-street interviews ("It sucks", says one guy, whose choice of pronoun indicates he thinks of Shakespeare as a thing, not a person). And he acknowledges that a problem with Shakespeare's history plays is that the characters, who were as familiar as pop stars to the Elizabethans, are largely unknown to modern American audiences.[17]

Pacino in the mid-1990s was a familiar celebrity to the North American audience, and therefore an exemplary vessel through which an American version of Shakespeare might be transmitted. Although Shakespeare features briefly as a character in the film, he does not appear similarly personified in the film's posters or trailers, which focus instead on the American Pacino's dialogue with Shakespeare and British high culture. Ebert's implicit reference to Prospero is also significant because *The Tempest* is the one play that may be read as Shakespeare himself interrogating the relation between Old and New World, as Jerry Brotton argues in the context of American new historicist readings of *The Tempest*:

> In claiming an exclusively American context for the play's production, American new historicist critics overinvest something of their own peculiarly postcolonial identities as American intellectuals within the one text that purports to establish a firm connection between America and the culture which these critics analyse with such intensity: early modern England.[18]

The American academy's eagerness in the 1990s to appropriate the one Shakespeare text that potentially references their nation is paralleled by the playful appropriation of Shakespeare by New York City in the poster and trailer for *Looking for Richard*. The campaign suggests the need for continuity between colonial and post-colonial, Old England and New World.

Celebrity is of equal significance in the marketing of three 1990s filmed *Hamlet* adaptations. The poster for Zeffirelli's 1990 *Hamlet* emphasises *Hamlet* as a familial drama and indicates Zeffirelli's pioneering role in the casting of Shakespearian British actors alongside American and Australian celebrity film stars, a strategy emulated by Branagh. Franco Zeffirelli's casting of Mel Gibson as Hamlet, and Branagh's distributor's use of diverse celebrities including Kate Winslet, Billy Crystal, Robin Williams, Jack Lemmon and Judi Dench in the *Hamlet* trailer, is marketed towards a broad audience demographic, comprising those familiar with the stars' work in either high or popular cultural productions, and promoting both the Shakespeare brand name and the contemporary stars. Despite the presence of many other celebrities of lesser stature, the foregrounding of Mel Gibson in the poster for Zeffirelli's *Hamlet* and of Al Pacino in the poster for *Looking for Richard* reassures the audience that the films are celebrity vehicles for those stars as much as they are 'Shakespeare movies', and hence familiar territory. Gibson and Pacino's ability to perform Shakespeare, indicating that Shakespeare can be both high art and Hollywood, is also implied. The stars are also, of course, making a statement of reverence towards Shakespeare as a high cultural text worthy of their thespian endeavours. Shakespeare endows Pacino and Gibson with high-culture status and they in turn make Shakespeare 'cool', indicating another manner in which the marketing of filmed Shakespeare adaptations is distinguished even from the marketing of other literary adaptations: it makes a definitive statement about Hollywood's ability to incorporate high art, as Shakespeare is the ultimate high art figure. One of the two poster images for Zeffirelli's *Hamlet* thus focuses exclusively on the protagonist Mel Gibson in close-up, clutching a sword. The close-up emphasises Mel Gibson's iconic action movie attributes: acting not thinking, good looks, decisiveness and masculinity, rather than Hamlet's traditional attributes: thinking not acting, inability to make up his mind, satire, tragic humour and feigned madness. Gibson's popular celebrity status complements Hamlet's high-culture credentials and characteristics to create a rich, if potentially contradictory, semiotic image.

Celebrity forms a significant component of the marketing campaign for Branagh's *Hamlet*, albeit in a different manner for the poster and the trailer. Whilst the theatrical trailer for Branagh's *Hamlet* emphasises the presence of both Branagh and an exceptionally high quantity of recognisable celebrities in lead and cameo roles, the poster focuses upon Branagh, using close-ups of him and juxtaposing him with massed, indistinguishable courtiers. Branagh's *Hamlet*, as with *Looking for Richard*, has different promotional posters for the film in North America and the UK.[19] The poster for both the advance and video release of *Hamlet* in North America is the same: a rear view of Hamlet facing the court in an interior shot of Elsinore. The poster is headed by the caption 'William Shakespeare's Hamlet, A Kenneth Branagh Film'. The UK poster image instead assembles a montage of two images separated by text: the top image a close-up of Hamlet and Gertrude and the lower image that of the advance of Fortinbras's army. The army gives the poster the added resonance of a war movie, broadening its potential generic appeal, and also situates it as an 'event' movie, with the appropriately high level of spectacle. It is tempting to infer that in the US the film was sold as a classy celebrity vehicle for both Branagh and Shakespeare, and as a Hollywood epic, whilst in the UK the dual status of *Hamlet* as both epic and domestic drama is emphasised instead.

Discrepancies between the reverential, epic tone of the posters for Branagh's *Hamlet* and the frequently postmodern qualities of the film

Poster for Kenneth Branagh's William Shakespeare's *Hamlet* (PHOTOFEST)

must next be investigated, as they provide an instance of posters and trailers arguably displaying greater conservatism and reverence than the films they are employed to market. The posters for the film situate the film as epic. A diptych image is used in the UK poster campaign to market *Hamlet*, and the decision to emphasise the battle scene in one half and, in the other half of the poster, Julie Christie with Kenneth Branagh, also draws upon the cultural resonance of epic battle films and Christie's most famous role in *Doctor Zhivago*. Insistence upon the authenticity of Branagh's interpretation of the *Hamlet* play text leads to a corresponding reverence in the poster and trailer to market the film. Although Branagh's *Hamlet* contains populist elements, such as the cameos by Billy Crystal as the Gravedigger and Robin Williams as Osric, they are excluded from the poster and trailer, which instead focus on the film's homage to two forms of high culture: the Shakespeare play texts and classic epic cinema such as *Doctor Zhivago*. Thus, it may be concluded, Branagh's *Hamlet* is eager to retain its high-culture status in both the UK and the US, in both film and marketing material.

'Yet sell your face for five pence and 'tis dear'[20]: the celebrity close-up

Branagh's employment of celebrities in cameos is one of his trademarks, established in *Much Ado about Nothing*. The fetishising of the celebrity commodity in close-ups must next be investigated. The use of the close-up is particularly salient in the poster campaigns for Almereyda's *Hamlet* and Julie Taymor's *Titus*. Distributed by Miramax in 2000 as a follow-up to the success of that distributor's 1998 film *Shakespeare in Love*, Almereyda's *Hamlet* makes significant use of the close-up in its poster and television ads. The UK poster for Almereyda's *Hamlet* is a brooding close-up head shot of the star, Ethan Hawke, which makes visual reference to the iconic Greta Garbo photograph in which she pulls her hair away from her pale, unmade-up face. The poster's visual reference to Garbo places the film semiotically in a venerable Hollywood film tradition as well as the position it already occupies as a filmed Shakespeare adaptation and as a filmed *Hamlet* adaptation. Lorne M. Buchman theorises the use of close-up in film in a manner also relevant to film marketing: 'the close-up implicitly communicates to the viewer that he or she is somehow privileged [and] can look at a world normally unseen, or seen only within the context of a more comprehensive picture'.[21] The viewer's sense of privilege functions well as a marketing tool, as it creates the desire in the viewer of the close-up shot on the poster or trailer to see it in its full context. Deployment of close-up in the poster also emphasises characteristics of *Hamlet* that film audiences might be expected to readily comprehend: introspection, heightened emotion and an intimate connection between protagonist and audience.

Isolation of an individual star's look and personality provides a means of establishing the star's unique celebrity aura. Bela Balazs, appropriately in the context of an analysis of the semiotic import of *Hamlet*, describes close-ups of actors' faces as a 'silent soliloquy',[22] emphasising their rich signifying potential in a useful contribution to the idea of their power on posters. The visual homage to Garbo employed in the *Hamlet* (2000) poster also illustrates that viewing and reading images such as posters may be understood as a learned, cumulative experience on the part of their audience. *Looking for Richard* and Almereyda's *Hamlet* both employ postmodern pastiche, self-referentiality and alienating or incoherent images in their posters and trailers in a manner that consolidates the positioning of the films towards the arthouse rather than the multiplex. Interestingly, although the Almereyda film's visuals draw upon global consumer culture in numerous scenes, particularly those in which the ghost of Old Hamlet disappears into a Coca-Cola vending machine and Hamlet's soliloquy in the Blockbuster video store, these scenes are excluded from the trailer. This may indicate unease on the part of the film-marketing team: that it would be indecorous, or possibly merely incomprehensible in such a capsule format, to draw attention too aggressively to the corporate nature of their enterprise. Instead, the trailer emphasises the Almereyda film's meta-cinematic awareness: in trailer clips of Hamlet's film of *The Mouse Trap* and the video footage he watches of his father. The poster and trailer for Michael Almereyda's *Hamlet* market the film's celebrities as prominently as the poster and trailer for Branagh's *Hamlet*. Whilst the North American poster for both films focuses solely on Shakespeare's most famous protagonist, feeding off the celebrity resonance of Hamlet and of Kenneth Branagh and Ethan Hawke simultaneously, the trailer employs other celebrities in its marketing strategy: rising filmed Shakespeare star Julia Stiles as Ophelia is particularly focused upon.

In the marketing campaign for another filmed Shakespeare adaptation released in 2000, the posters for *Titus* represent the lead Anthony

Hopkins visually in a manner that insistently recalls his role with the highest recognition factor: as the cannibal Hannibal Lecter in *The Silence of the Lambs*. One poster for *Titus* has a picture of the principals above a montage of images of ancient Rome, in which Hopkins impassively stares forwards, as Lecter does. There is also one poster for the film featuring a close-up of Jessica Lange as Tamora and one poster featuring a close-up of Anthony Hopkins as Titus, both in full armour. The sumptuous armour is offset by dirt and wounds, emphasising the film's generic diversity, as heritage film, horror film and war film. The muddied and bloody shot of Hopkins in battle regalia also recalls the strikingly similar still of Branagh used in the *Henry V* poster campaign. Hopkins and Lange are both actors, significantly, associated with both arthouse and popular film, theatre and cinema, enabling them to function as double signifiers in the posters for this film, providing celebrity signs in which the hybrid facets of their thespian backgrounds may be drawn upon. This rich semiotic mix again draws attention to the complex blend of sacred and profane in the texts under study. Titus is, indeed, Hannibal Lecter, cannibalism having a significant part to play in the text, but he is also a Shakespearian tragic hero.

Decorum of representation has always been a particularly pressing issue in relation to the performance of *Titus Andronicus*. In a display of the tension between radicalism and conservatism in late 1990s filmed Shakespeare adaptation, Desson Howe, reviewing *Titus*, argues that 'this modernization-of-Shakespeare fever (so the MTV generation can appreciate the Bard's utter dudeness) has become so banal a filmmaker could practically earn the appellation *enfant terrible* by adapting a Shakespeare play without such frills'.[23] In an interesting inversion of the customary dynamic, it is suggested, albeit ironically, that it is the trend-pursuing adaptations of Shakespeare that are conservative and that simply venerate a new tradition, that of postmodernism. Howe's use of the American colloquial term 'dudeness' also exhibits an anxiety with Hollywood's 'dumbing down' of Shakespeare.

Although Julie Taymor's modernised *Titus* did not perform well at the US box office, it is significant that a low-budget, even more radical version, only released to video outlets, made a relative profit. *Titus Andronicus*, written and directed by Christopher Dunne, is a film that elects to emphasise the violent and sexual elements of the play. The poster for the production is a cartoon illustration of a Rambo-style character

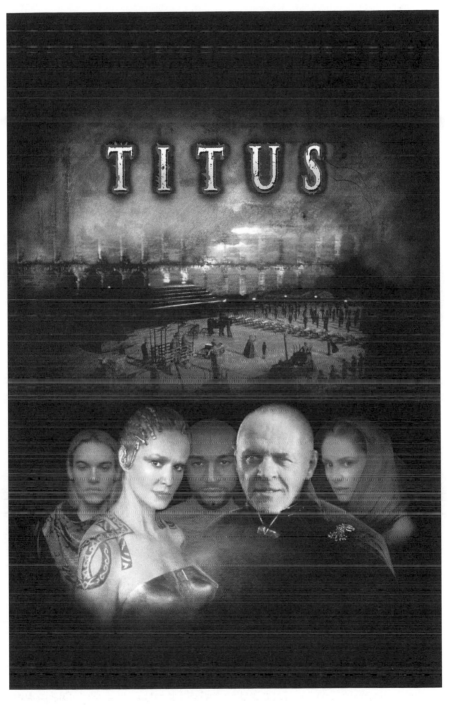

Poster for Julie Taymor's *Titus* (PHOTOFEST)

clutching a severed head in one hand and a shotgun in the other. At the base of the illustration is a decomposing corpse. The caption that heads the poster reads, 'William Shakespeare's savage epic of brutal revenge', and then, in much larger font, '*Titus Andronicus*', and at the base of the poster, a further caption reads 'The entire bloody tale! A new cult horror classic'. Dunne describes the process of making and promoting the film in the following manner:

> I had produced a commercially successful stage version of *Macbeth*, in a very lurid style, and I saw the commercial potential of adapting *Titus* to film. There has been a resurgence of interest in The Bard in this past decade, and Shakespeare was heating up when I completed my shooting script in 1992. It took until 1997 to schedule and complete the shoot [. . .] Interestingly, Julie Taymor's big budget version was a huge financial bomb, which is bad for her and ClearBlueSky, but leaves me feeling (as an outsider) a little smug since we are doing fine. The key is "don't spend too much money on a niche product" up front.[24]

The reference to Shakespeare as a 'niche' in the market is particularly interesting and raises the questions, which niche and what size? Certainly some producers of Shakespeare in the 1990s were ambitious to reach something broader than a 'niche' in the market. Christopher Dunne, within the confines of a small independent production, utilised his background and contacts network in advertising to promote the film in 1998, and employed the marketing tactics of word-of-mouth and graphic images in the posters and press pack for the film:

> Our lurid approach attracted a color photo mention in *Time* magazine of October 1998, and mentions in many lurid/exploitation media outlets in print and on the Internet here and in Europe, India and Hong Kong. I think it is very amusing that some Shakespeare scholars don't "get" what I was trying to do [...] which was what Shakespeare was trying to do [...] produce entertainment. Judging by our fan mail, I am also pleased that my film, warts and all, has stimulated interest in the reading of Shakespeare's works among people who otherwise wouldn't.[25]

In this account, Dunne arguably fails to acknowledge that 'lurid/exploitation media outlets' are not regulated to the same extent as Hollywood films prepared for theatrical release, curtailing a director such as Julie Taymor's ability to convey 'lurid' content, and indicating one relatively insuperable present boundary between arthouse and multiplex content. The concern of distributors is to reach a broad-based public, read by the distributors as more conservative in their tastes than niche markets such as those catered to by Christopher Dunne. However, as we shall see, the prevalence of sex as a marketing tool in posters and trailers for more mainstream filmed Shakespeare adaptations indicates that it is not the inclusion of sexual content in marketing but the manner of its representation, once again necessitating high/low hybridity, which governs its use in such films.

Selling Shakespeare with sex

Sexual elements are evident in the trailer for Branagh's *Hamlet*, which includes a brief scene of Hamlet and Ophelia making love. Branagh justifies the inclusion of the love scene in the film itself by saying 'if he were a thirteen-year-old who'd been dragged to a bloody four-hour *Hamlet*, he'd be very grateful for an occasional nude scene'.[26] Teens, as Branagh is well aware, need a sexually sugared Shakespeare pill. Thus, Branagh simultaneously stresses the educational value his 'authentic' *Hamlet* possesses (why else would the reluctant teen be attending the film at all?), but markets the 'sweetener' of graphic sexuality left to the imagination in early printed versions, and in so doing threatens to infantilise his mass audience. Another sexual scene in the North American full-length cinema trailer displays Claudius and Gertrude carousing together then retreating to their bedroom. Although this scene arguably has more legitimate derivation from Shakespeare's play than the love scenes between Hamlet and Ophelia, the decision to include it contributes to the argument that the trailer's sexual content functions as a marketing tool, to offset the film's 'boring' high-culture connotations.

Explicit sexual content traditionally tends to position a film as minority interest rather than multiplex-orientated in the American market, in this instance non-explicit scenes are employed to emphasise accessibility and modernity. Although within his *Hamlet* film Branagh chose to ignore the Freudian reading of an Oedipal relationship between Hamlet and Gertrude, espoused by both Olivier and Zeffirelli, the UK posters do imply such a relationship, with a large image of Hamlet and his mother positioned suggestively together. This raises the significant point that posters and trailers may make promises that the film itself does not deliver, including the suggestion of a higher sexual content. Meanings are thus attached to films through marketing before they reach the cinema. In the case of many films, they are marketed to the public on the basis of images that are not reproduced in the same form anywhere in the films, but it is the marketing, in the first instance at least, that must attract as many as possible to the cinema. Reverence will appeal to some, the 'purists', irreverence to others, the 'radicals'; some, the 'hybrids', may like a bit of both. Posters and trailers succeed where they offer something to each of these constituents, even if the film itself does not. The most significant goal when creating posters and trailers is to ensure that audiences buy tickets and see the film, not to accurately reflect the content of the film in marketing material.

Sexual content also formed a notably prevalent element in the promotion of *Shakespeare in Love*. A publication note that accompanies the review in the *New York Times*, a standard device in American cinema reviews to offer more detailed guidance than the rating alone, states that: '*Shakespeare in Love* is rated R (under 17 must be accompanied by parent or adult guardian). It includes nudity, bawdy humour and torrid sexual situations'. The voice-over for the post-Oscar trailer begins by describing it as 'the sexiest movie of the year'. The magazine *Glamour* published an article on sexual dysfunction that begins by alluding to *Shakespeare in Love* as a 'passionate film', and relates how:

> Viola [...] loses her virginity to the Bard [...] After a night of enviably satisfying love-making, Viola is awakened by her nurse announcing, "It's a new day". "No", the radiant Viola says with a knowing smile, "it's a new world!" Lucky Viola. More than one quarter of women and 7 per cent of men between the ages of 18 and 39 are unable to achieve orgasm during sex.[27]

It is the contemporary resonance of the sexual content of the film that is being employed to market it to a late twentieth-century audience. The trailer for *Shakespeare in Love*, a generically hybrid product, is also keen to emphasise its cultural significance, its related status as an event movie, and its sense of fun. Gender relations are prominent in the *Shakespeare in Love* campaign as they are in the campaigns for *William Shakespeare's Romeo + Juliet* and Branagh's *Hamlet*. Viola De Lesseps's (Gwyneth Paltrow) period of 'misrule' in *Shakespeare in Love*, when she dresses as a boy actor, is excluded from both the poster and the theatrical trailer, which focuses exclusively on the heterosexual romance between the two leads. A striking poster image of Fiennes and Paltrow embracing ran throughout the poster campaign, initially as an isolated image and, post-Oscar nominations on both UK and US poster images, centred between images of Oscar winners Geoffrey Rush, Ben Affleck and Judi Dench. The only scene in the trailer in which Paltrow still retains part of her male disguise comes in a love scene where Will Shakespeare unwinds her from the cloth she has used to flatten her breasts. Hollywood's conservatism regarding both the representation of homoeroticism in mainstream films, and genre conservatism in terms of emphasis on the film as a romantic comedy, is evident in both poster and trailer for *Shakespeare in Love*. Miles Thompson and Imelda Whelehan, in their essay in the volume *Talking Shakespeare*, comment upon the decisive removal of sexual ambiguity in *Shakespeare in Love*.[28] Of equal significance, however, is the exclusively heterosexual marketing of the film, in which the gay actor Rupert Everett, playing the gay playwright Christopher Marlowe, is excluded, and Gwyneth Paltrow's male disguise, sported for a significant quantity of the film, is not shown in posters or trailers. Reviews for the film and secondary articles remarking on its romantic qualities also overwhelmingly present it in exclusively heterosexual terms.

The trailer for *William Shakespeare's Romeo + Juliet* employs sexual images in a different manner, by presenting the film as an erotic thriller. Shots of the stars seen through a fish tank and shots of them embracing underwater are used twice in the trailer, giving an impression of the two bodies merging into one. The repeated underwater shots are combined with three shots of speeding cars to enhance the impression of danger which the trailer soundtrack, featuring DiCaprio screaming Juliet's name in despair and the sound of female screaming, also emphasises. Fred Goldberg has indicated that fear of alienating female audience members led to the exclusion of many fight scenes in the *Rocky* marketing campaign, and an alternative focus on the film's 'simple but appealing love story'.[29] This parallels the decision by the distributors of the video trailer of *William Shakespeare's Romeo + Juliet* to remove the car chase and gun-battle scenes of the theatrical trailer and instead focus exclusively on the love story.

The trailers for Branagh's *Hamlet* and *William Shakespeare's Romeo + Juliet* seek to achieve a similar balance between action and romance, to broaden the base of their generic appeal, but their nature as filmed Shakespeare adaptations also necessitates confrontation and reappraisal of the films' high-culture content. When Shakespeare is quoted in the trailers, the film marketers ensure that it is during highly charged moments, when the meaning of the language is readily comprehensible and the audience is reassured that the production is both 'authentic' Shakespeare and also exciting and accessible. Thus, for example, a fleeting shot of skyscrapers is accompanied by a voice-over saying 'in fair Verona where we lay our scene', and a shot displaying DiCaprio gazing lovingly at Danes is accompanied in voice-over by the words 'a pair of star-crossed lovers take their life'. The poster and trailer for *William Shakespeare's Romeo + Juliet* employ aspirational wish-fulfilment to appeal to the teen audience: Clare Danes and Leonardo DiCaprio provide a powerfully attractive image of good looks, romantic love and style. Doomed love was also a significant factor in the marketing campaign for a filmed Shakespeare adaptation in the previous year, Oliver Parker's *Othello*. Print advertisements used by Columbia Pictures to promote the film describe it as an 'erotic thriller', backing up the initial impression created by the poster, and the theatrical trailer includes a love scene.

In the North American one-sheet poster image used to promote *William Shakespeare's A Midsummer Night's Dream*, sexual content is absent. This absence may have contributed to the failure of the film's marketing campaign to produce box-office dividends. The visually featured stars are Michelle Pfeiffer, Rupert Everett, Calista Flockhart, Kevin Kline and Stanley Tucci, mature Hollywood actors rather than the younger stars such as Anna Friel. Michelle Pfeiffer's casting appropriately enables her to signify her Titania-like status as Hollywood royalty, foremost amongst actresses of her age in terms of profile and physical attractiveness. Her most celebrated role as Catwoman in *Batman* ought to have allowed her to market her sexiness to the audience, but in the poster she is demure, her body obscured. Calista Flockhart's celebrity rests upon her starring role as a sexually active woman in an adult television comedy/drama, *Ally McBeal*, but she is also presented on the poster in an asexual, buttoned-up image. The poster image, which was reproduced for newspaper and magazine advertisements, displays the names Rupert Everett, Calista Flockhart, Kevin Kline, Michelle Pfeiffer and Stanley Tucci along the left-hand side of a sunlit wood scene, with two large dragonflies and the silhouette of a figure with ass's ears retreating into the distance. On the right-hand side, from top to bottom, head shots of Kevin Kline, Michelle Pfeiffer, Stanley Tucci, Calista Flockhart and Rupert

Everett are illustrated, all smiling and bathed in golden light. The full title, *William Shakespeare's A Midsummer Night's Dream*, is picked out in the same elegant white font as the featured stars' names, and the tag line 'Love makes fools of us all' appears underneath the title. The impression created is one of a heritage movie, as both Kline and Flockhart wear visibly Victorian/Edwardian period costume, and of a magical fantasy. The name William Shakespeare appears in slightly smaller font than the stars' names but it is still made prominent by its presence in the centre of the illustration, directly beneath the silhouette of Bottom, suggesting a desire to employ Shakespeare as a marketing device but to temper the impact with the reassuring promotion of well-known Hollywood celebrities. Securing the right balance between the two can be seen as the marketers' major problem as they work across both the popular and the highbrow.

Younger, sexually attractive stars that might be expected to appeal to the key teen audience, Christian Bale and Anna Friel, are not in the foreground of the poster. Although the trailer makes more use of its ensemble cast, Calista Flockhart is the star who appears in the largest number of shots in the film's trailer. The fusion of 'high' and 'low' celebrities employed in the trailer for Branagh's *Hamlet* fails in this context because the stars lack strong resonance in *William Shakespeare's A Midsummer Night's Dream* than the US (Flockhart) or UK (Friel) domestic market. Furthermore, the attempt in the trailer to give all the major characters screen time and to emphasise plot points such as the conflict between the four young leads at length creates a pedestrian and rather confusing product. Possibly to create a dream-like atmosphere, the sequence of events presented is rapid and fragmented in the trailer, and there are no striking, memorable moments. Bottom's revelation of his ass's ears, for example, is presented in four very rapid shots and ends with his companions fleeing rather than his reaction, failing to capitalise on one of the play's best-known, and loved, moments. *Empire's* review of the cinematic release praises the performances by Rupert Everett and Dominic West and states of the adaptation that 'the general rule of thumb is whenever anyone goes in the woods, their clothes come off. And the chicks mud-wrestle. Otherwise this is largely an "aren't we cute" rampage through extravagant sets and over some sublime verse'.[30] None of the elements *Empire* focuses on are in evidence in the poster and trailer. *Empire's* recognition that nudity is a selling point was not capitalised on by the makers of the film's trailer or poster.

The *Empire* review is accompanied by a still of Tucci and Everett gazing lovingly into the middle distance with the suggestive caption 'Tucci and Everett are blown away by Kevin Kline's exquisite Bottom', in a possible joke reference to Everett's homosexuality, once again promoting sexual content in a manner avoided by the poster. *Empire*'s review of the video release of the film reduces its rating of the film from three out of five for the cinema release to just two out of five stars, but praises the stand-out performance by Kevin Kline and reiterates that 'you do get to see Flockhart and Friel in the first documented case of Shakespearean mud-wrestling, which in some people's eyes would justify the rental price alone'.[31] The persistence with which this point is made indicates that limited sexual content in filmed Shakespeare adaptations may be adopted as a selling point by reviewers even when it is largely absent from the primary marketing. Although *Empire* plays on the irreverence and eroticism of including the traditionally sexual spectacle of female mud-wrestling in a Shakespeare film, the trailer edits the scene to play as comedy, simply displaying Calista Flockhart being helped from the mud in an undignified manner. The trailer does, however, incorporate other sexual images, including a shot of Calista Flockhart and Christian Bale in bed together and a shot of the four lovers in the woods together semi-clothed. The trailer thus draws upon reassuring images of heritage film quality but blends them with the suggestion that the film also represents an urbane sex comedy, in a more appealing hybrid form than the poster.

Marketed with insufficient clarity concerning the target audience it was seeking to attract, *William Shakespeare's A Midsummer Night's Dream* was distributed by Fox Searchlight (who had also distributed *Looking for Richard*) and promoted as a costume piece and an 'authentic' adaptation. Although, in a form of cross-marketing, *William Shakespeare's A Midsummer Night's Dream* was advertised with both posters and trailers in cinemas showing *Shakespeare in Love* in North America, it was a commercial disappointment, grossing just 16.07 million dollars in North America and 1.18 million pounds in the UK, in comparison to, for example, the 1998 box office for *Shakespeare in Love*, which grossed 100.24 million dollars in North America and 20.08 million pounds in the UK. A review of the video release of the film in *Flicks* criticises too high a degree of fidelity to the text: a 'heavy-handed and unimaginative version' by a director 'too intimidated by the text' combined with the claim that 'many of the parts are badly miscast'.[32] Evidently, reverence unmediated by an imaginative, flexible and (post)modern approach to the text can fatally limit the audience for such a film. Thus, although the degree to which certain elements such as Shakespeare's name were summoned altered during the 1990s, both sexuality and celebrity persisted throughout the decade and beyond as key marketing devices for securing a mass audience.

The marketing role of film soundtracks in trailers

For trailers and posters seeking to attract a multiplex as well as an arthouse audience, the strategy of flattering the audience into a sense of sophistication is not as crucial as accessibility and familiarity. In the campaign for *William Shakespeare's Romeo + Juliet*, an MTV special was used to promote the film as accessible and familiar, and a music-video style is used in the trailer for the film, with rapid shots and heightened visuals as well as rock music. Beyond the significant marketing factor of familiarity, a further rationale exists for using popular music in the soundtracks and trailers for teen filmed Shakespeare adaptations that is of crucial relevance to this study. Popular music provides a space for both appealing to the vital teen audience and a means of introducing irreverence and contemporary resonance for that audience whilst retaining a sense of authenticity in the language and storyline of the films. Trailers are finished before even the film music is completed; let alone the final film, which is still being edited when the trailer is released. The trailer for the war film *K-19: The Widowmaker*, for example, accordingly used the appropriately militaristic *Gladiator* music in its trailer because its own music was not yet complete.[33]

Music plays a significant role in the trailer for *William Shakespeare's Romeo + Juliet*, ensuring both clear narrative exposition and positioning of the film to its teen audience. The soundtrack used on both the theatrical and the video trailer highlights the dramatic tension of the film, alternating between the love theme and a hard rock soundtrack. The full theatrical trailer also frequently employs the sound effects of gun fire and rotating helicopter propellers to enhance the sense of jeopardy and excitement and to make aural reference to action-movie trailers. These marketing strategies suggest a calculated attempt to entice a teen audience by referencing other genres popular with that audience, such as action films, rather than genres that might not be expected to have such appeal for that audience, such as heritage or art films. The advent of televised music videos created a target audience very similar to the key target audience for film marketers, and film distributors soon became aware of the power of the music video, or 'music trailer', as a marketing tool. As Jeff Smith, a film-soundtrack expert, indicates: 'since a music video could include either actual or additional footage from a film, it gave potential filmgoers a better idea of the film's stars, narrative, genre, and visual style than an accompanying single or album would'.[34] This connection is forged in *William Shakespeare's Romeo + Juliet*, as the switch from love theme to rock soundtrack coincides with the appearance of the anti-hero, Tybalt, and with scenes of the lovers separated and in the tomb together. Jeff Smith identifies a chronological trend in the relationship between film and soundtrack marketing: 'between 1989 and 1993 the market for soundtracks stabilized [...] The mid-nineties, however, saw a major upsurge in soundtrack sales that recalled the industry's salad days of the early eighties'.[35] This upsurge coincides with the inception of the teen filmed Shakespeare adaptation.

Corroborating my contention that the marketing of Shakespeare on film became increasingly postmodern, as reflected in its detachment from an appeal to heritage and Englishness during the late 1990s and into the new millennium, the trailer for Michael Almereyda's 2000 film *Hamlet* foregrounds its postmodern status. The trailer is a collage of images, and follows the film by frequently separating voices from bodies, creating an alienating effect, but significant disjunctions also exist between the film and the trailer. Almereyda's film abounds with logos, advertisements and product placement, but these are absent from the trailer, suggesting a desire both to streamline the trailer narrative without introducing some of the film's more complex statements, and to dissociate the film from a corporate context. In the film there is little music, but the trailer is characterised by a rock soundtrack throughout, which heightens its impact in the brief screen time it enjoys. Composed by Carter Burwell, the Almereyda *Hamlet* soundtrack subtly reflects Hamlet's troubled mental state throughout the film. The trailer for Almereyda's *Hamlet*, however, employs other music and resembles the trailer for Luhrmann's *William Shakespeare's Romeo + Juliet* in its insistent homage to the rapid editing and narrative style of music videos and in both its visual and aural styling. It would appear that the trailer soundtrack for Almereyda's *Hamlet* was created to situate the film in the successful teen filmed

Shakespeare adaptation genre, thus broadening its appeal, rather than adopting the more risky strategy of emphasising the film's 'indie' feel and rather downbeat tone. The commercial success of *William Shakespeare's Romeo + Juliet* had also indicated that a filmed Shakespeare adaptation marketed by an irreverent appeal via popular teen media could succeed as much as, or even outperform, one marketed as a more 'traditional' heritage adaptation.

The elements of postmodern pastiche in the Almereyda film's trailer include a paraphrasing of Shakespeare in musical shorthand. The film trailer uses popular music to elucidate the narrative, as the words provide exposition to guide the viewer through the abbreviated Shakespeare plot. Approximately halfway through the trailer, the music changes to a pop cover of a David Bowie song by the American rock band The Wallflowers, which does not feature in the film itself, in which the discernible lyrics concern kings, queens and heroes. These lyrics are accompanied by juxtaposed visual images of Kyle MacLachlan as Claudius and Ethan Hawke as Hamlet, posing the question of the rightful heir to the throne and representing the ephemeral nature of the power and status of all the main players in the play/film. Although some trailers use music that also features in the film, thus marketing the film and the soundtrack simultaneously, in this example the trailer's music was selected in order to convey the basic 'story' of *Hamlet*. Positioning itself towards a more mature target audience than *William Shakespeare's Romeo + Juliet*, the use of music as exposition in the *Hamlet* trailer arguably provided a more sophisticated means of plot retelling than the mapping of the story scene by scene in the theatrical trailer for *William Shakespeare's Romeo + Juliet*.

The *Hamlet* trailer's use of popular music enhances the sense of the film's relevance for its potential audience. The director Almereyda states in his published screenplay of the film that in the last weeks of editing, when he still wanted to reshoot some scenes, 'our friends at Miramax – busily dreaming up alternative titles for the film – were unwilling to throw us more money',[36] and he also observes that 'the Elizabethan language, coming thick and fast at the outset, confused our early audiences. (A test screening organised by Miramax yielded the second worst scores in the company's history.)'[37] The trailer removes these objections by employing pop music for clear narrative exposition and keeping Shakespearian quotation to a minimum. In one minute and fifty-six seconds, only sixty-two words are spoken. The limited dialogue is supplemented by text onscreen that summarises the plot. By the time of this film's release, the type of Shakespeare content which had been reinterpreted in one-word soundbites in the MTV special for *William Shakespeare's Romeo + Juliet* had been replaced with pop-music exposition, an arguably still more irreverent means of marketing Shakespeare.

Shakespeare's presence in poster tag lines

One of the most significant forms of film-marketing shorthand of all, the tag line for a film, is a one- or two-sentence distillation of the film which markets its most important features or, to use film-marketing terminology, 'high concept', often in a witty and memorable fashion in posters and other marketing material. Analysis of whether the text in the posters and trailers quotes directly from Shakespeare indicates the film marketers' degree of confidence in the Shakespeare brand name to market their products. Poster art must be considered in conjunction with the text that is also included on all film posters. Michael Wiese's useful description of the functions of the copy line and tag line merits full quotation:

> There are two primary copy elements: the copy line, which comes before the logo, and the tag line, which comes after. The copy line is used on ads and one-sheets for a film before it opens and before reviews appear. *The copy line sets up the picture* and grabs your attention. […] When the reviews come in, the best quotes from reviewers can replace the copy line in the ads. *The tag line comes after the title* and accentuates it.[38]

The font size and style of the title, and the selection of which film critics' comments to print upon the poster, are amongst the significant textual elements that interact with the visual art. The confluence of word and image gives indications concerning the meaning of the poster, as well as the film, and what elements of the poster are meant to take priority, each detail implying an attitude towards potential audiences. As we have already seen, in the case of Shakespeare adaptation, how to exploit Shakespeare's highbrow reputation while blending it with reassuringly accessible images is the difficult task facing the marketers. Unsurprisingly, they do not always seem to have achieved the perfect balance.

One of the most effective techniques in advertising is to draw upon a familiar topic, to serialise a concept and build brand recognition upon audience knowledge of that theme. 'Graphic conventions' are thus a significant element in poster art, and both the font, or type design, and the meaning of the text of the tag and copy lines necessitate analysis, as both elements are used to create a certain image of the film being sold. The title treatment for *Shakespeare in Love* is large and in cursive-style script, suggestive of Elizabethan secretary hand, and emphasising the film's status as both a heritage film and love story. *10 Things I Hate About You*, an adaptation of *The Taming of the Shrew*, uses a large, block-lettered title treatment in primary colours with a y-chromosome skewering the zero of '*10*', thus emphasising an aesthetic of the 'girl power' embodied by the female protagonist Kat and a comedic sense of fun with its big, colourful lettering.

The 1991 film *Prospero's Books*, directed by Peter Greenaway and based on *The Tempest*, did not use Shakespeare in its tag line. However, like the film itself, the tag line retains a sense of reverence to Shakespeare's universality, whilst also providing a useful plot synopsis: 'A magician's spell, the innocence of young love and a dream of revenge unite to create a tempest'. Such faux-Shakespearian quotation interestingly displays film marketers foregrounding the issues they want to emphasise, then couching those concepts in Shakespearian terms. In the mid-1990s filmed Shakespeare adaptations were frequently marketed with a mixture of Shakespearian and non-Shakespearian tag lines. Richard Loncraine's 1995 *Richard III* has four tag lines. Two are non-Shakespearian, but possess a pseudo-Shakespearian, proverbial quality: 'power conquers all' and 'what is worth dying for ... is worth killing for'. The other two quotations are Shakespearian: 'I can smile, and murder whiles I smile', from *Henry VI Part 3* and 'I am determined to prove a villain, and hate the idle pleasures of these days ... '[39] Both trailer and poster for *William Shakespeare's Romeo + Juliet* use the familiar Shakespearian quotation 'my only love sprung from my only hate' as their tag line. This tag line functions as an indication that the film as a whole is in Shakespeare's language, and it also displays consistency with other elements of the film's marketing campaign such as the MTV special in which 'love' and 'hate' are amongst the words described on the bodies advertising the picture. However, the film also uses two other non-Shakespearian tag lines in its campaign: 'The classic love story set in our time' and 'The greatest love story the world has ever known'. This film emphasises the resonance the Romeo and Juliet story possesses in Western culture, allowing their celebrity to exceed even that of Shakespeare. The two non-Shakespearian tag lines also emphasise both the modernity and the universality of Luhrmann's adaptation simultaneously, another consistent feature of the marketing campaign. While the profane 'nowness' of modernity is attractively dynamic, the recognition of continuity with the best of the past is attractively reassuring.

Oliver Parker's 1995 *Othello* employs a non-Shakespearian tag line that places the film as both an erotic thriller and as a store of 'universal', eternal emotional preoccupations: 'envy, greed, jealousy and love'. *A Thousand Acres*, directed by Jocelyn Moorhouse and released in 1997, is based on a successful novel which adapted *King Lear*, but the film was marketed with a non-Shakespearian tag line: 'Best friends. Bitter rivals. Sisters.' The tag line thus emphasises the 'universal' theme of familial disintegration rather than the specific disintegration of Lear's family and kingdom. The 1996 film *Twelfth Night: Or, What You Will* has the tag lines 'Before Priscilla crossed the desert, Wong Foo met Julie Newmar and the birdcage was unlocked, there was … ', thus situating the film in the genre of transvestite comedy rather than filmed Shakespeare adaptation. This gives the target audience a hook in terms of a minor genre trend in 1990s cinema, and emphasises the resonance of *Twelfth Night* to a modern audience by relating it to late twentieth-century gender politics, as well as referencing sexuality, despite the absence of overt homoerotic activity in the film itself. Although based on *Hamlet*, *In the Bleak Midwinter* is not marketed with Shakespearian quotations. The marketing team instead emphasises the film's status as a thespian farce: 'The drama. The passion. The intrigue. And the rehearsals haven't even started.' In conclusion, the marketing teams for *Prospero's Books*, *Richard III*, *In the Bleak Midwinter*, *A Thousand Acres* and *Twelfth Night: Or, What You Will* sought to extend their appeal beyond a relatively limited arthouse audience, by marketing the films as more than simply Shakespeare adaptations.

The American tag line for Hoffman's 1999 *William Shakespeare's A Midsummer Night's Dream* represents the film primarily as a romance, 'Love makes fools of us all'. Once again, faux-Shakespearian quotation by film marketers permits them to provide a one-line plot précis non-existent in the Shakespeare canon but still suggestive of a Shakespearian 'flavour'. The alternative tag line, 'Love looks not with the eyes, but with the mind; and therefore is winged Cupid painted blind', quotes from the play,[40] implying that the production is also 'authentic' in terms of its approach to Shakespeare's language. The web site used to promote the film upon release described it as 'shot on location in Italy, *William Shakespeare's A Midsummer Night's Dream* is a 400-year-old whimsical romantic comedy as it's never been seen before'. The trailer and poster, however, provide little to persuade their audience of the film's novelty. In a film review of *William Shakespeare's A Midsummer Night's Dream*, Samuel Crowl believes the director wanted to 'appropriate a daring excess in translating Shakespeare into the language of films'[41] from Baz Luhrmann. This goal presents irreverence, even transgression, as a marketing tool: it is a 'daring excess' to rework Shakespeare for a cinema audience. Crowl reiterates that it is paradoxically daring for a film-maker to retain Shakespeare's verse rather than updating the language into modern prose, rap, or song, for example, and he is also referring to the 'daring excess' of Luhrmann's visual style. However, there is no such irreverence in the marketing campaign for *William Shakespeare's A Midsummer Night's Dream*, which instead sold the film solely as a reverent heritage film, contributing to its box-office failure.

Julie Taymor's 1999 *Titus* has two tag lines: 'The fall of an empire. The descent of man' and 'If you think revenge is sweet … taste this'. The first tag line does not quote Shakespeare but has an archaic, epic tone suited to the heritage film genre. The closest approximations to the latter quotation within the play *Titus Andronicus* are 'O sweet Revenge, now do I come to thee', and 'I know thou dost; and, sweet Revenge, farewell'.[42] The tag lines form one salient example of an uncertainty more broadly manifested in the marketing of Taymor's film, also exhibited in the marketing of Hoffman's *William Shakespeare's A Midsummer Night's Dream*, regarding the balance between reverence and irreverence. The marketing team's emphasis in the poster art work and poster tag lines is upon the film as a historical revenge tragedy, and as a film for highbrow Shakespeare enthusiasts, rather than as a bold and postmodern reworking that fuses images of ancient Rome with futuristic visual motifs. However, confusingly, reviews of *Titus* often criticise it for being too irreverent: for example the *Washington Post* review, which expresses hostility to director Julie Taymor's style, claiming that it 'doesn't interpret Shakespeare so much as make an amateurishly postmodern spectacle of itself'. The reviewer is negative about the film's irreverent approach to Shakespeare, and displays anxiety that coherent, faithful adaptation has been replaced by postmodern indeterminacy. The crucial hybrid balance has been tipped too far from reverence and evocation of high cultural forms in the poster tag lines and too far in favour of postmodern fragmentation, at least according to the film review, to succeed in the competitive climate of the late 1990s multiplex.

Although there were several other reasons for the exclusion of Shakespeare from the tag lines for late 1990s teen filmed Shakespeare adaptations, which will be analysed in the fourth chapter, they also conform to the model I have established of a movement away from Shakespeare quotation both in the late 1990s and in studio pictures as opposed to arthouse pictures. Teen filmed Shakespeare adaptations display interesting variations in their tag line uses of Shakespeare. *10 Things I Hate About You* reworks an Elizabeth Barrett Browning poem in one tag line: 'How do I loathe thee? Let me count the ways'. The line selected has sufficient resonance in popular culture and the classroom for the punning to be accessible to the majority of the target teen audience. The second tag line, 'They're spitefully romantic', is also non-Shakespearian, the third tag line, 'Romeo, O Romeo, Get out of my face', a paraphrase of 'O Romeo, Romeo, Wherefore art thou Romeo./ Deny thy father and refuse thy name', from *Romeo and Juliet*, and the fourth, 'I pine, I perish', is taken from *The Taming of the Shrew*.[43] The gender politics of 'Romeo, O Romeo, Get out of my face' is worthy of remark, as the quotation is rewritten in order to promote a girl-power ethos rather than a patriarchal discourse. Hence, although teen Shakespeare posters notably never advertise their Shakespeare content in the visual images, they often make punning and oblique reference to it in the tag lines. This cleverly provides humorous stimulation for members of the teen audience who recognise the references, but does not alienate those teens who read the tag lines without recognising the source.

Never Been Kissed, a 1999 filmed adaptation of *As You Like It*, has three tag lines, which all exclude mention of Shakespeare: 'The class clown just turned chic', 'A comedy with class' and 'She's never been hip. Never been cool. Never been in … until now'. However, if viewers of the film are aware of its borrowings from *As You Like It*, then these tag lines arguably market Shakespeare as a means of attaining cool status, since it is the heroine's knowledge of Shakespeare in the film that enables her to display intellectual virtuosity and to attract the amorous attention of her English teacher. The 2001 film *Get Over It* has four tag lines, none of which quote from Shakespeare: 'Young, free and single. Again', 'Would you dump this guy? She did. She wouldn't', 'Let the party begin!' and 'Split happens'. The choice of tag lines indicates that the marketing team deem the film's generic categorisation as a teen film more important to foreground than its more specific generic categorisation as a teen filmed Shakespeare adaptation.

O, a teen *Othello* adaptation made in 1999 but released in 2001, has three non-Shakespearian tag lines: 'Everything comes full circle', 'Trust. Seduction. Betrayal.' and 'Nothing comes between two people's love, like one person's jealousy'. The closest match in the Shakespeare canon to the first tag line is provided by Edmund's words in *King Lear*, 'the wheel is come full circle: I am here'.[44] In a similar manner to the tag line for *10 Things I Hate About You*, although the tag lines for *O* do not quote Shakespeare, they exhibit pseudo-Shakespearian characteristics. In this context, the tag line's semblance of Shakespearian quotation provides sonorous gravitas, but like the film itself updates the sentiment to modern English. The 2002 romantic comedy, *Romeo and Juliet Revisited*, which was marketed primarily towards a teen audience, has the tag line 'You'll See "Dead" People … Living Happily Ever After!' and a plot outline suggesting: 'This is the story of what happens to the star-cross'd lovers after Shakespeare's famous play ends'. The tag line makes reference to Haley Joel Osment's iconic line from the film *The Sixth Sense*, 'I see dead people', and thus simultaneously makes a movie in-joke and indicates an irreverent reworking of Shakespeare's play. Thus, in the course of the 1990s through to the new millennium, direct quotation of Shakespeare in poster tag lines became less and less prevalent, a trend which may be ascribed to a number of factors, including the decline in the 'straight' heritage movie in favour of more hybrid postmodern forms such as *Shakespeare in Love*, and the growth of the teen filmed Shakespeare sub-genre, in which, despite its literary *kudos*, the overt presence of Shakespeare was viewed as a potential problem in attracting the teen audience by film marketers.

Chronological distinctions emerge in this chapter between the marketing of Shakespeare as heritage film in the early to mid-1990s through to the marketing of Shakespeare as postmodern cinematic spectacle in the late 1990s and the new millennium. Methods of ensuring accessibility in posters and trailers and achieving a wide appeal in poster graphics are further discussed in relation to marketing to a teen audience in Chapter 4, where it will be seen that these graphics were frequently also employed on DVD and video boxes and on the web sites promoting teen films. Posters and trailers destabilise any reductive high/low binary, and defy attempts to disentangle art from commerce. Although it is evident that issues related to working across a high/low binary are inescapable in Shakespeare's manifestations in popular culture, and that even within the category of posters and trailers some depend more upon high-culture connotations than others, it is those film-marketing campaigns that effectively blend high with popular elements that prove the most commercially successful.

CHAPTER THREE

Kenneth Branagh's filmed Shakespeare adaptations

T HE SYMBIOTIC RELATIONSHIP exhibited between veneration and irreverence in the marketing of Kenneth Branagh's filmed Shakespeare adaptations contributed significantly to what I have identified as the distinctive, hybrid nature of the marketing of filmed Shakespeare adaptations from 1989 to the present day. Branagh grew to be constructed as a marker of a particular version of Shakespeare, himself becoming a brand name associated with a potent blend of Hollywood multiplex entertainment and fidelity to standards of quality and authenticity. Branagh's appropriation of Shakespeare fashioned his career in Hollywood and consolidated Shakespeare's position in the American corporate and cultural marketplace. In effect, the Branagh brand succeeded in more or less demolishing the either/or high/low cultural barrier in filmed Shakespeare adaptations, born of Branagh's desire to break into the Hollywood market and to maximise Shakespeare's availability to mass audiences. Alison Light has remarked that 'Branagh's public commitment to a "life-enhancing populism" is premised on just this moving between high and low', perceptively adding that 'his version of both is always old-fashioned',[1] suggestive of a conservative thrust behind his high-low blend. The pre-sold qualities of the heritage movie genre, notably the 1980s Merchant Ivory films, were also significant in paving the way for Branagh's Shakespeare adaptations, but it was Branagh's *Henry V* that marked a new ambition to reach the broadest possible audience.

It is already widely acknowledged that Branagh occupies a seminal place in Shakespeare film history and that the release of *Henry V* in 1989 marked the beginning of a decade of unprecedented production of filmed Shakespeare adaptations in Hollywood. The release of *Henry V* indicated to an industry cautious since the commercial failure of Roman Polanski's *Macbeth* in 1971 the possibility that Shakespeare could be good box office. It is no exaggeration to state that without Branagh's timely commercial/artistic intervention, the 1990s Shakespeare-on-film phenomenon would not have happened, and it bears repetition that this was as much a marketing and commercial intervention as it was an artistic one. The distributors of Branagh's films sensed that money could be made out of Shakespeare if both adaptation and marketing achieved the right balance between deployment of popular ingredients necessary for audience interest, a proper respect for the Bard as supreme artist and intense commercial exploitation of Shakespeare's unmatched, global canonical status.[2] Even hostile critics would accept that Branagh is an extremely astute self-marketer, and invitingly self-reflexive about his work.

Although described above as a commercial success, it is, of course, the case that Branagh has had mixed fortunes in his Hollywood career. The diminishing returns enjoyed by Branagh's filmed Shakespeare adaptations from the beginning to the end of the 1990s may be ascribed to several factors specifically relating to marketing as well as the more common reasons presented by Branagh scholars such as his 'populism'. Branagh's films, for example, did not always avail themselves of new marketing technologies such as web sites and DVDs to the same degree as, for example, teen filmed Shakespeare adaptations. The varying degrees to which Branagh's films have achieved commercial success and demonstrated an ability to capture the consumer Zeitgeist must be investigated in relation to the distinctive political and social climate in which they were marketed, as well as the form taken by that marketing. Although the potential of filmed Shakespeare adaptations to reach a mainstream audience was rarely questioned by the late twentieth century, when *Henry V* and *Much Ado about Nothing* were released, their potential for moving from the arthouse to the multiplex rested on sales, marketing and distribution factors such as the willingness of mass-market cinemas and pay-per-view cable-television channels to risk screening them, and on the ability of film marketers to reassure audiences that the product would not be dull or incomprehensible. Branagh's films failed to follow the crucial trend of moving out of the heritage genre, and beyond even the Shakespeare on film genre, to become marketed in the hybrid manner of such multi-genre successes as *William Shakespeare's Romeo + Juliet* and *Shakespeare in Love.*

The rhetoric of crossover between the sacred, reverent and high and the profane, accessible and low is particularly in evidence in the marketing of Branagh's films. I would contend that this is the key marketing problem, the Holy Grail of marketers seeking to work across the high/low cultural boundaries, and the Branagh industry has been both the most and least effective in finding this Holy Grail. Reasons why film marketing can vary so widely in its degree of success are of particular interest and significance for this book. That Branagh is fully conscious of the dangers as well as the opportunities involved in adapting high cultural material for Hollywood is clear from the introduction to his script version of *Much Ado about Nothing*, where he writes of the performance style of his Renaissance Theatre Company that: 'We wanted audiences to react to the story as if it were in the here and now and important to them. We did not want them to feel they were in some cultural church. We made the same attempt in film'.[3]

Here, Shakespeare is represented as a secular religion, a sacred text, but one that may be made comprehensible and relevant by judicious deployment of twentieth-century media. If religion can be sold, in a secular age, then so can Shakespeare, but only with the aid of effective marketing techniques. Suzanna Thomas argues that 'what distinguishes cultural artefacts, from other purveyors of ideology (identified ... as the Church, family and school) is the greater extent to which they have been penetrated by capital and thereby transformed into commodities'.[4] Cultural commodities nevertheless employ the rhetoric of the Church and school in order to maintain their cultural circulation. 1990s Hollywood was operating in a semantic space reminiscent of J. G. Ballard's postmodern business park, Eden Olympia, an 'ideas laboratory for the new Millennium', where the employees make no distinction between the traditionally sacred and profane: 'somewhere in the office buildings ... staring at their screens, designing a new cathedral or cineplex, or watching the world's spot prices'.[5] Branagh's films were inevitably penetrated by capital, as the act of taking them to Hollywood, to secure the maximum audience, ensured that their production was dictated by profit-driven values, which could threaten the artistic integrity of the work. This balancing act was something which lay at the heart of the Branagh project, and hostile critics have, of course, been quick to argue that the balance tipped too far towards commercial interests. This is a reciprocal process whereby wants are systematically produced by the Hollywood film industry but the production of wants is never fully under the control of Hollywood hegemony, and hence marketing is always to some degree an imprecise practice. Branagh's films exemplify the complex process whereby filmed Shakespeare adaptations both catered to audience expectations and determined those expectations to some extent.

This chapter focuses only on the five filmed Shakespeare adaptations which Branagh directed himself: *Henry V*, *Much Ado about Nothing*, *In the Bleak Midwinter*, *William Shakespeare's Hamlet* and *Love's Labour's Lost*, which is why analysis of *Othello*, which he starred in but did not direct, has been excluded. Kenneth Branagh has acted in, directed, produced and adapted as screenplays two of his filmed Shakespeare adaptations: *Love's Labour's Lost* and *Much Ado about Nothing*, and acted in, directed and adapted, but not produced, two further filmed Shakespeare adaptations: *William Shakespeare's Hamlet* and *Henry V*. Branagh also directed a 1987 film of *Twelfth Night*, but this was a filmed version of a theatrical performance and does not have a comparable marketing campaign to the campaigns of films analysed in this chapter, and has therefore been excluded. This chapter simultaneously centres on the role of postmodern homage, appropriations and pastiche in the marketing of Branagh's films and on the depiction of Englishness in the marketing of Branagh's Shakespeare adaptations.

The postmodern elements of Branagh's approach are not prominent in the marketing until the campaign for *Love's Labour's Lost*, as they have the potential to threaten the aura of authenticity that Branagh's film distributors carefully cultivate. Branagh's postmodern, irreverent stance to the Shakespeare text, characterised by pastiche and intertextual references to other film and stage versions, is strategically concealed for commercial reasons. For example, Branagh made extensive cuts to the play text for all his films except *Hamlet*, and he employs the alternative, postmodern strategy of adding scenes that broaden the meta-cinematic frame of reference, strategies that enable Branagh to maintain control over his controversial version of Shakespeare's meaning. These changes are rarely mentioned in promotional interviews with Branagh. Although cast as a disinterested purveyor of Shakespeare to the masses, Branagh acts as mediator and translator, creating a specific version of Shakespeare palatable in Hollywood popular culture. As the marketing of a film to the general public forms part of the mandate of a film's distributor, responsibility for the manner in which Branagh's filmed Shakespeare adaptations are sold rests on a corporation rather than Branagh the individual. The marketing decisions made by Branagh's film distributors support my contention that the tension between veneration and irreverence reveals the socio-political determinants behind the sale of Shakespeare by Hollywood to the cinema audience.

Investigation of the manner in which the marketing of filmed Shakespeare adaptations worked in the 1990s indicates that non-American directors such as Kenneth Branagh (British) and Baz Luhrmann (Australian) ceded Shakespeare to Hollywood, which in turn benefited from the iconic version of Anglicised culture represented by Shakespeare. It is necessary to export Shakespeare primarily because America is the global benchmark for a film's success in its initial box-office release. Whilst Branagh's *Henry V* was marketed as a British 'giant-killer' film successfully exported to Hollywood, and *In the Bleak Midwinter* was a self-funded production that irreverently satirises and makes a fetish of the British love affair with Shakespeare, Branagh's other filmed Shakespeare adaptations were a US/UK amalgamation from their inception, in terms of financing, casting and target audience. The transatlantic version of Shakespeare that the Branagh brand name grew to represent made a particularly significant contribution to the commercial history of Shakespeare on Hollywood film. More broadly, Branagh's films may be subject to a neo- or post-colonial reading: Shakespeare is ceded by Britain to its stronger partner America. Branagh's films are sold as British heritage films conquering corporate America, with an appeal in the marketing to the educative value of the films as 'authentic' reproductions of the Shakespeare text, whilst simultaneously marketing the films as accessible commercial pictures.

Branagh's biographical relationship to Britishness must also be examined in order to determine his place in the process of selling Shakespeare to Hollywood, and to determine if his supplying of the compromised British response arises from his own Britishness. Branagh's relation to Anglocentric culture is not straightforward, and, operating from a liminal cultural trajectory, Branagh arguably possesses an outsider's perspective on British heritage that enables him to identify the most 'exportable' qualities of a British literary icon. Branagh is both close to bardolatry, having attended RADA and worked at the RSC, and distant from it, as Hollywood is, producing in Branagh a similar mixture of veneration and irreverence. The post-colonial concept of hybridity is relevant to this process of an Irishman of humble origin exporting the most celebrated British author to an ex-colony, creating a veneration purporting to be unrestrained by commercial imperatives. Branagh states that when he first encountered a television version of Shakespeare he lacked the cultural competence to access the plays' full meaning: 'I was eleven years old and from a background (Irish, Protestant, working-class) which had given me little preparation for watching Shakespeare'.[6] Hence, Branagh claims to have a degree of intellectual as well as geographical distance from Englishness, and he states that his Irishness provides a degree of alienation. However, the political situation in Ulster exemplifies that nationalism is commonly most intense in liminal areas, and may ironically have provided Branagh with the most complete identification possible with Englishness.

Branagh's public image itself combines irreverence and veneration, as a working-class lad made good and the uneducated purveyor of the pinnacle of Western culture. Branagh deploys a discourse of irreverent veneration towards *Hamlet* in his preface to the published screenplay that neatly represents his own constructed image and that of his Shakespeare film adaptations and their marketing:

> As the great soccer manager Bill Shankly once said, describing the importance of football, "It's not a matter of life and death. It's much more important than that." Certainly for me, an ongoing relationship to this kind of poetry and this kind of mind is a necessary part of an attempt to be civilized.[7]

The reverent tone is offset by the linking of Shankly, a working-class football icon, and a highbrow art form, which combines seriousness, play and populism. Constantly maintaining the fluidity of his relationship between high and low, Branagh's praise of the civilising benefits of poetry is prompted by lionising an ostensibly low cultural activity. Branagh's Irish background and the accusations levelled at him of money-making Thatcherism might arouse an expectation of irreverence towards Shakespeare, but his RSC training and his rhetoric of impassioned commitment when describing his agenda in making filmed Shakespeare adaptations suggest the converse. The tension between Branagh's bardolatry and his desire to Hollywoodise Shakespeare is shared by Baz Luhrmann, who as an Australian arguably possesses even greater licence for post-colonial and carnivalesque irreverence towards the sacred British text. Both directors share a degree of reverence both heightened and untrammelled by the proximity of English bardolatry.

Henry V: *pugilism and patriotism*

Branagh's relatively low-budget *Henry V*, distributed by Samuel Goldwyn, grossed 10.16 million dollars at the US box office in 1989, or, as Russell Jackson indicates, 5 million dollars negative cost. Russell Jackson continues by explaining succinctly that 'one yardstick of box-office success is that a film should make at least two-and-a-half times the cost of making the master negative'.[8] According to Michael Posner, Samuel Goldwyn by the early 1990s had a 'reputation for the successful handling of smaller pictures'.[9] Accustomed to introducing low-budget, quality Anglo-American films to a wider audience, Samuel Goldwyn also went on to release *Much Ado about Nothing*, and had distributed *Peter's Friends* in North America, which had a 3.2 million dollars box-office gross, 1.3 million dollars rental gross, and a 2.4 million dollars spend on press and advertising.[10] Stephen Evans, Branagh's financial broker, brought personal friends into the deal to finance *Henry V* in 1988, and he secured a contract with the BBC that advanced 2 million pounds for the shooting of the film. The success of Branagh's performance as Henry V on stage in 1984 in the Adrian Noble production was a significant determining factor in Branagh's ability to gain funding for a film version. The BBC financing emphasises that the *Henry V* project began as verifiably more 'British' than any of the Branagh films that would follow. The film was released on the eve of Veterans' Day in America, which coincided with the seventy-fifth and fiftieth anniversaries of the outbreaks of the First and Second World Wars. This display of deference to the latter-day victims of war, and preservers of British autonomy, indicates the reverence towards British institutions of monarchy and statehood that characterises the marketing of *Henry V*. The marketing of Branagh's version combines commemoration with a mandate to disseminate an updated version of both medieval history and Shakespeare.

In a promotional interview with the critic Michael Billington published immediately before the film's theatrical release in North America, Branagh influences the marketing of his film by describing the ideal cultural fusion and audience he is seeking: 'to make a popular film that will both satisfy the Shakespearean scholar and the punter who likes *Crocodile Dundee*'.[11] The crucial interplay between Shakespeare's sacred educative power and his powerful if complex popular appeal when correctly packaged is encapsulated in this quotation. Branagh positions himself as a Shakespeare-like figure, capable of fusing high and low culture in order to entertain all audience members, from royalty to groundlings. Thus the 'universal Bard' gives way to 'universal Branagh', as their genius transcends social, economic and cultural boundaries.

Part of the promotional activity for *Henry V* in America was determined by the manner in which the film was released. Samuel Goldwyn initially released the film on just a small number of screens, increasing the number until it had reached 103 screens in 124 days. Known in marketing terms as 'platforming', this limited run provides a means of building positive word-of-mouth from a specific demographic and thus, in film-marketing expert Fred Goldberg's words, 'is a way of building positive consumer awareness and interest in the other markets'.[12] The relatively conservative, strategic number of screens upon which *Henry V* was released was a significant component of the successful marketing campaign. *Henry V* was marketed as a quality picture that was anticipated to have the potential to slowly gain box-office momentum by way of strong word-of-mouth and critical acclaim. The release figures imply a further significant point about the campaign. The film was not marketed as a blockbuster; rather, it enjoyed break-out success and belied the idea that filmed Shakespeare adaptations had purely niche appeal.

One of the reasons for the film's break-out success is its dual appeal both as a stirring, patriotic British film and as a gritty Hollywood war film. Although Branagh's film of *Henry V* arguably contains anti-war elements, they are generally countered and contained by more straightforward patriotism in the marketing. Subversion and patriotism are open to marketing techniques aimed to attract a broad audience, appealing to both sceptics and patriots, and in tune with a late twentieth-century audience, the pragmatism, dark cynicism and horror of war are emphasised, for maximum marketing appeal, alongside the jingoism associated with Laurence Olivier's classic film version. The Englishness and patriotism of Olivier's 1944 film of *Henry V* is emphasised from the opening credits, with their dedication 'to the Commandos and Airborne Troops of Great Britain, the spirit of whose ancestors it has been humbly attempted to recapture in some ensuing scenes'. Deborah Cartmell usefully notes that Branagh's employment of nostalgia in *Henry V* similarly exhibits him 'cunningly consolidating Shakespeare as an ideological force [...] the fighting spirit of the British combined with the eternal words of the Bard provide an ideal British export, a force to be reckoned with (or marketed) abroad'.[13] This is nevertheless a vision of Englishness mediated through American cultural imperialism, as it was Branagh's commercial success at the American box office with *Henry V* that brought him international recognition and which granted him a significant cultural platform from which to diffuse his cultural orthodoxy. Both Branagh's *Henry V* and his filmed *Hamlet* may be termed postmodern epics, large scale and ambitious but also playfully aware of their own generic status and aspirations, and wary of overt flag-waving nationalism or glorification of war and empire. However, the more modest commercial aspirations of *Henry V* allowed it to enjoy a proportionately far greater success than Branagh's four-hour *Hamlet* film project.

Branagh's distribution company sought to encapsulate and distil the most marketable elements of the film in its campaign, and the poster provides a strong example. The American poster image for *Henry V* illustrates a muddied and vulnerable individual which frustrates the aesthetic expectations of the poster-viewing audience concerning the visual depiction of royalty; nevertheless with his heraldic dress and look of steely determination the king's image makes an appeal to patriotism. The UK poster image also appeals to patriotism, in which a triumphant, armour-clad Branagh stands above his cheering troops in the foreground, whilst in the background there is a heroic image of him, sword aloft, rearing up on his horse against a backdrop of flames. A caption above Branagh reads 'The great adventure of a king who defied the odds to prove himself a man', and beneath the film title are the words 'A bold new film by Kenneth Branagh'. The striking, brightly coloured image focuses on the adulation of royalty and on Branagh's youthful good looks and virility. By way of contrast, the poster used for the Spanish market shows the tiny figure of the king standing in semi-darkness, viewed from behind and framed by a huge doorway. It conveys a sense of vulnerable individuality quite different from the bold forward-facing close-up of

Henry used for America. These contrasting images indicate that filmed Shakespeare adaptations perform a range of what Graham Holderness terms 'specific commercial and cultural functions within the economic and ideological apparatus of a bourgeois-democratic society'.[14]

Graham Holderness usefully interprets Branagh's reworking of *Henry V* as 'postmodern patriotism',[15] and the marketing made it clear that whilst the film *Henry V* may be situated in the genre of post-Vietnam Hollywood war films, in which war represents waste and futility as frequently as glory and patriotism, the historical figure Henry V represents a bygone age of chivalry and courage. Branagh's natural eye for marketing stunts had led him to consult with Prince Charles at Buckingham Palace on the emotional experience of monarchy during preparation for his stage version of *Henry V*. As Michael Skovmand argues, these consultations 'were seen by the British intelligentsia as just another instance of Branagh's capacity for entrepreneurial, unprincipled self-promotion',[16] indicating how politically sensitive Branagh's exploitation of British cultural commodities could prove.[17] The text on the retail video box for *Henry V* focuses on regal courage and victory, rhapsodising that:

> The battle scenes are spellbinding, from the siege of Harfleur and Henry's stirring exhortation to his small army to go "Once more unto the breach", to the dramatic victory at Agincourt. In addition to his own extraordinary performance as King Henry, Branagh elicits brilliant work from a stellar cast.

The cover art for the *Henry V* video box is a close-up of the King crowned, whilst the DVD cover illustrates Branagh in full battle regalia in close-up with a large sword in his hand. Together these graphics emphasise both the cinematic power of medieval battle and ceremony and the dominance of the central performance by Branagh. The American trailer is still more jingoistic, with no sense of pastiche. Accompanied by dramatic music, the solemn American voice-over intones:

> It was a time of courtiers and kings. It was the turning point for the English throne. It was one of history's greatest adventures, led by a soldier who would not retreat, a lover who would not give up. A leader who upheld justice. A rebel who would not give in. A king who defied the odds to prove himself a man. The Samuel Goldwyn Company presents a bold new film by Kenneth Branagh.

This potent combination of British history and Branagh's populist genius is fused with Shakespeare's 'greatest hits' in the verse used in the trailer: Branagh shouts 'once more unto the breach, dear friends, once more', and excerpts from the St Crispin's day speech visually accompany battle scenes. The opening shot of the trailer shows Branagh sweeping through a doorway in full regal garb. A subsequent shot of the hanging of Bardolph, a moment that undermines positive response to Henry in the film, is sanitised in the trailer by voice-over reassurances that this was a just and manly king.

It may be concluded that complex negotiations took place between Branagh and the transmission of Shakespeare as English high culture to Hollywood. The extensive cuts Branagh made to the play text were rarely referred to by him in promotional interviews, except when indicating that he had cut some of the comic scenes, notably the 'leek' scene, because they were not funny to modern audiences, arguably American audiences in particular. This is a necessity for marketing the films to Hollywood, which proved receptive to Branagh's hybrid conservative-but-updated version of heritage Britain, and which might have been particularly alienated by Elizabethan references to British regional prejudices. Branagh is thus positioned as the arbiter of the multiplex audience's taste, an audience that is wary of academicism and outmoded humour. Roger Ebert, part of the small circle of American film critics who have a substantial impact on cinema-going opinion and hence word-of-mouth film marketing, observes that 'Branagh is nothing if not a film director of high spirits and great energy. His *Henry V* was a Shakespeare history filled with patriotism and poetry'. [18] Although patriotism is at times subverted by the realpolitik and ugly battlefield slaughter of Branagh's *Henry V*, the pre-eminent American film critic of the 1990s is left with the impression of a film with mass appeal. Thus, although at times in his film Branagh resisted overt nationalism, his resistance was ultimately outweighed by a palpable appeal to British heritage and patriotism in the film's marketing. Peter Drexler perceives that the function of such 'familiar film codes' as individual heroism and the horror of war in *Henry V* is to 'reconcile the film's message with the audience's viewing habits'.[19] This was also a function of the distribution company for *Henry V*: to provide an image of a medieval English king that would be appealing to a contemporary American audience, employing familiar film codes such as the horror and the heroism of war. The potent iconicity of the Shakespeare brand formed another powerful mode of conveying that The British Were Coming.

As Deborah Cartmell indicates, just as with teen filmed Shakespeare adaptations, a bid for longevity via the school market is a significant goal for Branagh's *Henry V*: 'it is designed with an eye to providing a marketable teaching resource, a teaching resource which inspires appreciation (rather than 'understanding') of Shakespeare'.[20] This quotation recalls Jameson's distinction between connotation and representation.[21] Branagh produced a film that, in an instance of postmodern marketing, is both sold as a teaching resource and as an individual's free-handed adaptation and vision. Branagh is also adapting medieval and early modern historiography. Even in the light of its box-office success and appeal to the educational market, however, when *Henry V* was released on DVD in July 2000, it was with no extras or special features, as is also the case with the DVD of *Much Ado about Nothing*. Furthermore, despite initial claims that it would be released in June 2001 on DVD, the planned double-disc special edition of *Hamlet*, containing numerous special features, was removed from its release schedule by the distributor Warner Home Video and is now intended for release in 2006, to coincide with the tenth anniversary of the film's cinematic release. It is a significant omission in the history of the marketing of Branagh's films that his distributors have not fully deployed the powerful new medium and marketing tool of DVD.

One fundamental claim underlying the *Henry V* marketing campaign is that Branagh himself is capable of making decisions about how much of the text to include to make it as comprehensible as possible. He has become the self-proclaimed mediator between the now arcane, obscure or dull parts of Shakespeare and those parts that can be most readily adapted to become 'cinematic'. 'Branagh' came to form a powerful, branded shorthand for both filmed Shakespeare adaptation and the heritage movie genre, but Branagh was to threaten the status of his own brand name over the next decade or so by experimenting with less evidently 'authentic' adaptation in films such as *Love's Labour's Lost*. Branagh's appropriation of Shakespeare is characterised by an explicit transfer of Shakespeare's cultural capital from England to Hollywood, where Shakespeare could be marketed and re-exported to as broad and large an audience as possible. In the process, the Englishness of Shakespeare is both paid homage to, and reinterpreted back to a British, and global, audience through the prism of Hollywood film. Branagh integrates such film genres as the lavish heritage movie and the epic romance with a purported mandate of academic rigour. The outstanding Branagh marketing phenomenon was ultimately Branagh's own self-promotion as the mediator of Shakespeare to American cinema audiences, and his perception of Hollywood and Shakespeare as possessing equal cultural status, rather than the success of his films at the box office. Branagh's cultural politics and his reinterpretation of English history are well attuned to Hollywood's simultaneous search for cultural *kudos* and commercial success.

Alan Sinfield compares the deconstructive and appropriative ability of the Elizabethan stage to undermine 'the mystique of the crown' by stripping privileged monarchical symbols of their aura and putting them into 'broad cultural circulation' within the Shakespeare industry. Drawing upon a related theory, Walter Benjamin's concept of aura, it can be argued that Branagh's *Henry V* represents a post-auratic loss of mystique. In the same piece, Sinfield continues by arguing that the subjection of 'high culture to a market ethos' by what he terms 'the New Right' both 'undermines the mystique of cultural hierarchy and hence one of the convenient sources of state legitimation (the same thing has been happening to the UK royal family)' and produces two different genres of filmed Shakespeare: 'the determinedly inoffensive "commercial" Shakespeare films of Kenneth Branagh [and] dissident versions'.[22] To transpose this argument from a British political context, Branagh's films had to be on one level 'determinedly inoffensive' in order to be 'commercial' in the conservative cultural climate of Hollywood in the late 1980s. However, the broad circulation of *Henry V* in American cinemas reaffirms rather than deconstructs the sanctity of the monarchy, as the romance, pageantry and military elements within Branagh's adaptation of medieval and early modern historiography are the elements emphasised in the American marketing campaign. Although the film itself at times interrogates patriotism and nationhood, the selling of *Henry V* to the American market entailed celebration without subversion of the glamour of English monarchy and history. Although suppressing contemporary politics in *Henry V* might be considered more difficult than in some of Branagh's later filmed Shakespeare adaptations, the focus of the film's marketing is nevertheless on 'universal' themes to be found in Shakespeare, the horror of war, the redemptive power of love and courage, rather than upon any specific recent conflicts. The conservatism of the representation of Shakespeare is yet more strongly in evidence in Branagh's next filmed Shakespeare adaptation, *Much Ado about Nothing.*

Much Ado about Nothing: *from kingship to Keanu*

The marketing campaigns for *Much Ado about Nothing* and *Henry V* emphasise the significance of the distributor, Samuel Goldwyn, in determining the promotion of Englishness. Samuel Goldwyn distributed about eight to ten films annually and specialised in producing British films that purported to offer what Tino Balio terms 'an alternative to commercial Hollywood product', for example, 'Kenneth Branagh's *Henry V* (1989) and *Much Ado about Nothing* (1993), popular Shakespearean adaptations in the heritage film mould'.[23] Goldwyn recognised the potential profitability of a particular 'heritage' film version of Englishness in Hollywood, and Branagh's films form part of a long lineage of such heritage pictures that have proved to be successful exports to Hollywood. Englishness has a tradition of selling well in Hollywood in the guise of the heritage film genre from the 1930s onwards. Peter Wollen has observed that following the success of Alexander Korda's 1934 British-made film *The Private Life of Henry VIII* at the US box office, there was a notable proliferation of Hollywood films set in Britain and 'films which fell into what we might now label the "British costume heritage" sub-genre [. . .] largely based on classics of English literature or on adventure stories drawn from Britain's imperial past and present'.[24] The British costume heritage sub-genre peaked from 1935 to 1940, when George Cukor released his *Romeo and Juliet* as well as the Dickens adaptations *A Tale of Two Cities* and *David Copperfield* and the Reinhardt and Dieterle *Midsummer Night's Dream* was released. Goldwyn was the best-placed distributor for Branagh's work because of the company's track record in successfully distributing such pictures. On a budget of 8 million dollars, *Much Ado about Nothing* grossed 2.43 million pounds in the UK and 22.55 million dollars in North America on its initial cinematic release. The film thus exceeded the box-office success of *Henry V* in the key North American market.

Analysing the Branagh phenomenon in 1994, Michael Skovmand perceived the hostility he identified within British academia to Branagh as being based upon precisely the type of 'pervasive unease with his "politics" [...] crypto-Thatcherite, an entrepreneur with essentially commercial intentions' rather than 'his popular, anti-avant garde approach to Shakespearean film'.[25] Avant-garde films such as *Prospero's Books* could not excite the interest of a Hollywood studio as easily as the judiciously broad-based appeal of *Much Ado about Nothing*. Branagh's description of his priorities when filming *Hamlet* may be aptly introduced into analysis of *Much Ado about Nothing*, as those priorities remained unchanged from *Much Ado about Nothing* to *Love's Labour's Lost*:

> The style is a development of my other Shakespeare film work. Among its principles are a commitment to international casting; a speaking style that is as realistic as a proper adherence to the structure of the language will allow; a period setting that attempts to set the story in a historical context that is resonant for a modern audience but allows a heightened language to sit comfortably. Above all, we have asked for a full emotional commitment to the characters, springing from belief that they can be understood in direct, accessible relation to modern life.[26]

The following paragraphs will demonstrate how stringently Branagh's principles regarding casting, language, and the fusion of accessibility with a sense of historical authenticity were adhered to in the marketing of *Much Ado about Nothing*.

The marketing of Branagh's films foregrounds Shakespeare's accessibility and permeation of popular culture by emphasising set-piece speeches and soliloquies with dramatic music, camera work and close-ups. These cinematic techniques have the effect of alerting the audience to 'Shakespeare's greatest hits' within the film's narrative. Kenneth Branagh provides the most evident example from the 1990s of a director who employs Shakespeare's celebrity status to enhance his own reputation, as critics of his films have long observed. For example, Hal Hinson in his review of *Much Ado about Nothing* identifies Branagh's adaptation as collapsing the high/low binary in favour of the latter, to the detriment of the former:

> All the emphasis seems to have gone into making a movie about which the director-star could say, "Look, see how much fun Shakespeare is?" As a result, the film works moderately well as modest light entertainment. But after "Henry V", we had every reason to expect more from Branagh than Shakespeare dumbed down for the masses.[27]

Much Ado about Nothing does not 'dumb down' any more than *Henry V*, if the benchmark for 'dumbing down' is taken to be textual cuts or inclusion of populist elements. The marketing campaign for *Much Ado about Nothing*, however, was moving beyond selling a high culture and heritage movie to an emphasis on generic diversity and 'crowd-pleasing' elements, particularly physical comedy and spectacular settings.

Much Ado about Nothing marked the beginning of Branagh's extensive employment of American film stars, which functioned partly as a marketing strategy, and the casting of Keanu Reeves, most familiar from teen films, as Don John can be seen as an intelligent commercial decision rather than as a moralising, depoliticised statement about the play's tone. Branagh says of his decision-making process:

> I was determined, however, not to cast only British actors. I wanted a combination of elements that would exploit the novelty of doing Shakespeare on film [...] In crude terms, the challenge was to find experienced Shakespearean actors who were unpractised on screen and team them with highly experienced film actors who were much less familiar with Shakespeare. Different accents, different looks. An excitement borne out of complementary styles and approaches would produce a Shakespeare film that belonged to the world. As a long-time admirer of American screen acting, I naturally wished to include some US actors. In place of events, much of the action in this piece comes from the characters' emotional volatility. The best American film acting has always had this emotional fearlessness.[28]

Unlike *Henry V*, which stars all British actors, *Much Ado about Nothing* seeks to appeal to the US market through casting. Aesthetic aspects of the directorial decision-making process are highlighted by Branagh, whilst there is a reluctance to concede, in the context of Shakespearian screen adaptations, that Hollywood film-making is governed by how much money a film can make. This is part of a broader attempt at concealment of a film's financial objectives, a concealment paradoxically stemming from commercial imperatives, and it encourages film-makers to employ Shakespeare as a legitimising 'high art' element, capable of vindicating their commercial enterprise. Trinh T. Minh-Ha, a film-maker as well as a cultural-studies critic herself, observes of commercial cinema that it functions by 'eschewing the financial determinations of its images (or to hide it only to better validate it; hence the common habit of looking at films as "low budget" and "big budget") so that they can function more effectively as phantasy'.[29] The commercial aspects of film production are thus masked in favour of the aesthetic in a complex interaction between art and money that far predates Hollywood film. Shakespeare's unparalleled high-culture status provides a relatively straightforward means of veiling finance with 'phantasy'.

The American and British video and DVD boxes for *Much Ado about Nothing* differ in the genres they promote. The British version uses the poster image for its cover sleeve, emphasising the sepia-tinted heritage film look of the picture and displaying its ensemble cast. The American version for both VHS and DVD foregrounds the celebrity couple Kenneth Branagh and Emma Thompson, emphasising the film's status as a romantic comedy, and reducing the focus on British character actors, less familiar to a US audience, by picturing them as smaller. In the American image, Branagh and Thompson are the largest figures at the front, then, in receding order, the American film stars Keanu Reeves, Denzel Washington and Michael Keaton, and then a much less familiar couple are less visible at the top of the image – Kate Beckinsale (in her first film appearance) and Robert Sean Leonard. The video release of *Much Ado about Nothing* carries just one trailer before the feature presentation, for *The Piano*. *The Piano* matches the quality costume-piece marketing angle that characterises how *Much Ado about Nothing* was packaged for an Anglo-American audience, and both films mingle arthouse with blockbuster qualities. Both films also arguably cater for a post-teen female audience. *Much Ado about Nothing* is designed to create a particular 'look': bright (as opposed to the dark 'look' of, for example, *The Piano*, or *Henry V*), and that brightness is strongly in evidence in the poster and trailer for the film. This bright, accessible look facilitated the film's expansion beyond arthouse to mainstream; completing the process initiated by *Henry V*, and marks a move towards a more explicit catering for American audiences.

The trailer for *Much Ado about Nothing* reverently implies its consoling validity as an adaptation of Shakespeare in its insistence on the importance of listening to the play's language, a strategy mimicked in the combination of spoken and written words in the trailer for *In the Bleak Midwinter* analysed later in this chapter. A key theme of the play, the central critical issue in New Critical readings, was thus employed by Branagh: the actual Elizabethan pronunciation would have been 'Much Ado about *Noting*', and the play focuses on overhearing, spying and the power of words. However, awareness of contemporary critical readings of the play is an insignificant motivating factor in comparison to the reassurance for the audience that the play's language is not sacrificed or desecrated, even though large portions of the text are cut. A strategy of suppressing the difficult and dark elements to an even greater degree in the marketing of *Much Ado about Nothing* than in the marketing of *Henry V* was rewarded with greater box-office receipts, suggesting that the more conservative and generically identifiable the adaptation in the early 1990s, the greater the economic return in Hollywood.

The poster for *Much Ado about Nothing* in both America and the UK is a photographic image of all the principals, and is headed by the caption: 'Romance. Mischief. Seduction. Revenge. Remarkable.' This tag line sanitises the basics of the Shakespearian plot and ultimately reduces them to a broad cross between a romantic comedy and a thriller. The poster subtly exhibits the Shakespearian content by featuring William Shakespeare's name inscribed just beneath Kenneth Branagh's head, which forms the centrepiece of the poster. Branagh's name appears in the same-sized font as Shakespeare's, and that of the other stars of the film which appear above either Branagh or Shakespeare. Whilst the poster might suggest that it is Branagh rather than Shakespeare being employed as a brand name, Branagh's brand name in turn depends strongly upon his association with Shakespeare.

The marketing campaign for *Much Ado about Nothing* excludes any potentially disruptive elements from the film in favour of marketing a bright, scenic, pastoral film in the romantic-comedy genre. The film's marketing removes darker elements of the play, such as Hero's slander, from the sunny Tuscan ambience. A 'problem play' is transmuted into a problem-free play and the marketing, with its strong generic identity, plays a key role in this normalising process. Hence the marketing campaign focuses on the sunny fantasy world of Tuscany and the comic possibilities it embodies. In his review of *Much Ado about Nothing*, Roger Ebert notes that 'the film's action is a progression through a series of picnics, communal bathing, banquets, dances and courtships. Branagh sets the pace just this side of a Marx Brothers movie'.[30] Ebert situates Branagh's film version as a sanitised and at times farcical romantic comedy. The trailer for the film strongly consolidates this generic categorisation: the selected scenes emphasise 'banquets, dances and courtships' almost exclusively. Branagh's apparent commitment to the dictates of Hollywood genre entails a corresponding sacrifice of fidelity to the mixed tone of Shakespeare's play, in order to make a film that may be situated in commercially viable genres. Although this is a stark illustration of the limits of reverence, Branagh might argue that he is keeping faith with Shakespeare's own willingness to work with the grain of the popular theatre. The rarity of filmed adaptations of those other Shakespeare 'problem plays' *Measure for Measure* and *Troilus and Cressida* may be explained by their resistance to the easy generic classification and packaging sought by film distributors who feel the need to satisfy rather than to frustrate or challenge the generic expectations of the target audience. Sarah Keene, the PR for *Much Ado about Nothing* in the UK, worked to a brief from the Publicity/Marketing Director at the film-distribution company, Entertainment Films, and states that:

> In answer to whether Shakespeare is a help or a hindrance – obviously it's impossible to pretend that the films are anything other than adaptations of Shakespeare although if one is hoping to attract the biggest cinema-going audience (18–25 year olds) then Shakespeare is almost certainly a hindrance rather than a help. With "Much Ado" we felt that the film was so hugely enjoyable and with such a starry cast of names that would appeal to a younger audience (e.g. Keanu Reeves), that we would partially overcome the negative attitude to Shakespeare by good word of mouth and good reviews.[31]

Keene expresses the significant belief that Shakespeare is potentially a marketing impediment, particularly to young people, and she indicates that selling the film as 'hugely enjoyable' rather than educational or improving, less enjoyable qualities of Shakespeare, and as a vehicle for Hollywood film stars, is the best means of overcoming Shakespeare's negative connotations. Her remarks must also be situated in the context of the marketing of late 1990s teen filmed Shakespeare adaptations, which endorsed the same path of emphasising the pleasure of the viewing experience rather than, for example, the high-culture *kudos* of Shakespeare.

The voice-over for the trailer for *Much Ado about Nothing* accordingly positions the film generically as a Branagh film and as a romantic comedy rather than as a Shakespeare adaptation. It initially provides Branagh's directorial pedigree, 'He brought you *Henry V* and *Dead Again*', and continues by stating that Branagh will bring his 'unique excitement and vision to one of the great romantic comedies of all time'. This phrasing ensures that a wide range of genres are being deployed, not only the 'Branagh film' genre, but the historical, heritage picture, the noir thriller and the romantic comedy, assuring the audience of a directorial range that ensures *Much Ado about Nothing* will be a Hollywood film rather than an academic text. Branagh is also effectively equated with Shakespeare in this voice-over: it is his vision and adaptation of a timeless story and his genius is moulding his source material in much the way that Shakespeare did. 'Excitement' is illustrated visually by a fire-eater at a ball, and the trailer opens with the scene at the film's start in which the horsemen arrive in Messina, paying tribute to *The Magnificent Seven*. Hence, whilst being positioned as a timeless romantic comedy, the generic distinction is elided by the inclusion of action sequences that pay homage to the Western film genre, ensuring cross-gender and age-group audience appeal.

Neil Taylor places the success of *Much Ado about Nothing* and *In the Bleak Midwinter* in the broader context of genres that proved successful in Britain in the preceding decade, genres that Branagh emulates and successfully exports to Hollywood:

> The revival of British cinema in the early 1980s was characterised by nostalgic period films drawing on classic literature about upper-class life, precise and loving photography of sites of national heritage, and a focus on male rivalry and bonding. That sounds a reasonable description of *Henry V* (where the Chorus paces the white cliffs of Dover and the band of brothers bond with their king). For all that it was shot on location in Tuscany against scenes of Italian heritage, it will do well enough for *Much Ado about Nothing* (1993) too. And as for Branagh's *In the Bleak Midwinter* (1995), a lightweight comedy about some actors mounting a production of *Hamlet* on a shoestring, it is more about Ealing comedy Britishness than it is about Shakespeare's play.[32]

This quotation usefully reiterates the significance of the heritage movie genre, notably the films of Merchant Ivory, in paving the way for Branagh's Shakespeare adaptations. However, as will be seen in my analysis of the next three Branagh pictures, drawing upon the heritage tradition when marketing the films became insufficient as a stand-alone selling point in the postmodern climate of the late 1990s and new millennium.

In the Bleak Midwinter

In the Bleak Midwinter, as Branagh indicates, allowed him more room for experiment than his other filmed Shakespeare adaptations because it was a self-funded production: 'I loved making that film. I had complete creative freedom, having paid for it myself thanks to *Frankenstein*'.[33] Branagh somewhat disingenuously suggests that his personal project granted him 'complete creative freedom', implying that his sense of fidelity to Shakespeare constrained him from exhibiting that freedom in his other adaptations. The film is also an anomaly as it is not a full adaptation of a Shakespeare play; instead it incorporates scenes from *Hamlet* into a comedy scripted by Branagh. Released on 1 December 1995 in the UK and on 16 February 1996 in America, it grossed the modest sum of 346,839 dollars in the US. Released in American cinemas as *A Midwinter's Tale*, the alternative title's pun on Shakespeare's play *A Winter's Tale* makes the film's frame of reference more explicit for an American audience. The American poster for *A Midwinter's Tale* is a photographic image of all the principals, all wearing sunglasses with the sole exception of Joan Collins, by far the most familiar of the stars to an American audience and consequently visually emphasised. The film's trailer similarly indicates that Joan Collins's presence is one of the key marketing tools for the film in America. She is in the final two shots of the trailer, addressing the audience for *Hamlet* and emphasising her presence, while in the trailer for the British release, Collins features mainly as a spectator and Michael Maloney, a British stage actor little-known in America, is the actor who appears most frequently in the trailer. Joan Collins is not only a celebrity, she is a celebrity better known from popular cultural contexts, most notably for her role as Alexis Carrington in the long-running 1980s soap opera *Dynasty*. Her role in that soap ensures a high recognition factor for Collins amongst both British and, more importantly, American audiences, who are less likely to recognise featured British television celebrities such as Julia Sawalha.

When one of the film's characters, Mollie, learns about her brother's intention to produce *Hamlet*, her misgivings provide a fictional parallel to the difficulties Branagh faced in attracting a large cinema-going audience to his filmed Shakespeare adaptations in the 1990s: 'Great. Hello kids. Do stop watching Mighty Morphin' Power Rangers and come and watch a four-hundred-year old play about a depressed aristocrat. I mean it's something you can really relate to'.[34] This screenplay extract is a striking expression of Branagh's attitude to the challenge of marketing Shakespeare to a broad audience, and to the key teen audience, on stage or film. Branagh's solution to the problem of making *Hamlet* accessible is to combine reverence with pastiche. Branagh's two versions of *Hamlet* also display postmodern characteristics: *In the Bleak Midwinter* is a radical reworking and Branagh's four-hour 'full text' *Hamlet* interpolates sufficient scenes to significantly reinterpret the received wisdom about elements of the text. In a film with markedly more modest commercial aspirations than his other Shakespeare adaptations, Branagh is evidently at liberty to interrogate the framework of mega-entertainment and consumerism in relation to sacred literary values with more freedom than in films, such as *Much Ado about Nothing*, where his dissociation from consumerism is far less apparent.

Branagh's borrowings from other text and film sources are signposted much more clearly in the trailer for *In the Bleak Midwinter* than in the trailers for his Shakespeare adaptations that are marketed as more faithful. Whilst the viewer must identify *The Magnificent Seven* and Kosintsev as influences for themselves in the trailers and posters for *Much Ado about Nothing* and *Hamlet* respectively, the trailer for *In the Bleak Midwinter* chooses instead to focus on Branagh's 'magpie genius'. Thus, the whole trailer has the appearance of a silent movie, including written inserts, and theatrical clichés appear in the trailer that also appear in *Shakespeare in Love:* a lead actor complaining about coughing in the audience, as Will Shakespeare does, and a sign says 'the show must go on!' Once financial constraints were virtually removed, Branagh's distributors dared to make his anxiety of influence a marketing tool, and the film is marketed as 'A new film by Kenneth Branagh', rather than Branagh's re-working of *Hamlet*. Even so, when the trailer segues from auditions to performance, an explanatory sign saying 'the play' appears on screen, reassuring the audience that when *Hamlet* is performed there will still be the requisite degree of homage to Shakespeare's art. The trailer for the American market is driven by critical approval; it contains three quotations from critics: 'Spinal Tap for the Shakespeare set', 'Kenneth Branagh has crafted a masterpiece' and 'delightfully different and altogether wonderful'. These quotations perform the multiple functions of indicating that the film was well received by critics and of positioning the film reverently and irreverently: as a 'mockumentary' like *This is*

Spinal Tap, as a Kenneth Branagh masterpiece and as a novel and wonderful oddity. Such lauding of the production is replaced in the British trailer by genial eccentricity. The mannered irreverence towards Shakespeare exhibited in the marketing of *In the Bleak Midwinter* was replaced by a far more reverent campaign for Branagh's next Hollywood film production, *Hamlet*.

Hamlet: 'authenticity' and epic cinema

Branagh's four-hour *Hamlet* was released in America on Christmas Day 1995 and in the UK in early 1996, and distributed by Rank. In the period from 1993 to 1996, between the release of *Much Ado about Nothing* and *Hamlet*, significant restructuring took place amongst the largest Hollywood movie studios. As Tino Balio relates, not only was Goldwyn acquired by Metromedia International Group in December 1995, but in November of the following year, 'New Line Cinema and its art-house subsidiary Fine Line announced an operating loss of $19 million and soon after were put up for sale by their new owner Time Warner'.[35] This process of consolidation marks a broad commercial trend, continued by Miramax, particularly in the acquisition of part of its distribution network by Disney, in which art films were produced by studios rather than independents. The corporate power rebalance coincided with a change in Branagh's distributors, and with his move into more mainstream Hollywood film production.

Branagh's introduction to the published screenplay of his *Hamlet* suggests that he had difficulty finding finance for a filmed adaptation of the play:

> My attempts to finance a film version had been in motion since the opening of *Henry V*, but the perpetual reluctance of film companies to finance Shakespeare had frustrated each attempt. In 1995 Castle Rock Entertainment finally agreed to follow this dream, by financing a full-length version that would perhaps be followed by an abridged version at a more traditional length.[36]

Branagh's claim forms part of a much broader narrative, also employed by Miramax in their campaign for *Shakespeare in Love*, that depicts bringing Shakespeare to the screen as a labour of love by the director/auteur Branagh or fledgling, risk-taking studio Miramax, a labour resisted by the indifference or hostility of the major Hollywood studios, who inevitably privilege commerce over art. Ian McKellen's description of his search for funding in the 1990s suggests that Castle Rock may have been observing the profitability of filmed Shakespeare adaptations in the mid- to late 1990s rather than 'following a dream':

> Branagh's success with *Henry V* and *Much Ado about Nothing* and Franco Zeffirelli's *Hamlet* starring Mel Gibson were fresh in the minds of financiers whom I hoped to interest in another film based on a very popular Shakespeare play, which could be screened in mainstream cinemas round the world.[37]

As McKellen remarks in the press kit for *Richard III*, 'this project took off because film people got excited about the script. Whether they realised it or not, the person who excited United Artists was Shakespeare. I'm happy to be his agent'.[38] McKellen, a celebrity himself, positions Shakespeare as the authentic 'star' in this statement. He is also dismissive about the aesthetic sensibility of the 'film people', interestingly implying that Shakespeare's genius has the power to move them subconsciously with its magic despite their secular focus on money. McKellen, like Branagh, positions himself as the necessary mediator or agent between the sacred Shakespeare and the profane Hollywood studio, represented in this instance by United Artists. Indeed, film critic Mick LaSalle praises McKellen's *Richard III* for combining 'a shrewd understanding of Shakespeare with a healthy, low-brow approach to cinema', and concludes that 'the result is the best Shakespeare on screen since Kenneth Branagh's *Much Ado about Nothing*'.[39] It was the commercial success of Branagh's 'mainstream' filmed Shakespeare adaptations that made further film financing possible rather than his artistic vision. Castle Rock Entertainment had also distributed *In the Bleak Midwinter* and produced Oliver Parker's *Othello*, in which Branagh plays Iago. Thus, despite Branagh's claims that it was difficult to secure funding for Shakespeare films in the mid-1990s, Castle Rock was willing to finance Branagh's highly ambitious and risky epic project, suggesting that finding funding for filmed Shakespeare adaptations was no more difficult than finding funding for other film projects. However, Branagh's depiction of Shakespeare as a sacrosanct body of texts that film-makers have a duty to disseminate ensures that reluctance by Hollywood to finance Shakespeare films can be castigated as philistinism, inexplicable but 'perpetual reluctance'. Branagh's self-characterisation resembles that of Henry V, a visionary leading a small band of devoted followers to glorious victory against the odds. A parallel is also evident with Shakespeare's own mythologised biography; a Stratford bourgeois pushing at the limits of the London commercial theatre, much to the chagrin of the university wits.

Branagh's four-hour *Hamlet* was commercially unsuccessful in comparison to *Henry V* and *Much Ado about Nothing*: on a budget of 18 million dollars, low for a film of such epic scale, it grossed only 4.42 million dollars at the US domestic box office. The *BFI Handbook* lists *Hamlet* as the sixteenth least profitable film of 1997, with a profit to cost ratio of 0.471, whilst *William Shakespeare's Romeo + Juliet* was the twelfth most profitable film of 1997, with a profit to cost ratio of 7.1.[40] The box office for Branagh's *Hamlet* also compares unfavourably to the 1990 Zeffirelli *Hamlet*, which grossed 20.7 million, and was distributed by Warner Brothers, although the 2000 filmed *Hamlet* adaptation, directed by Almereyda, made on a budget of 2 million dollars, grossed only 1.57 million dollars. Reviewing Branagh's *Hamlet*, Richard B. Woodward suggests that, 'clocked at three hours 58 minutes (not counting intermission), this most faithful film version of *Hamlet* should bring the Shakespeare express to a screeching halt'.[41] Woodward rejects Branagh's quest for authenticity, and suggests that the earnest rather than postmodern playfulness of the project, signified by commitment to a 'full' text, were fatal to the film's commercial success, and more broadly to the profusion of filmed Shakespeare adaptations in the 1990s. Although subsequent history proves Woodward's contention regarding the 'Shakespeare express' wrong, *Hamlet* marks a turning point in the attitude of the press towards Branagh, obvious by increasing scepticism and a desire to query the potential profitability of his films. Certainly the sheer length of Branagh's *Hamlet* made distributors wary of giving it a wide release, one reason Russell Jackson compares *Hamlet*'s commercial failure with the success of *William Shakespeare's Romeo + Juliet*:

> Luhrmann's *Romeo + Juliet*, with its youth appeal and Leonardo DiCaprio as Romeo, must have seemed like a winner from an early stage. Although its budget was a relatively modest $14.5m., it was given the "wide" opening regularly employed with much bigger films: the distributors opened it on 1,276 screens in the USA, grossing over $11m. in the first weekend. (In the same season Branagh's *Hamlet* opened on three screens initially, and made

only $148,000 in its first weekend, although more cinemas showed it and more money was made in subsequent weeks.)[42]

In contrast to Luhrmann's *Romeo + Juliet* and other 1990s filmed *Hamlet* adaptations Branagh's *Hamlet* exhibits postmodernist elements but also possesses a self-consciously modernist epic scale. Branagh's justification for his version of *Hamlet* in the screenplay suggests that it is secular scripture. Branagh describes his initial encounter with *Hamlet* reverently:

> In the play itself and chiefly in the character of Hamlet I experienced the insistent hum of life itself […] I felt I had encountered a genuine force of nature, and on that journey home and for sometime afterwards, its memory made me glad to be alive.[43]

The focus in the press marketing on the film as full text and four hours in length also implies the existence of a Bloomian sacred Shakespeare text from which to work: stable, transcendent and universal.

If Branagh's *Hamlet* is contrasted with Michael Almereyda's, the epic aspirations of the former become apparent. The Branagh epic film is shot in 70 mm, creating a sense of quality and epic, whilst the Almereyda film is shot in 16 mm and is less than two hours' long. The final scene in the Almereyda film lasts about five minutes compared to circa twenty minutes in the Branagh, and although Almereyda's film does not modernise Shakespeare's language, its extensive cuts indicate that no attempt is being made at presenting a full-text version. However, Branagh's claim that his film represents an authentic full script is a marketing ploy rather than a scholarly reality, as his screenplay conflates the *First Folio* and elements of the *Second Quarto* such as the 'how all occasions' soliloquy, which only occurs in the *Second Quarto*. Although differences between versions of the *Hamlet* texts are an academic distinction unlikely to be noted by the majority of the audience for Branagh's *Hamlet*, their interest for this study lies in Branagh's desire to make an appeal to educational validity, whilst still providing the audience with the quality of verse and the set-piece speeches they would expect from a full text. The awkward combination of scepticism and pragmatism exhibited in Branagh's decision-making on the script indicates that, although marketing imperatives determine the degree of 'full-text' accuracy, the legitimate question of why it was stated to be the full text in the first place must be raised. Branagh's difficult project of reconciling scholarly accuracy with popular accessibility, as Shakespeare is famed for doing, produced a mixed achievement in the novel concept of a full-text *Hamlet* screenplay.

Branagh's *Hamlet* displays an attitude of defiance to both Hollywood conditions of cultural production and to the reverence/irreverence relationship. The full play text reconstruction of *Hamlet* was employed as a marketing point, and the American, but not the UK, poster advertises 'William Shakespeare's' *Hamlet,* even though the film's title in cinemas was simply *Hamlet.* This uncertainty in the film title branding process suggests that Branagh's distributor was particularly keen to emphasise the film's authenticity to the American market, but was willing to adopt a shortened title version for cinemas, perhaps on the assumption that anyone at the cinema would already be aware of the film's source text. Sarah Keene states of the campaign for *Hamlet* that:

> With *Hamlet*, the film was positioned as a classic version of a classic text. As there had been several other screen versions of the play, we needed a unique selling point for this version and so we did not shy away from the fact that Branagh's version was the full text on screen for the first time, a four-hour version. I hoped that the marketing and advertising would make a virtue out of this necessity by positioning the film as an "event", in other words I wanted them to stress the length so that audiences would approach it as a very special night out. However I don't feel that this actually happened in the marketing/advertising and I am sure the film would have drawn a bigger audience if it had.[44]

Unfortunately, the unique selling point of Branagh's *Hamlet* was not packaged in a manner appealing to a mass audience. Keene shrewdly notes that an appeal to improving high culture is insufficient in itself to ensure box-office success, and that it must be combined with an emphasis on the film as spectacle, or as she terms it, an 'event'.

Ironically in light of the repeated emphasis on the full-text nature of Branagh's filmed interpretation, by 2001 a two-hour version of Branagh's *Hamlet* was in circulation. Writing in that year, Bernice W. Kliman indicated that 'so far the shorter version has not been released in the USA or Canada but has been seen on Spanish television'. Her explanation of the rationale behind the decision was that 'according to pre-release interviews, Branagh had no artistic stake in the shorter version; Castle Rock Entertainment stipulated it for non-English markets and for airline screenings'.[45]

Such commercial logic on the part of Branagh's distributor casts a revelatory light on the attitude of the marketing team to the sacred text if it appears to be unmarketable. It also emphasises that the sanctity of the text breaks down in the crucial foreign markets, where fidelity to the English language 'original' text cannot function as a marketing tool. Ian McKellen's account of his quest for funding for a Hollywood film version of *Richard III* is relevant to this issue, both for its indication of the significance of celebrity in marketing Shakespeare and for the indication that films targeting a global audience cannot always rely on the traditional 'star' attributes of Shakespeare for their appeal, as:

> A large percentage of audiences for an English-language movie see it with subtitles or dubbed into their own language. So much for the selling power of Shakespeare's verse. Of course, if Ken or Mel or, best of all Arnie or Sly were cast as Richard, it would have been easier [to obtain funding for the film].[46]

Castle Rock's marketing ploy of a uniquely 'authentic' full-text film was replaced in favour of a more accessible, shorter film suited to the foreign markets and contexts such as airlines where a four-hour film might prove impractical. However, since, as indicated above, even the four-hour *Hamlet* film made unrealistic claims to authenticity, the distributor's reduction of the film's run time for accessibility must not be dismissed simply as Hollywood philistinism triumphing over the director's artistic vision. Commercial viability is arguably as important an indicator of the success (in this context a problematic term, blurring as it does both commercial and artistic judgement) of a filmed adaptation as aesthetic achievement, and maintaining a hybrid balance between high and low formed one means of fusing the commercial with the aesthetic. Peter and Will Brooker group Branagh's *Hamlet* with *Batman Forever*, *CutThroat Island* and Ian McKellen's *Richard III* as exemplary postmodern Anglo-American films, on the basis that they 'pick and mix' historical signifiers and poach self-consciously from earlier cinematic texts.[47] However, the postmodern qualities of Branagh's *Hamlet* are not emphasised in the marketing campaign, at a time when other marketing campaigns such as *Looking for Richard* and Luhrmann's *William Shakespeare's Romeo + Juliet* use their film's postmodern assimilation of other media as a selling point. It will next be indicated that *Love's Labour's Lost* also fails to marry its appeal as postmodern pastiche with its culturally accredited status as a filmed Branagh Shakespeare adaptation.

Love's Labour's Lost

Love's Labour's Lost repeated the poor commercial performance of *Hamlet* on its theatrical release in America, grossing 284,291 dollars. In the UK the film grossed 527,000 pounds. It was the first film made by Branagh after the formation in late 1999 of the Shakespeare Film Company, a production company dedicated to making films based on Shakespearian classics, with each film intended to be budgeted at about 16 million dollars. *Love's Labour's Lost* would appear to be an obscure and unlikely choice of play for a filmed Shakespeare adaptation. However, its minor place in the canon and relative unfamiliarity to a Hollywood audience compared to *Hamlet* or *Romeo and Juliet* enabled Branagh to make changes to the source material without sacrificing the aura of authenticity, at least outside the academy. The American poster campaign for *Love's Labour's Lost* makes it clear that Branagh is attempting a more irreverent, Luhrmann-style modern dress filmed Shakespeare adaptation. The four male leads wear black trousers and white tank tops, while the female leads wear party dresses, in a rejection of the heritage film period costume. The caption for the posters reads: 'a new spin on the old song and dance', a particularly striking example of film marketers translating the Shakespeare play and the musical into a fashionable postmodern pastiche. The full-length screener of *Love's Labour's Lost* released for video retailers in North America advertises the film as 'sexy all-star fun' on the box. Such use of eroticism as a marketing tool is emphasised in the trailer for the film, which features footage of the female leads dancing around chairs in corsets and fishnet stockings. The US poster features the four couples locked in embraces and grasping at each others' thighs. The overt sexuality of these scenes, as in the trailer for Branagh's *Hamlet*, is merely implied by the Shakespearian source material (for example, in the bawdy puns of *Love's Labour's Lost*), indicating that the foregrounding of sex is primarily a commercial decision, as it was in the marketing of *Shakespeare in Love.*

Love's Labour's Lost was released on DVD in the UK on 11 September 2000 and the disc includes five deleted scenes, the trailer, out-takes, featurette and a commentary. This marks a much more elaborate DVD production than previous DVD releases of Branagh's filmed Shakespeare adaptations, an indication of the huge increase in significance accorded to DVD extras in the film-marketing industry even in the years between the release of *Henry V* and *Love's Labour's Lost*. The American video-rental edition of *Love's Labour's Lost* also promotes the soundtrack in a trailer before the feature. Branagh employs a similar hedge to that employed in his *Much Ado about Nothing* and *Hamlet* for his casting of *Love's Labour's Lost*: a combination of British and American actors. The poster and trailer foreground the latter, particularly Alicia Silverstone and Matthew Lillard, stars of the successful teen movies *Clueless* and *Scream* respectively.

The visual employed on both the official site, poster and video cover for *Love's Labour's Lost*, which depicts a blindfolded Alicia Silverstone dancing with Kenneth Branagh, is also erotic, and significantly, the text employed for the tag line, 'Let's face the music and dance', is a quotation not of Shakespeare but of Cole Porter. The rumoured relationship between Branagh and Silverstone during the shoot also formed an incidental means of marketing the eroticism of the picture. Cole Porter is a home-bred American, significantly emphasising that where one expects a British Shakespeare to be, there is an American in his place. This arguably forms an instance of America and Britain's 'special relationship', a joint, and interchangeable, civilisation. John Drakakis interprets the use of Shakespeare quotations to be characteristic of postmodernism: 'with the endless circulation of Shakespearean quotations now sharing the same status as other forms of representation, we have entered the realm of the postmodern'.[48] The use of non-Shakespearian quotations to advertise a Shakespeare film takes the postmodern frame of reference one step further.

In an interview, Branagh's description of what he wanted from the tone and mood of the picture emphasises a kitsch Hollywood pastiche of Englishness, and safe, 'authentic' creative decisions regarding sets and costumes:

> Definitely something heightened, an atmosphere that was romanticised, highly glamorous, a safe world. I wanted it to feel like a terrific holiday romance which is interrupted by the real world, by the news that the King of France has died and by the advent of World War II. I liked the idea of that between the wars world of fading glamour. We wanted to build a sort of fantasy Oxbridge in which the power of love has the effect of increasing

the intensity of everything. So the colours are very heightened and so are the sets, the make-up, the clothes. I wanted the audience to enjoy a visual escapism that is also part of the fantasy of romantic love.[49]

The first sentence of this quotation could just as aptly describe the stylistic approach adopted in the making and marketing of *Much Ado about Nothing*. An idealised version of Englishness, Shakespeare and learning is presented in both films.

The film makes explicit a trend in the marketing of Branagh's films that is also evidenced by the casting of *Much Ado about Nothing* and *Hamlet*: a transatlantic set of aesthetic and marketing criteria. The film's PR campaign embraced this concept, as Sarah Keene describes:

With *Love's Labour's Lost* we had a very unusual film – a Hollywood musical from a Shakespeare play. We also had a very starry cast and we exploited them as much as possible. We stressed the singing and dancing in an attempt to convince the audience that this was an unusual and ambitious idea that was a unique film experience. But I think the combination of classic text and Hollywood song and dance routines was just too difficult an idea for the cinema-going public to embrace and the film did not perform well.[50]

Keene indicates that, although marketing a film as multi-genre can broaden its audience, the risk of confusing the audience is high. The campaign was characterised by a focus on the film's hybrid nature, to the detriment of box-office figures. Carol Hemming, one of the two hair and make-up designers on *Love's Labour's Lost* describes her intentions in the Studio Production Notes for the film in terms that have broader implications for the way it was marketed: 'it's a fantasyland, so we were creating a fantasy somewhere between Hollywood and the rest of the world and it's fantasy mixed with the 1930s. Some of it seems to be American, some of it Hollywood, some of it English'.[51] This description of fantasy also characterises fantasy representations of Shakespeare in Hollywood, an amalgam of venerable heritage with modern accessibility and provincial Englishness with global cultural imperialism.

John Drakakis relates this process to the loss of aura attendant upon the reproduction of art forms as postmodern parody, as 'parody *can only be* respectful to "cultural values" in a purely relativistic sense, since what it evinces is an implicitly politically inflected approach to an original rather than an identification with its cultural value'. He differentiates this process from 'that which asserts a continuity between the original and its subsequent incorporation into the structures of contemporary experience, in short, its iconic value'.[52] The process outlined by Drakakis is echoed by Christine Battersby's concern, centred on an accusation of patriarchal bias, that postmodernism feeds upon the canons of Great Texts and Authors formed by Modernism and its precursor Romanticism, leading to a situation in which 'established authors and *oeuvres* are dismembered and decentred via a process of rereading, reinterpretation and parody that fractures both *oeuvre* and tradition into discontinuity'.[53] Branagh's version of postmodernism follows this 'parasitic' process of dismembering the Shakespeare text but ultimately reinforcing the status of Shakespeare rather than actively deconstructing it. Although Branagh's films are marketed as authentic, Branagh's vigorous cutting and reinterpreting of the texts of *Henry V, Much Ado about Nothing* and *Love's Labour's Lost* conforms to Battersby's description of postmodernism.

Unlike the *Hamlet* campaign's assertion of iconic value in its marketing, the marketing campaign for *Love's Labour's Lost* stresses pastiche. Irreverence towards the Shakespeare text arguably reduced the film's audience: its drastic cuts reduce its value as an educational or highbrow Shakespeare rendition whilst its status as a filmed Shakespeare adaptation excludes it from the genre of light-hearted musical comedy. Branagh's distributors failed to exploit the rhetoric of generic diversity and high/low cultural crossover with the success that they had enjoyed with *Henry V* and *Much Ado about Nothing*. Marketed as perhaps a partial response to the success of Luhrmann's irreverent approach to interpreting Shakespeare on film, *Love's Labour's Lost* failed to capture an equally sizeable audience. This failure may be attributed to an inability to replicate the impression of reverence and authenticity that forms one key note of Branagh's carefully cultivated brand. Branagh's attempt at rebranding and belatedly moving with the times after the hubris of his *Hamlet* project resulted in commercial failure for a second time. In the case of *Hamlet* the full-text enactment is necessarily presented as a positive attribute in the marketing campaign, but in *Love's Labour's Lost* Branagh openly concedes that much of the Shakespeare play text has been cut for the film and replaced by Cole Porter dance numbers.

An on-set press preview promoting Branagh's filmed adaptation of *Love's Labour's Lost* notes that it seems 'only fair that, given the length of his relationship with Shakespeare, Branagh should ride the wave. But he could have been swept away. Lillard says reading a scene with Branagh is "like shooting hoops with Michael Jordan", but also that in Branagh's company, "I'm sitting with the grandfather of the Bard". It is a double-edged compliment.[54] The compliment is double-edged as Lillard draws attention to the unattainable nature of Shakespeare's status for Branagh whilst ostensibly paying homage to Branagh's attainment of celebrity status through his affiliation with Shakespeare. This passage creates an inverted lineage of celebrity: with Shakespeare as the successor of Branagh who is both on a par with a sports star such as Michael Jordan and prepared to impart his celebrity clout to furthering the career of his protégés Shakespeare and Lillard. Celebrity as popular cultural discourse appears in contexts such as the *Love's Labour's Lost* preview as a means of forming a desired opinion – that Shakespeare is a marketable commodity – to readers and viewers alike. In summary, with *Love's Labour's Lost*, the customary hedge is employed in the positioning of the film not only as a Shakespeare adaptation and a Branagh film, but as an addition to a venerable Hollywood genre as well. However, the Cole Porter musical form has insufficiently broad-based appeal to guarantee an audience in a Hollywood environment where reworking of the musical form, such as Baz Luhrmann's *Moulin Rouge*, is expected to be increasingly postmodern.

'Is he not able to discharge the money?'[55]: Branagh's diminishing returns

A 1999 feature in the American magazine *Newsweek* concludes that the Shakespeare brand name had unprecedented power in Hollywood by the turn of the millennium, as 'After 400 years of being merely the greatest of all writers, Shakespeare is suddenly an adorable guy and a pop icon'. This quotation depicts Shakespeare's popular culture status as recently acquired. The feature listed the most 'talked about' recent or current Shakespearian releases, such as Ethan Hawke's *Hamlet*, 'set in the contemporary corporate world. Hamlet's mother Gertrude, and stepfather, Claudius, says Hawke, are 'in a kind of Ted Turner-Jane Fonda situation'. Such parallels between Shakespearian characters and contemporary celebrities represent a marketing strategy intended to flag Shakespeare's universal significance. The article continues:

Meanwhile Branagh has formed the Shakespeare Film Company [...]

Branagh will do *Macbeth* with the Scots fun couple as a power-thirsty duo on Wall Street after the Millennium. And finally, *As You Like It* set in Kyoto, Japan. "Producers and financiers are much more savvy about this stuff", he (Branagh) says. "Going into a room and saying 'Hey, guys, I'd like to make a musical version of an obscure Shakespeare comedy' isn't as hard as it used to be".[56]

The article attributes this shift in attitude to the success of first *Henry V*, and then particularly *William Shakespeare's Romeo + Juliet*. Branagh alludes to both the significance of marketing a Hollywood film as part of a fashionable genre (the romantic comedy of *Much Ado about Nothing* has more obvious appeal to Hollywood studios than the largely outmoded musical form) and the significance of choosing a well-known rather than an 'obscure' Shakespeare play when trying to pitch a filmed adaptation of it.

However, by 2001, the outlook for Branagh's filmed Shakespeare adaptations appeared to be less auspicious, as Branagh deferred the production of two further planned films, adaptations of *Macbeth* and *As You Like It*. This was widely reported in the British press as a result of the relatively poor commercial performance of *Hamlet* and *Love's Labour's Lost*. The *Belfast Telegraph* suggested that:

> The Shakespeare film boom might be over … Branagh's films of *Henry V* and *Much Ado about Nothing* were widely acclaimed but his last Shakespeare film, *Love's Labour's Lost*, a Thirties-style song and dance, cost £8.5m to make but only took £527,000 at the box office.[57]

This apparent downturn in the fortunes of Branagh's filmed Shakespeare adaptations did not correlate to a broader downturn in Hollywood production and profitability. The domestic (North America: US and Canada) gross box office posted a new high for the ninth consecutive year, as receipts for 2000 reached a record 7.66 billion dollars. However, competition also increased over the previous decade: there were 410 theatrical films released in North America in 1990, but 478 films were released theatrically in North America in 2000.[58]

The average marketing costs of new feature films also rose very steeply in the decade 1990–2000 according to the Motion Picture Association of America's *2000 US Economic Review*. In 1990, in millions of dollars, the average total print and advertising costs for a film were 11.97:1.73 for the print and 10.24 for the advertising. In 2000, again in millions of dollars, the average total print and advertising costs for a film were 27.31:3.30 for the print and 24.00 for the advertising. Even more significantly in the context of this book, the marketing costs for the Motion Picture Association of America subsidiaries and affiliates rose steeply. This category comprises the studio 'classics' divisions, including Sony Picture Classics, Fox Searchlight, New Line and Miramax. As recently as 1998, in millions of dollars, their average total print and advertising costs for a film were just 5.47:0.62 for the print and 4.86 for the advertising. In 2000, those figures had almost doubled to average total print and advertising costs for a film of 10.14:1.18 for the print and 8.96 for the advertising, indicating that the increased number of screens that films such as *Much Ado about Nothing* were released on also carried greatly increased prints costs, and hence greater financial risks if they failed to make an impact at the box office. Distributors such as Miramax consequently had to cover their cost base by distributing profitable 'quality' pictures such as *Shakespeare in Love* and *Chocolat* rather than commercial disappointments like *Love's Labour's Lost*. These statistics place the postponement of Branagh's two further planned Shakespeare adaptations into a broader socio-economic context, and indicate why failure at the American box office is as proportionately costly as success is profitable.

Branagh implied in a 2001 magazine interview that a press conspiracy was responsible for reports that *As You Like It* and *Macbeth* had been shelved indefinitely. He countered that he planned to conduct a private workshop in summer 2001 with some actors on the screen adaptation for *Macbeth*, and that he 'hoped' to shoot it towards the end of 2002. He continued by indicating that 'once again, the media seem to have made up my mind for me. Reports of my premature retirement are grossly exaggerated'.[59] Although *Macbeth* remains on the back burner, Branagh's *As You Like It* is currently scheduled for production in 2006, with Bryce Dallas Howard slated to take the role of Rosalind. Three filmed Shakespeare stalwarts, Brian Blessed, Kevin Kline and Adrian Lester, are also on board for the film.

The media arguably conspired to ensure Branagh's success to an equal degree when he made *Henry V*, however. Furthermore, Branagh's box-office success merits interrogation. In the early 1990s it was based partially upon his ability to produce filmed Shakespeare adaptations on time and within budget, unlike, for example, Orson Welles in his film production of *Othello*, or the financial difficulties that prevented Olivier from filming *Macbeth*. Despite Branagh's claims that financing for his films was difficult to acquire, Castle Rock and Miramax were content to accept a smaller rate of return on *Hamlet* and *Love's Labour's Lost* respectively (*In the Bleak Midwinter* is excluded from this argument as it was funded by Branagh himself). Although this decision by distributors was based partly on the success of *Much Ado about Nothing* and *Henry V*, there was also a broader agenda. In exaggerating the commercial achievement of Branagh's films the distributors not only saved face on loss-makers in the domestic market, but also, as I argue throughout this book, Shakespeare provides Hollywood with 'cultural capital', countering the claims of 'dumbing down' with action films and summer blockbusters that Hollywood faced in the 1980s and early 1990s. Miramax in particular employed Shakespeare and other sources of literary adaptation to facilitate its transition to major Hollywood player in the late 1990s, as Chapter 5 of this book describes in detail.

Furthermore, by 2001, Hollywood's filmed Shakespeare adaptations were so copious that the specific Branagh brand name was a superfluous source of intellectual validation for Hollywood if Branagh was producing loss-making films. The omission of 'William Shakespeare' as well as the use of 'Kenneth Branagh' as a brand name in the marketing of Branagh's filmed Shakespeare adaptations must also be explored. Despite the desire to lay claim to authenticity in his filmed Shakespeare adaptations, Branagh entitled his filmed *Frankenstein* adaptation *Mary Shelley's Frankenstein*, whilst he did not preface his filmed Shakespeare adaptations with the title 'William Shakespeare's … '. This may be partly the result of the large number of B-movie Frankenstein horror films, which Branagh felt must be distinguished from his 'authentic' version in a manner not required by his Shakespeare films. Hollywood's apparent reluctance in the early 1990s to use Shakespeare's name in film titles was replaced by a vogue for using Shakespeare's name in film titles in the mid- to late 1990s. In the history of Hollywood, the Shakespeare brand name has never formed a marketing impediment in itself, and production of Shakespeare films has taken place throughout every decade of the Hollywood studios' existence, albeit with varying degrees of success.

The *idea* of Shakespeare as a marketing impediment is, however, widely employed by film marketers in case films under-perform – the Shakespearian subject matter can be blamed. The Shakespeare brand name paradoxically represents a hedging of risk, as marketers can cite successful Shakespeare adaptations in their defence if filmed Shakespeare adaptations fail, but if they succeed, the marketing of Shakespeare can be portrayed as a difficult obstacle overcome by good marketing. What actually failed was not the marketing of the Shakespeare brand name but the marketing of the Branagh brand name, a form of labelling which is essential for marketing and has been, as Braudy and Cohen demonstrate, from cinema's inception:

> Films needed to be distinguished from each other so that they could be recognisable to exhibitors and audiences, so that they could attract their particular fragments of the mass audience. Increasingly, narrative forms settled into genres, recognisable from posters, reviews and gossip, if not named by a specific label. Increasingly, the supposed personality of the performer became a means of describing or specifying a particular film.[60]

'Branagh' came to form a powerful, branded shorthand for both filmed Shakespeare adaptation and the heritage movie genre in the 1990s, but Branagh threatened the status of his own brand name by experimenting with less evidently 'authentic' adaptation in *Love's Labour's Lost* and in the posited Japanese *As You Like It*.

In an interview with Ramona Wray and Mark Thornton Burnett, Kenneth Branagh suggests that:

> The 1990s represented the end of an era in Shakespeare filmmaking. There was the end of, and a reaction to and a move away from Welles, Olivier, Kurosawa (a certain kind of Shakespearian film-making), which seems to have been reborn and freed up, so we might see a significant amount more.[61]

Branagh implies that Shakespeare on film was established as a valid cultural interpretation by a succession of talented predecessor directors, leaving him a cultural space in which to popularise the films. This space was also opened up by the need for Hollywood, and America, to claim to represent civilisation, a major reason for appropriating a cultural icon such as Shakespeare, as it had been in early Hollywood, when he was adapted as a means of culturally validating the new medium. In 1910, as Roberta E. Pearson and William Uricchio indicate in an extract from *Moving Picture World*, filmed Shakespeare adaptation was praised as it 'elevates and improves the literary taste and appreciation of the great mass of the people'.[62] Such self-legitimating belief in the educative and improving power of Shakespeare for the masses was reinvigorated by Branagh from 1989 to 2001. Branagh is a member of the universalist school of thought regarding Shakespeare's cultural resonance, as exemplified by Allan Bloom's 1964 claim that 'Shakespeare's humanity was not limited to England or to making Englishmen good citizens of England'.[63] Branagh's appropriation of Shakespeare as cultural capital is characterised by an explicit transfer of such capital from England to Hollywood, where Shakespeare can be marketed and re-exported to an audience as broad in composition and as large in size as could be attained. In the process, the Englishness of Shakespeare is both paid homage to, and reinterpreted back to a British, and global, audience through the prism of Hollywood commercial film. Significantly, Branagh's films are marketed as much as films in certain Hollywood traditions such as the heritage movie and the film noir, as they are as 'Shakespeare adaptations'.

Branagh's successful integration of popular forms with a purported mandate of academic rigour was intended to reach a mass audience base, and did so with considerable success until 1996, when the pendulum was allowed to swing too far from a popular to an elitist agenda with his four-hour epic *Hamlet*. Branagh's filmed Shakespeare adaptations form a model of Western cultural hegemony operating at the particular historical epoch of the run-up to the new millennium. The outstanding Branagh marketing phenomenon was ultimately Branagh's own self-promotion as the mediator of Shakespeare to American cinema audiences, and his perception of Hollywood and Shakespeare as possessing equal cultural status, rather than the commercial success of his films as measured by box-office receipts. Whilst the Shakespeare brand name proved more resilient than Branagh's at the box office, Branagh's (cultural) politics had shown themselves to be well attuned to Hollywood's search for the elusive combination of commercial success and cultural *kudos*.

CHAPTER FOUR

Hollywood teen Shakespeare movies

T HE TEEN AUDIENCE is a prime target for film marketers. Although the unprecedented quantity of teen Shakespeare adaptations in the second half of the 1990s onwards may be partially ascribed to Shakespeare's status as a teaching aid, producing a captive audience of sorts, an equally significant counter-current exists in marketing, exhibiting contradictory anxiety at Shakespeare's potentially off-putting high-culture status. This provokes a marketing strategy that could encapsulate the best of both worlds, in which both reverence and irreverence could be used to sell Shakespeare to the teen audience. The teen filmed Shakespeare phenomenon is a recognisably distinct genre from 1996 onwards, the year in which Baz Luhrmann's landmark film *William Shakespeare's Romeo + Juliet* was released, and the marketing of these films demonstrates the growing postmodern irreverence that characterises the latter half of the decade. The presence of Shakespeare at all in these films, however, also rests on the apparently contradictory argument that Hollywood can provide art forms to the teen market which contain high cultural capital. The five films focused upon in this chapter appeal in their marketing to the teen audience's assumed knowledge of Shakespeare, through in-jokes and quotation, although the same films' marketing evinces a contrary current, anti-intellectual and revelling in its own self-conscious irreverence, and appealing to the 'teenager as rebel' stereotype. The trends mapped in this chapter consequently indicate the necessity of revisiting Deborah Cartmell's conclusion that 'the film industry needs to confirm Austen and

Shakespeare as belonging to "British heritage"; accordingly, they must be marketed as conservative icons'.[1]

The marketing of teen Shakespeare adaptations promotes their status as postmodern parodies of their literary source material, but also demonstrates anxiety to market the films as exponents of the source text. This chapter offers a critique of definitions of the teen audience within film marketing, followed by an in-depth analysis of the marketing of three Hollywood studio pictures which purport to adapt virtually entire Shakespeare plays rather than lengthy excerpts from them: *William Shakespeare's Romeo + Juliet*, *10 Things I Hate About You*, and *O*, followed by analysis of two other significant 'free' adaptations: *Never Been Kissed* and *Get Over It*. Interrogation of the nature of the cultural or reading positions offered by the teen films must be accompanied by analysis of the extent to which the teen audience may be identified, and, more importantly, created, and read in terms of neo-Gramscian hegemony and post-Jameson postmodern theory. Even though the 'ideal' teen audience for a film marketer is not composed of marginal or oppositional youth subcultures, but the more conformist majority, skilled marketers are fully aware of the attraction of the non-conformist in the teen market. Furthermore, the tendency in, for example, both Angela McRobbie and Dick Hebdige's work on youth subcultures to automatically equate 'subordinate' youth culture with resistance is not a formulation borne out by the film-marketing model posited here, although it does overlap with the appeal to the rebelliousness of youth in the notion of irreverence.

The aspects of film marketing to the teen audience I will focus upon are web sites, the educational market and the use of Shakespeare in the classroom, both real and fictional, titles, VHS and DVD packaging and extra features, and reviews. Analysis of the marketing of teen filmed Shakespeare adaptations provides the opportunity to investigate whether the fusion of 'popular' and 'elite' modes of discourse may fulfil Hollywood's commercial and ideological objectives.[2] Analysis of teen filmed Shakespeare adaptations encourages interrogation into why 1990s Hollywood studios deemed Shakespeare an appropriate cultural product to market to the teen audience. Study of the marketing of teen filmed Shakespeare adaptations indicates that Shakespeare's texts were often presented in a diffuse or disguised form, in comparison to, for example, the presence of Shakespeare in the marketing of Branagh's films or *Shakespeare in Love*. Why Shakespeare was at times presented in this form is one of the questions I will address, by exploring suggestive connections between teen filmed Shakespeare adaptations and the place of Shakespeare in late twentieth-century education. Decorum of representation of Shakespeare in the popular media is a central issue in this book, and in the adaptation of Shakespeare for teen films even more was at stake than the retention of Shakespeare's aura: the whole manner in which teens, a supposedly particularly impressionable market segment, were educated in classic literature was placed under the cultural microscope, and with it, the issue of Hollywood's role as a responsible purveyor of culture.[3] The primary focus upon postmodernism within this chapter, as in my penultimate chapter on *Shakespeare in Love*, is the appeal of ironic knowing and how that appeal is transmitted through marketing to the teen audience. Hegemony theory is also relevant in determining to what degree the teen audience controls the output of Hollywood. The opinion of Jerry Bruckheimer, a highly successful Hollywood producer, is illuminating in this context:

> Often Pettigrew [Bruckheimer's screenwriter for *Top Gun*] would see Bruckheimer standing on the boardwalk, looking at the teenage boys and girls sprawled sunbathing on the sand. On one of these occasions he said to Bruckheimer, "I see. What you're doing is trying to get inside the heads of these teenyboppers and figure out what they want to see". Bruckheimer seemed honestly surprised. "Oh no", he replied. "You've got it backwards. Don [Simpson – his co-producer] and I *dictate* what they want to see".[4]

In Bruckheimer's polarised Hollywood industry insider opinion, it is Hollywood that dictates what teens see at the cinema, and the teens are not in control of the popular cultural forms they consume. Although his opinion may not provide an accurate indicator of the actual cultural transaction that takes place between Hollywood teen films and their audiences, it does provide an interesting insight from a significant influence on the marketing of Hollywood films concerning the relationship between Hollywood teen films and their audiences.

At this point some initial clarification of the definition of 'teen movie', as distinct from 'teen audience' may be helpful. When 'teen movies' are referred to in this chapter, the term does not signify films targeted at the teen audience, since those films constitute, as Jon Lewis describes, 'the vast majority of the mainstream product now that the industry has embraced the adolescent as its ideal audience'.[5] Rather, the smaller category of films both *for* and *about* teenagers will form the focus, specifically films about teenagers and high school that borrow from Shakespeare's plays. As an example of this distinction, despite the casting of teen film stars, such as the star of *Clueless*, Alicia Silverstone, and the star of the teen horror film franchise *Scream*, Matthew Lillard, in the Branagh film *Love's Labour's Lost*, the film was not marketed and positioned as a teen movie. The film lacks elements such as a high-school setting in its trailers, teen-orientated television advertising or a teen-orientated soundtrack: the film's Cole Porter music might be expected to appeal to an older audience. The difficulty of creating a taxonomy of teen filmed Shakespeare adaptations has been noted by some scholars of Shakespeare on film. Richard Burt's distinction between hermeneutic and post-hermeneutic manifestations of Shakespeare in popular culture leads him to argue that filmed Shakespeare adaptation, particularly teen adaptation, increasingly presents 'Shakespeare without Shakespeare'.[6] Burt's interesting 'post-Shakespeare' reading implicitly creates three different Shakespeares: the brand, the body of plays and the man. Such a tripartite structure helpfully undermines any stable concept of an 'authentic' Shakespeare. Adaptations in the 1990s spanned the first and second version and at times, as in *Shakespeare in Love*, the third as well. By analysing the degree to which these three versions of Shakespeare were marketed specifically towards teen audiences, Burt's methodological problem of taxonomy may be successfully overcome. The marketing of teen filmed Shakespeare adaptations, just like the marketing of *Shakespeare in Love*, indicates a highly complex frame of reference to and relationship with Shakespeare, best analysed in the context of the master binary, veneration and irreverence. It is next necessary to explore modes of defining the teen audience in more detail, and to relate them to the decision-making process for those marketing films to the teen audience.

Film marketers are of necessity concerned with identifying common interests among the young, to ensure their film has broad-based appeal. To some extent this overcomes inevitable market segmentation. It is well known that film marketing defines its audience in terms of 'niche markets', where groups of people are united by similar interests, tastes, disposable income and pursuits rather than simply age or gender. This is a useful distinction in this context, as the term 'teen audience' as I use it does not simply refer to people thirteen to nineteen years of age. Louise

Levison describes the relevant definition of the audience as constructed by film marketers in the following manner:

> Studios are particularly eager to make films for the teen and young adult market – usually defined as people between the ages of 12 and 24. Still the largest audience block, they made up 41 per cent of movie admissions according to the MPAA's 1999 "Economic Review". And those between 25 and 29 add another 12 per cent. Generation-X and Generation-Y tend to go see the same films.[7]

I employ the term 'teen audience' throughout this chapter to denote both the cinema-going audience and the target group that film marketing is aimed at. 'Teen adaptations' is the standard terminology within both journal and press analyses of filmed Shakespeare adaptations and marketing and scholarship analysing filmed versions of Shakespeare targeted at a high-school audience. The manner in which the teen audience is identified differs from one academic discipline and cultural context to another. In marketing and in a cultural-studies context, 'teenage' takes on a broader significance than the straightforwardly chronological. Lucy Rollin describes her decision to employ the word 'teen' in her research as determined by the fact that 'teen' 'seemed to avoid the over glamorizing of *youth*, the sociological tone of *adolescent*, and the negative Fifties overtones of *teenager*, while still suggesting all of the above'.[8] The teen audience is not a homogenous entity, it is multivalent and unstable. Regulation of the teen audience's use of the media by parental, academic and State forces must be linked to the Shakespeare phenomenon in the sense that the high-culture version of Shakespeare may be taken to represent a legitimate and laudable interest for teens to pursue.

The methodological problems inherent in determining the relationship between text and audience are most evident in analysing the teen audience. The difficulty of conducting meaningful ethnographic audience research is the most palpable factor in its under-researched status, but the constitution of the film audience is undoubtedly an area in which further research would be of use to both film marketers and academics surveying their output. This research would be most helpful and manageable with regard to specific target audiences, and could be complemented by further research on how film marketers attempt to 'construct' their audience to a certain extent, and how they reach their target audience through marketing. Although this chapter avoids extensive focus on audience reception in favour of close readings of marketing texts, further research could be helpfully supplemented by a survey of the teen audience which sought to analyse their preferences in terms of significant factors including 'viewing contexts', the type of venue or exhibition hall they attend, who they attend with, and their generic preferences in terms of content. This research would form a crucial extension of the work that has already been done on more easily verifiable aspects of audience such as age range and frequency of attendance, most notably by Kathryn Fuller, Rick Altman and Martin Dale. The useful statistical research conducted by the MPAA, particularly that organisation's 2000 *Motion Picture Attendance Survey*, although valuable, would be enhanced by a more in-depth study of audience tastes and preferences, and the degree to which particular marketing tools such as television spots and full trailers advertising films on youth television channels influence their choice of film.

In marketing terminology, the teen audience is a niche market: a group of people who share a strong particular interest, lifestyle or taste. Although fluid, this audience is inevitably regulated by the hegemonic forces of, for example, education and the media. A 'demographic' is a less specific tool to help define a niche, and specificity is appropriate in this context, in order for teen film audiences to feel a product is made for them. According to Angela McRobbie: 'without presenting youth as an essentialist category, there are none the less a sufficient number of shared age-specific experiences among young people which still allow us to talk meaningfully about youth'.[9] Nevertheless, it is McRobbie herself who acknowledges the significant methodological hurdle to be overcome in studying teen culture: universalism. Indeed, she argues that it is impossible to posit a homogenous 'cultural politics of youth in the 1990s'. Hence, whilst emphasising 'the importance of positioning young people as active negotiators and producers of culture rather than simply its consumers', McRobbie states that 'the very notion of a cultural politics implies a unity of focus and a direction which it is difficult to find in youth culture and which perhaps is not what we should be looking for in any case'.[10] I avoid an essentialist unity of focus in favour of the more productive theory of hegemony which informs McRobbie's argument. Paul Willis, David Buckingham and David Morley have all interrogated the idea that teens are duped and victimised by popular media, arguing instead that they possess a high degree of sophistication in their reading of cultural texts, a proficiency of which the media industry is very conscious. Their research forms part of a much broader debate which challenges the perception of consumers as easily manipulated.[11]

The interaction between the teen audience and teen films is hence a complex one which cannot be adequately explained in empirical terms, according to how many teens attend certain films, or by 'a theory of the ideal spectator inscribed in the text', to employ David Morley's phrase. Shakespeare's prominent place in secondary and higher education implies that he may be a 'pre-sold' product for the teen audience, but analysis of the marketing of teen Shakespeare adaptations indicates that this very factor in his appeal is also a source of anxiety for film marketers wary of alienating the teen audience with high-culture credentials. Targeting teens as the key cinema-going audience is partly based upon the concept that younger consumers are a more desirable marketing target because they have not yet formed brand preferences.

William Shakespeare's Romeo + Juliet

William Shakespeare's Romeo + Juliet is the film that in retrospect may be seen to have sparked the trend for adapting Shakespeare for teen films in the late 1990s, and it is the first filmed Shakespeare adaptation that positions itself towards the teen market in such an exclusive manner in its marketing campaign. Although *William Shakespeare's Romeo + Juliet* functions as a watershed in the marketing of (teen) filmed Shakespeare adaptations in the 1990s, it is distinguished from other films in the sub-genre as it lacks the social setting of the high school, and because it is more closely related to the Shakespeare text it adapts, despite extensive cuts and editing.

William Shakespeare's Romeo + Juliet names Shakespeare in its film title, and film titles are themselves both one of the foremost indicators of genre and a marketing tool. Luhrmann's use of Shakespeare in his film title has a twofold marketing effect, emphasising its close relationship with its source text and insisting on its 'authenticity', and drawing upon all the positive connotations that the Shakespeare brand possesses. The title selected for Luhrmann's film provocatively emphasises both veneration and irreverence: Shakespeare's *kudos* is invoked, but the playful use of the plus sign rather than 'and' indicates a desire to abbreviate and update the sacred material, placing it in an American teen vernacular. *William Shakespeare's Romeo + Juliet* indicates a space for radicalism within apparently conservative faithful adaptation in many more ways than its title, however.

The screenplay of the film, by Baz Luhrmann and Craig Pearce, was published by Hodder Children's Books, giving an indication of its intended audience. The introductory notes by Baz Luhrmann also target teens through irreverence, positioning the film as 'rambunctious, sexy, violent, and entertaining the way Shakespeare might have if he had been a film maker'. Luhrmann continues 'we have not shied away from clashing low comedy with high tragedy, which is the style of the play, for it's the low comedy that allows you to embrace the very high emotions of the tragedy'.[12] The repeated rhetorical trope in film marketing of referring back to Shakespeare's own popular culture status in early modern England to legitimise film adaptations emerges again here, and also underlies the claim to authenticity in the title. Luhrmann exhibits self-conscious awareness that he is operating on the boundaries of high and low culture, and that there are certain expectations of decorum that he is frustrating as an Australian director radically adapting the work of a British literary and cultural icon for a teen American mainstream audience. This awareness is helpful to those marketing the film as a successful fusion of high and popular culture. Luhrmann's book combines the screenplay with a version of the play. There are several possible meanings that can be ascribed to this form of marketing. The screenplay substantiates the argument that there is much conservatism in the adaptation, as it reverently juxtaposes Shakespeare's text with the film's abbreviated version. The inclusion of the play text emphasises that the screenplay can be used in an educational context, as a school study aid to be read in conjunction with the 'authentic' verse. It also situates the screenplay in the same high reading context as the play text, and it demands the same attention, signifying that this book is aimed at the high-school audience.

The educational audience for teen filmed Shakespeare adaptations in general may be envisaged as tripartite from a film marketer's perspective, as it includes those who know the play well already from study and who are most alert to alterations to the text, those who are approaching a film as an introduction to the play and those who are simply attracted to the high cultural resonance of the Shakespeare brand name. However, the mythical story of Romeo and Juliet's doomed teen romance has popular culture connotations that extend far beyond any direct relation to Shakespeare plays, and in the marketing campaign for Luhrmann's film, the 'classic love story' provides a crucial 'pre-sold' product for a teen audience: an aesthetically valued, educational literary text with an extraordinarily high cultural recognition factor. The text on the box for the VHS release of *William Shakespeare's Romeo + Juliet* depends on the audience's familiarity with the story being told, as it markets the film as a 'brilliant and contemporary retelling of the world's most tragic love affair'. This appeal to both the genius and the universality of Shakespeare's play is carefully complemented by focus on its bold contemporary relevance and the originality of Luhrmann's vision. Hence, the text on the VHS box also describes the film as 'dazzling', 'unconventional', 'futuristic', 'wildly inventive' and 'unforgettable'. The familiarity of the story rather than its status as a Shakespeare play is marketed, in conjunction with its postmodern reworking.

The two DVD releases of *William Shakespeare's Romeo + Juliet* in 2002 also exemplify the appeal of high/low hybridity to film marketers, as they position it as both a Baz Luhrmann film, directed by someone famed for his jouissance in appropriating high-culture forms (Shakespeare and opera) and transforming them into popular culture, and as a filmed Shakespeare adaptation. In conjunction with a DVD special edition of the film which includes bonus material created by Luhrmann as one of the special features, a collector's edition DVD box set of Baz Luhrmann's *Red Curtain Trilogy: William Shakespeare's Romeo + Juliet*, *Strictly Ballroom* and *Moulin Rouge* was also released. The marketing of these DVDs may also, however, be read as an appeal to generic diversity: the 'pre-sold' educational market for Shakespeare is combined with those who may be equally or more interested in the growing and Oscar-nominated oeuvre of Baz Luhrmann's films. Each disc is marketed with lavish DVD packaging and lengthy commentaries on the making of the films, creating the sense of a quality product which combines literary and cinematic high culture.

The DVD director commentary allows Luhrmann to revealingly explore his attitude to adaptation; in statements such as 'the idea in the whole film is to find modern day images and equivalents that could decode the language of Shakespeare'. Other crew members support Luhrmann's contention that the film blends reverence with accessibility, enabling 'Shakespeare's language [to] tell the story'. The production designer Catherine Martin states that 'ironically, the thing that was incredibly successful about this movie is that you [Baz] took the text as written by Shakespeare and because we clash it with a modern context, the language is clarified because it is articulated in familiar images'. These comments substantiate my argument that the film was sold as a way of 'reverently' and 'irreverently' leading audiences back to Shakespeare by decoding the text, placing it in modern contexts and using explicatory music and visuals. This sales pitch had worked very successfully for Kenneth Branagh earlier in the decade. A further piece of Luhrmann's DVD commentary parallels Shakespeare and Luhrmann's use of music for the purpose of narrative clarity, disingenuously overlooking music's significance as a marketing tool:

> One of the things about Shakespeare was that he totally stole popular culture or anything of the streets from low comedy but particularly he took popular music and just put them in his shows because that was a way of engaging his audience into the storytelling. Every choice we've made in terms of cinematic devices has been grounded in some reality of the Elizabethan stage. That has really been our motive in everything we've done here.

The profit motive was the equally significant motivator for both Shakespeare and Luhrmann which remains unmentioned. Luhrmann instead chooses to emphasise his concern with authenticity. Popular music forms one of the most potent means of marketing filmed Shakespeare adaptations to a teen audience: in addition to its stand-alone appeal, it performs the distinctive function within Shakespeare film marketing of reassuring the teen audience that difficult themes and language can be made comprehensible by judicious use of explicatory, familiar music.

Extending my second chapter's analysis of the significance of music in the trailer for *William Shakespeare's Romeo + Juliet*, the importance of music television in the film's campaign must now be examined. The film's British video release carries just one trailer, for *The Fifth Element*, a film that represents science fiction marketed to the MTV generation. This trailer is followed by an advertisement for music from *William Shakespeare's Romeo + Juliet*, primarily of the popular, 'indie' music genre. The popular music provides an accessible means of appealing to the teen market's cultural competence in both high-culture Shakespeare and popular music, and this soundtrack CD proved so successful that a second volume was released a year after the first in 1997. As Richard Burt records:

> The week before its U.S. release, the film sponsored the TV show in which Danes starred, *My So-Called Life*, with ads for the film blaring forth tracks from the first soundtrack CD […] That same week MTV itself aired a half-hour special on the film three times. The Special included segments that were introduced with semi-naked male and female bodies inscribed with the words "Family," "Honor," "Love," "Hate," and "Revenge" tattooed in Gothic script [...] It tries to reposition Shakespeare as something cool instead of something silly, feminine, or distasteful.[13]

The 'repositioning' was achieved primarily by the use of popular music on the soundtrack and by advertising on MTV.

Many characteristics of postmodernity are exhibited by the elements of the marketing campaign that the MTV campaign highlights: the blurring of different media forms, the combination of text and image in a dynamic relationship and the inseparability of cultural artefacts from their economic context. The inscription in Gothic characters of words that distil rather than quote from Shakespeare is a particularly potent demonstration of an apparent reverence to the Shakespearian text and its meaning that is really a pastiche of both the Shakespeare plot and the multiple signifier 'Elizabethan'. Soundtracks targeted at the MTV audience formed a significant aspect of the marketing and merchandising campaigns for *10 Things I Hate About You* and *Get Over It* as well as *William Shakespeare's Romeo + Juliet*.

The box-office success of *William Shakespeare's Romeo + Juliet* confirms that Shakespeare in the 'original' language can find a large teen audience, perhaps even more so than modernised adaptations with less guaranteed longevity as teaching aids, although visuals can replace or elucidate elements of the language to make the film more cinematic and comprehensible to teens. Another highly significant marketing tool was the official web site, which foregrounded Shakespeare and marked one of the first occasions on which a web site played a significant role in the marketing of a film.[14] Use of a web site in the mid- to late 1990s became a very significant new marketing tool for both studio films and independents. Jeffrey Zeldman, who created www.batmanforever.com in 1995, states of that site that 'it was the most popular movie-themed site of the year, and it not only helped market the movie, it helped market the

Web as a medium for entertainment'.[15] The medium was hence well established as a marketing tool by the following year when *William Shakespeare's Romeo + Juliet* was released. Young people are active consumers of the Internet, and the huge box-office success of the low-budget horror film *The Blair Witch Project*, largely due to word-of-mouth on the Internet, alerted Hollywood marketers to a significant new marketing tool.[16] The marketing of teen films emphasises the power of the individual teen audience member's consumer vote and opinion, through such devices as feedback icons on the film's web sites. Feedback icons grant the teen audience a 'stake' in the success of a given film, as well as providing a useful form of market research to film marketers.

However, simultaneously, film marketers strive to merge teen individuals into enormous target groups. The ethos of the film industry can in part be blamed for a reductive attitude towards the critical acuity of teens, as marketing rationales such as film-genre theory stress the primary significance of industry discourse and its hegemonic power over the cinema-going audience. If film marketers do represent a hegemonic domination, they must at least ensure that they appear to be catering to the needs and sensibilities of the teen audience at all times, rather than creating or containing that audience with their products. The biography of Shakespeare on the web site for *William Shakespeare's Romeo + Juliet* parodies teen-orientated advertising and adopts a colloquial tone, as the following extract indicates:

> the Bard's group was bad. They kicked ass so bad his competitors used to send out speed writers, shorthand artists and bribe other actors in his plays to try to make their own bootlegged copies of his plays. The unauthorized "boots" were known as "The Bad Quartos". (Weird but true.)[17]

An interesting implicit analogy is made with rap music in the term 'had the rhymes': rap is a subversive, irreverent medium associated strongly with teen culture. The web site also knowingly plays with the issue of textual controversy in Shakespeare, and inverts it in order to ironically affirm the play's universal authenticity. Thus, even inaccurately transcribed versions of Shakespeare's plays are reread as 'bad' in the sense of superior, cool and empowering.

Making a broader point that may be usefully applied to the film's web site, Deborah Cartmell reads the self-reflexive nature of 'successful adaptations' as producing:

a comment on their own constructions, either through self-reflective imagery or intertextual links to other screen adaptations of Shakespeare. Success is achieved not by rubbishing the original but by revering the original; the successful adaptation must make it clear that it is – and can only be – a pale version of the Shakespearean text.[18]

Although Cartmell's emphasis on reverence is appropriate, not all Hollywood filmed Shakespeare adaptations display such respect in their marketing. Cartmell also downplays the difference between the necessity of exhibiting a certain degree of humility towards Shakespeare when adapting him and the elitist idea that filmed Shakespeare adaptations cannot succeed on their own aesthetic terms. In the same manner, film marketing employs postmodern irony and pastiche in its promotion of Shakespeare but ultimately reiterates the supremacy of its original 'script source'; as the web site promoting *William Shakespeare's Romeo + Juliet* indicates: 'Shakespeare had the rhymes. Everybody knew it'. The web site for the film displays a complex mix of reverence and irreverence in its response to Shakespeare's cultural capital. The fundamental commercial consideration is whether this film can be marketed so that the teen audience is persuaded to see it at the cinema both because of, and, paradoxically, despite its source material. Marketed in popular cultural media such as MTV, the film has also been rapidly appropriated as a teaching aid in schools and universities.

The image that forms the centrepiece of the web site's home page notably places even more emphasis on the violent content of *William Shakespeare's Romeo + Juliet* than the trailers and posters for the film which I considered in my second chapter. The couple are placed in the centre of the image, kissing passionately beneath the flaming, fiery heart which forms a pervasive logo for the film throughout its marketing. On either side of the lovers, massed gunmen and disembodied hands holding pistols point their weapons towards the oblivious couple. The image forms a memorable means of conveying both the crux of the story, the preordained tragedy of Romeo and Juliet, and the hip modernity of the film's interpretation of that story: the juxtaposed image of guns and lovers recalls, amongst many other film posters and web site images, those created to promote the 1993 Quentin Tarantino film *True Romance*.

The official web site thus markets *William Shakespeare's Romeo + Juliet* as entertaining, but the educational value is also stressed. An entertaining and sensitively adapted version of *Romeo and Juliet*, which retains the original text, can form a successful educational tool by virtue of its ability to entertain and nurture an enthusiasm for Shakespeare in the teen audience. The web site contains an entire section on 'The Author', and positions him as an English celebrity whose success rests on his ability to combine popular culture with the culture of the elite in the manner of an American film or rock star, or indeed Baz Luhrmann. The 'Author' section features a parody of the Chandos portrait which displays Shakespeare wearing a baseball cap backwards inscribed with the word 'Bill', in the manner of a rap star. The picture recalls Al Pacino's baseball-cap-wearing in *Looking for Richard* and reiterates the equation the web site makes between Shakespeare and rock stars:

> Theatre of the time was enjoyed by commoners as well as the privileged. Often the audiences were completely illiterate. Public theatres like THE HOPE, THE FORTUNE, THE RED BULL and THE SWAN were "open air" so the players had to compete with livestock sales, screaming street hawkers, and the ubiquitous drunks. To reach this crowd Shakespeare could not rely on a large stack of amplifiers. He needed the most electrifying words and images ever created in the English language. Concepts that would galvanize common people and make them stop, lose themselves, rise above the muck for an hour or two. It was crass. It was business. It was art. And it was genius. Shakespeare had the rhymes. Everyone knew it.[19]

Highbrow, transcendent elements of the Shakespeare myth are emphasised alongside the concrete, bathetic realities of Elizabethan existence, blurring the indistinct boundaries between high and low culture and providing a version of universalism. Emphasis upon parallels between sixteenth- and twentieth-century entertainments averts the alienation factor of an unfamiliar historical milieu, and the well-established vision of Shakespeare producing high art within the popular forms of the day is reiterated. It is interesting that high-culture appeal appears to be pointedly omitted here; there is no reference to the court, monarchy or aristocracy as there is in *Shakespeare in Love*, and Shakespeare's original context is presented as entirely popular. Explicit transposition of Shakespeare from Elizabethan England to the advertising discourse of late twentieth-century America is of particular relevance to this book, as the use of Shakespeare as a marketing tool is made explicit through the language transition. Shakespeare's celebrity status is ironically subverted but subsequently reiterated, as, for example, his methods of writing and creative sources are mocked in order to reinforce his genius on the web site for *William Shakespeare's Romeo + Juliet.*

Luhrmann's approach to Shakespeare is legitimised by emphasising Shakespeare's own revolutionary approach. Describing Shakespeare's theatre as 'crass' and 'business' not only reinforces the negative set of connotations that commerce carries in relation to art but also grants Luhrmann's version of the celebrity Shakespeare a marketable rebelliousness. The web site provides further evidence that Shakespeare's status as an establishment figure is inverted in the marketing of teen Shakespeare films. Negative critical and academic responses to *William Shakespeare's Romeo + Juliet* centre on the accusation that reducing the intellectual challenges posed by engagement with the play is an inevitable corollary of updating the play for the MTV generation. Thus, for example, Desson Howe asks 'how far do you take such license before losing relevance to the play?', Stephanie Zacharek describes it as 'a travesty – a film that turns the play's characters into broad caricatures', and Mick LaSalle declares that it is a 'monumental disaster' in a piece entitled 'This "Romeo" is a True Tragedy, DiCaprio, Danes Weak in Shakespeare Update'.[20] These critical responses are not new arguments, and have been powerfully expressed from Leavisite hostility to popular culture onwards. A shared concern of Cultural Studies and English Literature, and beyond, in the late twentieth century focused upon the impact of mechanical reproduction and the fear of losing 'our' cultural inheritance. New media such as the Internet illustrate the challenges facing those retaining Arnoldian, Leavisite or Bloomian assumptions of high cultural and aesthetic purity. Shakespeare's simultaneous portrayal by film marketers as a genius and an individual operating within the inevitable confines of history, as in the extract from the web site for *William Shakespeare's Romeo + Juliet,* indicates ambivalence towards the aesthetic validity of popular culture. Richard Burt's attack upon the film exemplifies such ambivalence, as he argues that it:

> dumbs down Romeo and Juliet in order to show how their suicides issue from their participation in Verona Beach's gang banging, drug taking, party-all-night-long family feud rather than from their rejection of it, has literally to retard itself [...] in order to make its pedagogical point clear to its targeted teen audience. These American films and television episodes are not simply inane, I hope it is clear. But neither are they redeemable

through some kind of political analysis that would seek to convert ostensibly trivial texts into serious (i.e. political) texts.[21]

Burt's analysis of both teen mentalities and popular culture exhibits unease at their relation to high culture and education. His analysis furthermore demonstrates some of the methodological difficulties of critiquing a high-school Shakespeare film with the same set of criteria that are used to discuss a written, canonical text: such as whether it is intelligent, educational and 'faithful' to the original text.

William Shakespeare's Romeo + Juliet challenges the traditional binary between high and low culture, sixteenth- and twentieth-century media, by direct confrontation, using tools such as a television news framing device to explicate the film's narrative. These tensions are also extensively addressed in the marketing on both the web site and the poster. The 1996 film's marketing campaign marks a chronological transition point in the 1990s, in terms of both the degree of referencing of Shakespeare in its marketing, which reached its peak in this film, and the particularly patent use of hybridity, emphasising both highly irreverent appropriations of Shakespeare by Luhrmann and fidelity to the 'original' text. It is marketed as a film that can make Shakespeare appeal to a teen audience on an unprecedented scale. In its appeal to the teen audience and its careful maintenance of high/low hybridity, it is also a remarkably consistent marketing campaign, coordinated in a manner that ensures the key messages, that Shakespeare can be both high and low, British and American, and educational and fun, are conveyed forcefully. Subsequent teen filmed adaptations, appearing on the back of Luhrmann's success, display a much more cautious referencing of Shakespeare and a desire to market the films primarily as teen movies rather than Shakespeare adaptations. Discrepancies between the boldness of the marketing of Luhrmann's transformation and appropriation of Shakespeare for the teen audience, and the conservatism, caution and unease with which Shakespeare was introduced into the marketing material in the case of *10 Things I Hate About You* must next be investigated.

10 Things I Hate About You

Analysis of the marketing campaign for *10 Things I Hate About You*, a 1999 teen adaptation of *The Taming of the Shrew*, indicates the extent to which commercially driven interactions between high and low culture govern the inclusion of Shakespearian material in film marketing. Aspects of the shrew's taming which sit uneasily with late twentieth-century gender politics are adapted in the film and removed from the marketing for *10 Things I Hate About You*. Katherine's famous 'obedience speech' is partially inverted in a scene where Kat recites a sonnet in which she expresses her love for Patrick but also recounts occasions when he has behaved badly to her. The trailer excludes this scene, possibly in order to avoid revealing the final scene, but also positioning the film generically as a straightforward romantic and familial comedy. The trailer focuses on the blossoming love affairs of both Kat and Bianca, positioning it as a romantic comedy with broad-based appeal. The distributor of *10 Things I Hate About You* was risk-averse in avoiding any reference to the brutality of the taming that takes place in the film's source play. Spousal abuse is no longer considered a suitable topic for popular comedy as it was for an Elizabethan audience. Just as in Branagh's *Much Ado about Nothing*, excision from source text to film of putative disturbing elements was intensified in the transition from film to marketing campaign for *10 Things I Hate About You*. An acceptable modern-day Kat might be expected not only to resist taming but to fight back aggressively. The poster seeks to sell the film by reinforcing Kat's empowerment: her stance in the centre foreground of the assembled cast photograph displays her wilful display of superiority over the other featured characters, and she is the central figure towards whom the viewer's eye is drawn. The visual centrality of Kat also enables the marketers to draw on the cultural capital of Julia Stiles's (Kat's) celebrity.

The marketing campaign for *10 Things I Hate About You* broadly displays more hesitancy in referring to its borrowings and assimilation from Shakespeare than the campaign for *William Shakespeare's Romeo + Juliet*. Film marketers grounded the appeal of *10 Things I Hate About You* in recognisable yet socially desirable settings. Rather than being taught in the classroom, the Shakespearian plot is placed in school corridors, parties, cars, sports events and suburban houses in the trailer for *10 Things I Hate About You*. The closing scene exhibits Kat rewriting a Shakespeare sonnet to describe her own troubled love affair – an explicit appeal to the relevance of Shakespeare for the teen audience today. She successfully shifts Shakespeare into her own context, exemplifying adaptation and granting it legitimacy. The sonnet Kat recites also forms the source of the film's title, so it is sign posted in the film marketing. Such rewriting of high culture grants teens the illusion of empowerment, and control over the cultural products they consume.

Although there are numerous similarities between *The Taming of the Shrew* and *10 Things I Hate About You*, these common features are not replicated in the film's poster, trailer, web site, television spots and newspaper advertisements, the latter of which use the poster image for their graphic. In both play and film there are two sisters, the elder being unmanageable and short-tempered, the younger being the source of much adulation and more conventionally attractive in looks and personality. Just as *Shakespeare in Love* has a vast array of Shakespearian references, varying from obvious to obscure, so *10 Things I Hate About You* has Shakespeare references of varying subtlety within the film that serve the purpose of allowing those who spot them to feel knowledgeable whilst those who do not are not aware that they ought to be looking for them. The DVD box text describing the film does not mention Shakespeare, selecting instead to emphasise the following points:

> A cool cast of young stars is just one of the things you'll love about this hilarious comedy hit. On the first day at his new school, Cameron (Joseph Gordon-Lewitt – *Halloween: H2o*, television's *3rd Rock from the Sun*) instantly falls for Bianca (Larisa Oleynik – *The Baby-Sitters Club*), the gorgeous girl of his dreams. The only problem is that Bianca is forbidden to date until her ill-tempered, completely un-dateable older sister Kat (Julia Stiles – *Wide Awake*) goes out, too. In an attempt to solve his problem, Cameron singles out the only guy who could possibly be a match for Kat: a mysterious bad boy (Heath Ledger – *The Patriot*) with a nasty reputation of his own. Also featuring a hip soundtrack – this witty comedy is a wildly entertaining look at exactly how far some guys will go to get a date.

Despite the exclusion of Shakespeare from this text, the front cover art of the DVD box features the tag line, 'How do I loathe thee? Let me count the ways' prominently beneath the cover art, which, although paraphrasing Elizabeth Barrett Browning, has a faux-Shakespearian quality and deploys antiquated language which evokes literary adaptation.

In the film's marketing campaign, the level of referencing of the source material is evasive. The film's trailer, for example, is very high-school orientated, and in its brief thirty-second run time, the condensed trailer makes no reference to Shakespeare, instead showing the protagonists in settings including a sports stadium, a nightclub, an archery field and a paintball contest. These settings reassure the audience that the film is an irreverent teen comedy as well as a literary adaptation. The trailer also focuses upon the lead actress Julia Stiles. Stiles's celebrity power was considered strong enough to sell products in Hollywood. Her celebrity has been linked in other press reports to Shakespeare. One article pronounces Julia Stiles to be 'a one-teen Shakespeare explosion by herself';[22] a reference to Julia Stiles's other roles as Desi, the Desdemona character in *O* and Ophelia in Ethan Hawke's 2000 version of *Hamlet*. *Premiere* magazine expands upon the marketing of Stiles as a Shakespeare star:

> He may be a pillar of English literature, but William Shakespeare has also become Hollywood's hot new writing flavour – at least six of his plays are currently being adapted for the big screen. *Wicked* actress Julia Stiles is starring in half of them. "There's just so much depth to Shakespeare", Stiles says. "It's always going to be open to new interpretations". The eighteen-year-old actress especially relished her role as Kat, the anything-but-tame update's shrew. "She was such a strong thinker", Stiles says. "We need that in Hollywood now".[23]

Several significant, complex marketing tactics are employed here. Whilst Shakespeare's status in English literature is affirmed, his appropriation by Hollywood as a screenwriter is acknowledged to be a potential handicap to overcome. Shakespeare's 'depth' is read primarily in terms of his status as a mine for reworking, and the article also provides the opportunity to emphasise the reworking of *The Taming of the Shrew* to suit modern sensibilities. Kat's tough, opinionated, intelligent, feminist stance, emphasised in the poster, trailer, web sites and newspaper advertisements for the film, is a marketing theme replicated in the article.

The former editor of *Empire*, Emma Cochrane, confirms the significance of Stiles as a marketing tool: 'we are also due for the next generation of teen talent to break through, and their popularity will also spur these productions on. It helps to have a Leo or Julia Stiles in a leading role'.[24] The association with Shakespeare in turn assists DiCaprio and Stiles, granting them substance as actors who can 'do Shakespeare' as well as light entertainment. The research of P. David Marshall in the field of semiotic analysis of the cultural phenomenon of the, as he terms it, 'commodity status' of celebrity provides a theoretical model from which to 'assess the ideological function of the celebrity in the construction of consumer capitalism'.[25] Julia Stiles is branded as a celebrity partially trading off the fame of the greater celebrity William Shakespeare, a feat Kenneth Branagh had accomplished with such success in the early 1990s.

Film marketers equated the teen audience with resistance in the official web site, a resistance that can only be overcome by making Shakespeare fashionable. The film's distributor-created web site exclusively targeted a teen audience, to the extent that it commanded all adults to stay away, emphatically stating 'ALL POSERS STAY OUT! If you've already graduated and you're still coming to this site, get a life. To all moms and dads: Gestapo tactics don't work! If you want to know what we do, just ASK!'[26] This significantly suggests that graduates and similar 'posers' may have an interest in the site, perhaps because of the Shakespearian connection. The salient point here is that figures of cultural authority, such as parents and those who have successfully graduated from high school, are 'posers' if they continue to demonstrate an interest in the activities of teens. They are represented as trying unsuccessfully to recapture 'hip' youth culture. Thus the film marketers align themselves with teens in opposition to other authority figures attempting to impose a dull version of Shakespeare. Marketing to teen culture requires such hostility, as youth culture can only be defined in opposition to adult culture. Hostility here can take the form of aggressive reappropriation, alteration or recuperation of Shakespeare. Modernisation furthermore enables a fashionable and accessible version of Shakespeare to be saved from the 'posers' who wish to confine him to dull high-culture contexts.

The prominent *New York Times* film critic Stephen Holden, in a review significantly entitled '*10 Things I Hate About You:* It's Like, You Know, Sonnets and Stuff', notes that:

> Among the crop of recent teen-age movies whose plots parody stories from classic literature, "10 Things I Hate About You" [...] tries the hardest of any to season its screenplay with authentic Shakespearian touches. Students in a writing class at Padua High School (somewhere around Seattle) are asked to create sonnets. There is an Elizabethan-theme prom that inspires some fancy hairdos and fetching costumes. And every now and then the banter among the characters incorporates actual Shakespearian quotations. If it's all very clever for a teen-age film, it also feels terribly forced. One of the many delightful things about "Clueless",

the movie that started it all, was a glove-smooth fit of Jane Austen's "Emma" on a teen-age comedy of manners. You barely sensed Austen's presence.[27]

This review supports the possibility that teen filmed Shakespeare adaptations may be the film industry's response to the accusation that it is culturally illiterate, and encapsulates the censorious air some film critics and academics adopt towards teen movies, and those with the temerity to adapt Shakespeare into a popular cultural context. The use of the term 'parody' places Stephen Holden in the school of thought that objects to the postmodern updating of Shakespeare on film. This review also notes that these teen films borrow as much from each other as they do from classic literature, going on to cite a range of similarities, of varying persuasiveness, between *10 Things I Hate About You* and *She's All That*. These comparisons must be tempered by consideration of generic conventions, as film-genre expert Thomas Schatz emphasises: 'As a popular film audience, our shared needs and expectations draw us into the movie theater. If we are drawn there by a genre film, we are familiar with the ritual'.[28]

Holden concludes by noting that the film is 'rated PG-13 (Parents strongly cautioned) [as] it abounds with off-color humor'.[29] This certification crystallises the contention that Shakespeare is considered a means of making certain difficult topics such as bawdy humour 'safe', both morally and educationally, for a teen audience. The teen audience is catered for with 'off-color humor', but this is offset by the film's Shakespeare references. A *Salon* review detects the sanitising process required for *The Taming of the Shrew* to become a teen film:

> Although "Shrew" is easily one of Shakespeare's funniest works, it's also one of the hardest for modern audiences to wrap their egalitarian sensibilities around [...] For all the play's 16th century genius, its Stepford wife-style emotional lobotomizing doesn't quite float in the contemporary high-school genre. So instead, "10 Things" is a classic comedy of misunderstandings, false starts and, eventually true love – all tempered with the very 20th century point of view that if the guy is strong enough, the girl doesn't need to be weak [...] In basic plot points, "10 Things" doesn't differ too much from the mountain of other teen tales out there now [...] although the Bard's touch gives the movie a few added layers of complexity.[30]

The film's marketing exploits the film's 'girl power' message and its relationship to other teen films far more than its status as a Shakespeare adaptation. The review's unquestioning equation of '16th-century' with 'genius' is particularly striking, indicating the reverential stance towards Elizabethan heritage frequently expressed in reviews of filmed Shakespeare adaptations, as is illustrated further in my next chapter on *Shakespeare in Love*. The review suggests that incorporating Shakespeare content ensures that the film is set apart in a crowded genre in which originality is at a premium. The film is also, however, placed within the safe bounds of the easily identifiable and marketable teen-comedy genre. Above all, marketing must be swift and direct, accounting for the necessity of focusing upon generic recognition.

An appeal to their film's intellectual sophistication and literary references is not a significant method employed by film marketers to attract the teen audience to *10 Things I Hate About You*. Within the film, characters that quote Shakespeare are mocked because their dialogue is undigested: they have not reached that stage of intellectual sophistication yet when their love may be declared in their own witty in-language. By reciting Shakespeare they are ironically not conforming to the high standards of wit set by their peers, but simply reaffirming their social inadequacy and lack of social integration. In the trailers any quotation from Shakespeare is excluded, in favour of displaying the more self-assured characters that do not need to quote Shakespeare directly. Although cultural capital is crucial in forming social relationships for teens, it is proficiency in popular cultural forms such as rap music and paintballing rather than Shakespeare quotation which is celebrated in the trailer for *10 Things I Hate About You*. In the marketing campaign, then, a process of appropriation as legitimisation is enacted, signifying a desire to prove that Shakespeare need not seem incongruous in the setting of an American high school, or amidst the gang warfare of Verona Beach. Shakespeare provides a means of introducing high culture into the traditionally popular culture, American site of the teen movie. Finding the appropriate register for discussing this conscious juxtaposition and blending of high and low culture is an enduring challenge for marketers of filmed Shakespeare adaptations. Shakespeare as a 'great author' of Western literature is sold by film marketers as relevant, both timeless and contemporary, with regard to the teen audience's emotional and intellectual lives, and irreverence feeds into this idea of relevance.

O

O, a teen filmed adaptation of *Othello*, marks a turning point in the nature of the deployment of Shakespeare in the marketing of filmed adaptations of his plays. The campaign for the film makes even more limited direct reference to Shakespeare than *10 Things I Hate About You*, and indicates an increasing desire to sublimate or conceal Shakespearian content. Whilst reverence is accorded to Shakespeare by the use of him as script source, overt dependence upon him as a high cultural icon is replaced by irreverent commentary upon his receptivity to modernised adaptation. Although the filming of O was completed in 1999, and the marketing campaign began at that time, its release date was deferred by two years.

Miramax's Dimension Films, a genre subsidiary of Miramax, acquired the global rights to O with the initial intention to release it in October 1999, and with a prints and advertising budget of 10 million dollars. Miramax also owns the rights to the Michael Almereyda *Hamlet*. The prints and advertising budget indicates that Dimension Films was convinced by the success of other filmed Shakespeare adaptations that O merited significant marketing outlay. However, after failing to make its October 1999 release date, O remained unreleased for nearly two years before Lions Gate Film, an independent distribution (video and theatrical) and production company with offices in North America and Britain, purchased it. A release date in April 2001 was planned for ten cities, and the date was then moved again to August 2001 for a general release in 1,500 theatres. The delays in release may be attributed to several factors. The film was rated R by the MPAA for violence and a scene of strong sexuality, language and drug use, raising noteworthy issues concerning the representation of Shakespeare in teen filmed adaptations. The R rating also excludes the key PG-13 demographic, an essential component of both the teen audience and the educational audience in North America, from viewing the film. Studio doubts about the marketability of O were related to the fatal Columbine, Colorado high-school shootings in 1999, arguably indicating the need for marketers to adapt their campaigns in line with the prevailing social and political climate. An article in the *Washington Post* describing the delays addresses these issues:

> Other than the contemporary high-school setting, the plot closely follows that of the play, which ends in the deaths of the main characters. Green-lighted when high-school-age horror and suspense movies were all the rage, "O" was initially to be released in the fall of 1999. But after the massacre at Columbine High School in April of that year, studio executives grew nervous about releasing a film with a graphic rape sequence and a bloody series of murders that leaves four characters dead and one badly wounded [...] Miramax faces a problem in finding a way to draw an audience to "O".[31]

The article does not see a strict adherence to Shakespeare's plot as a marketing impediment, but the violent and sexual nature of some scenes in the film is more difficult to square with the film's marketing tactics and ideal target audience.

This difficulty may be related to Ian McKellen's account of his search for funding for his film of *Richard III* in the mid-1990s, which documents hostility amongst Hollywood studio executives to Shakespeare in a manner relevant to both *O* and to the exclusion of domestic violence from 10 *Things I Hate About You*. McKellen narrates how he:

> pointed out with confidence to polite, junior studio executives that, these days, filmed stage classics need not belong only in art houses and that this particular story of intrigue and murder could be universally popular. There was a general muted enthusiasm and some promises to consider buying the movie once it was made but with no suggestion of any loan in the meantime. One studio boss read the script and telephoned me to say that *Richard III* was "too dark: the public wants Pollyanna Shakespeare".[32]

Ironically, it is the 'intrigue and murder' that situates *Richard III* in the arthouse for the studio head, not its status as a filmed Shakespeare adaptation. The US and UK poster campaign for *O* focuses upon the themes of jealousy and love rather than violence and murder in *Othello*. The poster is illustrated with large, sultry head shots of Julia Stiles and Josh Hartnett in the top half of the poster. Beneath them, a smaller full-body shot of Mekhi Phifer nevertheless engages the viewer's attention because it cleverly shows him reaching to throw the letter 'O' in the air as if it is a basketball. The top of the poster is tinted red while the lower half is blue-tinted, emphasising both the sensuality of the illustrations of Stiles and Hartnett and the isolation of Phifer. The entire image is superimposed on a black backdrop and has ragged edges, resembling a frayed manuscript. The tag line 'everything comes full circle' is placed at the top of the poster whilst a second tag line, 'Trust. Seduction. Betrayal.' is on the right-hand side. The failure of *O* at the box office in comparison to the success of *10 Things I Hate About You*, with Stiles a confident, brash, comic heroine rather than a victim, would seem to support the statement that 'Pollyanna Shakespeare' is easier to sell, partly because it spans the attractive genres of romance and comedy.

One promotional web site indicates the angle from which *O* was being marketed:

> Trends wouldn't be trends if Hollywood didn't think there was an audience that wanted movies that followed them. This film, a teen adaptation of a Shakespearean tragedy set in a sports background combines three of the trends seen most in 1999 (teens, sports, and Shakespeare) [...] Shakespeare has been the inspiration for movies since Hollywood's earliest days. While some people might prefer more straight adaptations with his words intact, I suppose a well-done adaptation is preferable to a poor one, regardless.[33]

The web-site author might also have observed that in autumn 1999 both the trend for adapting Shakespeare in high-school films, and studio backing for Shakespeare after *Shakespeare in Love*, were at their 1990s peak. The marketing campaign for *O* indicates that the postmodern reworking of Shakespeare's plays for teen films has broader resonance. The actor playing Othello, Mekhi Phifer, was described as 'doing a contemporary riff on Shakespeare while resurrecting his basketball skills [...] [his] character Odin James is Othello in Air Jordans [...] We follow the story almost to a 'T' although interpreting it with contemporary language. I think we're doing the original justice'.[34] The explicit mandate is to modernise Shakespeare – 'Othello in Air Jordans' could form a tag line for the film, and the film is scripted in colloquial modern English, as is *10 Things I Hate About You*. This feature also promotes Phifer's television credits, rap album and writing projects, generating the 'buzz' (to employ a film-marketing term) that this young Shakespeare star is a true celebrity and a 'Renaissance man' in terms of his accomplishments.

The marketing campaign for *O* indicates that its film marketers are targeting a teen demographic. Mekhi Phifer's role as a young black cultural hero is presented in a stereotypical style: he raps, he is a good basketball player, and so on, situating him within popular culture for the teen audience, at odds with his role as a Shakespearian actor. *10 Things I*

Hate About You also features an English teacher, played by Daryl (Chill) Mitchell, who raps in order to teach his class Shakespeare's sonnets. Rap is a relatively new type of popular culture and, hence, to translate Shakespeare into the medium also inevitably involves 'updating' Shakespeare and, implicitly, making him more appealing to the teen audience as a consequence. Rap is also a language-based art form, within which deviations from mundane language use can be readily incorporated. Most significantly of all, rap is an art form that originated in the US, and its imbrication with Shakespeare may therefore be read in post-colonial terms.

Shakespeare's traditionally highbrow status is acknowledged and then confronted; the decision to adapt Shakespeare is grounded in terms of his claimed popular cultural relevance. Kat's appropriation of the sonnet form in *10 Things I Hate About You*, indicating that her instruction in Shakespeare grants her a sufficient degree of cultural competency to rewrite it, may be related to the casting of rap stars, both in *O* and in *Get Over It*. The casting of Mekhi Phifer may also be situated in the broader context of young actors familiar in popular culture being cast in Shakespearian roles. Setting an early precedent in the 1980s, Molly Ringwald played both Miranda in Mazursky's *Tempest* and Cordelia in Godard's *Lear*, but was chiefly known for starring in several of the best known 'Brat Pack' films of the 1980s: *Pretty in Pink*, *Sixteen Candles* and *The Breakfast Club*. Keanu Reeves, known for teen films such as *Bill and Ted's Excellent Adventure* when he won the role of Don John in Branagh's *Much Ado about Nothing*, also played Hamlet onstage, and one of the leads in the free adaptation of *Henry IV*, *My Own Private Idaho*. The cast of *O* is a commercially minded combination of budding teen stars such as Josh Hartnett, Rain Phoenix and Julia Stiles and an older and recognisable actor, Martin Sheen, to add gravitas, appeal to an older market and enhance audience recognition.

Casting forms an important means of ensuring that the 'risk' of employing Shakespeare in a high-school film is offset by certain standard marketing 'safety blankets' such as the foregrounding of stars familiar to the teen audience – required reassurances for those marketing teen filmed Shakespeare adaptations in the 1990s. A review in a 1999 issue of the film magazine *Premiere*, primarily targeted at a teen and twenty-something audience, carries a still from *10 Things I Hate About You*, depicting the two young lovers in an altercation, and argues that:

During her Shakespeare marathon, Stiles managed to avoid wearing the dreaded corset, but Michelle Pfeiffer, as Titania in *A Midsummer Night's Dream*, was not so lucky. "It's such a costume piece", Pfeiffer says of the latter, more faithful movie adaptation [...] Will audiences suffer Bard burnout? Josh Hartnett (*The Faculty*), who gets nasty as the Iago-based Hugo in *O*, thinks that would be, well, tragic. "If they are tired of it, they're going to miss out", Hartnett says. "I like that Shakespeare fella. He could write".35

Hartnett's colloquial tone masks a standard tribute to Shakespeare's eternal genius, and also indicates that he is an all-American teen idol willing to embrace Shakespeare on the basis of his powerful writing alone. Shakespeare figures as an iconic cultural phenomenon and celebrity 'personality' and he is described with familiarity and in terms of the relevance his work has in a (post)modern context. The costume genre is implicitly presented as tired and outmoded. Marketing such a familiar product as Shakespeare or his plays necessitates the perception that innovation is being provided to justify its reworking. It is also evident that many different generic categories are being referenced to broaden the films' appeal, including musical, costume piece, teen movie, female empowerment piece and suspense.

The most significant DVD special features on *O*, released on 19 February 2002, include audio commentary by Tim Blake Nelson, deleted scenes with commentary and a comprehensive analysis of key basketball scenes. A second disc features the 'newly restored classic film Othello': the 1922 Emil Jannings silent *Othello*. Although this inclusion appears to be an attempt to ground *O* in a venerable Hollywood tradition of filmed *Othello* adaptations, ironically such a film could be viewed irreverently by teens as a novelty piece or curiosity. These features form a typical 1990s film-marketing fusion of Shakespeare as sacred film text rather than play text, and the teen film as popular culture form in the analyses of basketball scenes. The teen audience, a highly significant cinema-going demographic, might also be expected to be amongst the most assiduous collectors of DVD and video. The inclusion of two versions of *Othello*, creating a pedigree of both film history and Shakespeare adaptation, may be read as a desire to tap into this collectors' market, amongst other complex intentions. However, although the DVD special features do make some mention of Shakespeare and include the 1922 *Othello*, Shakespeare does not receive any screen credit, in either the 'an adaptation of ... ' form or as the title form *William Shakespeare's O. O* marks a transition in the marketing of filmed Shakespeare adaptations, in which Shakespeare is sublimated and implied rather than emblazoned in the title and marketing material as he was in *William Shakespeare's Romeo + Juliet*. This does not simply mark a desire to hide Shakespeare, but may also indicate a flattery of the teen audience, suggesting that they are capable of recognising on their own that this film is a Shakespeare adaptation, with all the positive attributes the Shakespeare brand carries. Film marketers increasingly aimed to adopt a collusive relationship with the teen audience in the 1990s and new millennium.

Shakespeare's celebrity aura and brand name provide a positive image of quality in the context of the marketing of *O*. Stephen Brown, a marketing expert, points to the power of established brand names, of which Shakespeare forms an example:

> As anticipated by Baudrillard, the very ubiquity of hyperreality appears to have stimulated a countervailing desire for authenticity and heightened concern with *chronology*. Thus, we see periodic campaigns for "real" beer, bread, eggs [and] renewed interest in "authentic" music, films, books and cooking. [...] Emphasis on authenticity in advertising is paralleled, to some extent, in the branding arena, where longevity is considered to be all-important, especially at a time when the new product development rate is seemingly exceeded only by the new product failure rate [...] long-established brand names are *extremely* precious commodities. It would appear that in an increasingly uncertain, fragmented, disorientating and fast-changing world, they provide consumers with a point – an oasis – of marketing stability.[36]

Shakespeare's celebrity combines an aura of authenticity with film marketers' desire for a brand name to create stability and a store of value, exemplified in numerous marketing contexts, such as the use of Shakespeare's 'brand name' in film titles. Signifying the importance of both 'authenticity' and title in marketing filmed Shakespeare adaptations, *O* had an alternative working title of *Yo, What's Up with Iago?* which was abandoned, possibly because it exhibited too high a degree of irreverence. *O* as a title has a number of possible cultural resonances. It suggests the numeral zero, and hence invokes teen nihilism and a sense of inadequacy. It is reminiscent of the letters some rap stars use in their stage names, such as Jay-Z and Ice-T. There may even be an attempt to evoke the erotic classic *The Story of O* in the film's title, thus implying the existence of sexual content in the film. To produce an effective marketing campaign, as in all these films, the marketing team for *O* had to correctly maintain the hybrid balance required to maximise audience.

Never Been Kissed *and* Get Over It

It is next necessary to examine what two teen filmed adaptations of Shakespeare that did not refer to Shakespeare anywhere in their primary marketing, *Never Been Kissed* and *Get Over It*, indicate about the cultural activity of adaptation. *Never Been Kissed* is a free adaptation of *As You Like It* that frequently references the play, but mention of the play is often excluded in the film's marketing material, such as the poster and web site. *Never Been Kissed* draws solely upon the romantic and pastoral elements of *As You Like It* and bypasses any reference to themes such as exile and injustice, paralleling the excision of unsettling elements from *The Taming of the Shrew* by the screenwriters of *10 Things I Hate About You*. Arguably, taking genre into account, film marketers felt less comfortable overtly incorporating Shakespeare into a light-hearted, lightweight comic context than they did exploiting Shakespeare in the context of 'high tragedy'. Whilst the scarcity of direct reference to Shakespeare in the marketing of *O* arguably marks a desire to flatter the teen audience, the absence of Shakespeare from the marketing of these two films instead indicates an anxiety that the teen Shakespeare genre has run its course and that it is safer to emphasise the comedic aspects of the films.

Get Over It has a plot that revolves around an amateur musical production of *A Midsummer Night's Dream*, and the central love quadrangle pays homage to that of Helena, Hermia, Lysander and Demetrius. *Get Over It* was released in North America in March 2001 on a limited number of screens without advance screenings for critics, and the nature of the release implies a very conservative attitude on the part of the distributor and a concern that the film lacks commercial potential. This attitude is exemplified by the decision to market this film as a teen comedy rather than a Shakespeare film. The trailer for *Get Over It* makes no mention of Shakespeare, and although the school play is alluded to on several occasions the play's content and title are not specified. The trailer instead focuses upon broad physical humour and on the central teen romance, without drawing upon its parallels with the Shakespeare plot. Unlike *William Shakespeare's Romeo + Juliet* and *O*, the DVD release of

Get Over It had surprisingly limited special features, wholly devoted to marketing its teen celebrities rather than making any attempt to present the film as a teaching aid or Shakespeare adaptation. In addition to the standard components of scene selections and subtitles option, there is a selection of cast biographies and four trailers. The Miramax official site for *Get Over It* does, however, cross-market with another teen filmed Shakespeare adaptation by recommending *10 Things I Hate About You* as a film that will be enjoyed by teens who had enjoyed *Get Over It*.

Convention and even cliché are marketing tropes as significant as their opposite: the suggestion that a product is providing novelty or a new spin. One review of *Get Over It* highlights the extensive use of convention in the marketing of teen comedy particularly emphatically:

> You're given fair warning by the adverts, all featuring attractive people in "zany" poses, and the trailers, with the now-typical collection of the snappiest lines, plot developments and a dog humping a basketball. We're not in the realms of classic literature here. Not *exactly*, anyway … *Get Over It* boasts one or two more brain cells than your usual teen flick with literary knobs on and, despite having the target audience squarely in its sights, it still manages to be enjoyable for those who know what to expect.[37]

According to this review, whilst the trailers emphasise low-culture elements such as comical poses and the amorous dog, the film itself also provides a more intelligent frame of reference for those with the cultural capital to appreciate it. The trailer for *Get Over It* draws upon previously successful examples of the teen-movie genre and positions the film as the natural successor to those films. As in *Shakespeare in Love* and *William Shakespeare's A Midsummer Night's Dream*, which one reviewer claimed contained: 'the best trained mutt (uncredited) since *There's Something About Mary*',[38] there is a crowd-pleasing 'bit with a dog' in the trailer for *Get Over It*.

Timing is also a significant factor in the exclusion of Shakespeare in both these marketing campaigns. *Never Been Kissed* was released in 1999, at a time when the most commercially successful teen films were lewd sex comedies such as *American Pie*. Marketers decided to emphasise the film's status as a star vehicle for Drew Barrymore and as a romantic comedy instead of as a teen filmed Shakespeare adaptation, possibly to avoid direct comparison with *10 Things I Hate About You*, which was released at almost the same time and which had used Shakespeare in its campaign, albeit cautiously. *Get Over It* was released in 2001, when teen Shakespeare adaptations appeared to be waning in popularity, particularly after the difficulties surrounding the release of *O*. Emma Cochrane, then editor of film magazine *Empire*, confirmed this trend in January 2001: 'The trend for updating Shakespeare for the teen market seems to be over'.[39] In an interview later in the year, she substantiated her claim in the following terms:

> The trend is over but not dead [...] I think they will be continually popular. He wrote cracking stories and many people of school age have to study his work and want to see their own versions of the text. But there have been diminishing returns on Shakespeare films (e.g. *O*) so I think there will be a bit of a pause before we see a similar rash of releases at the same time. So anything that doesn't seem to be quite working will be killed in pre-production and stories will be developed more closely before they are filmed.[40]

Emma Cochrane correctly emphasises the need for the teen audience to feel that Shakespeare is 'customised' for them, in 'their own versions', in order to find them attractive. She also makes reference to two of the key elements of marketing campaigns for teen filmed Shakespeare adaptations: their educational value and the role of celebrities. Long-established attributes lend Shakespeare validity as subject matter for teen movies: an intellectually and morally elevating literary icon that fires the mind and imagination rather than numbing the teen audience. Nevertheless, if box-office returns for teen filmed Shakespeare adaptations diminish, then the commitment to Shakespeare and the appeal to high culture must be altered into a more marketable form.

The increasing use as school-teaching aids of a variety of media forms such as film and the Internet are contributing factors to the circumstances that made teen Shakespeare films commercially viable, as they ensure a ready-made educational market for the films. Preceding chapters have indicated that filmed Shakespeare adaptations provide cultural validation for both the films' makers and their audience: to know and to be interested in Shakespeare in any medium is broadly accepted in Western culture as a signifier of accumulated cultural capital. Film marketers are aware, however, that a teen audience does not necessarily share such veneration. By the end of the 1990s, driven by commercial imperatives, film marketers for Hollywood teen movies decreased their reliance on an adulterated Shakespeare branding as the principal marker of genre in favour of emphasising other genres deemed commercially safer. The marketing campaigns for *William Shakespeare's Romeo + Juliet* and *10 Things I Hate About You* demonstrate what could be achieved by a successful balance between esoteric, high-culture Shakespeare and an accessible Shakespeare reinterpreted through rap, pop music, images on the Internet and other popular media.

According to Tony Howard, filmed Shakespeare adaptations 'reflect Hollywood's globalization of film culture – the recycling of certain internationally recognisable cultural icons – and the targeting of high-school and college audiences familiar with canonical Great Books'.[41] Gary Taylor's anxiety about 'dumbing down', referred to earlier, focuses on dilution of the Shakespeare brand. He argues that 'even when Shakespeare's plays are good box office, what makes them good box office is not exactly Shakespeare'.[42] Taylor's anxiety may be misplaced, however, if the broad move I have identified in marketing from direct quotation of Shakespeare to more covert referencing is read as an assumption by marketers of postmodern audience sophistication and cultural competence rather than as 'dumbing down'. Taylor's critique is more convincing, however, in its indication that it is not only the presence of Shakespeare that determines the box-office failure or success of filmed Shakespeare adaptations, and that refusing to modernise Shakespeare's language and aiming for a broader audience than the educational market are not in themselves sufficient to silence criticism amongst certain academics of irreverent vulgarisation of Shakespeare. Indeed, criticism of filmed Shakespeare adaptation is full of complaints about lack of fidelity, although in more recent years this has been balanced by more positive critique.[43] Considering the frequency with which teen films that freely adapt Shakespeare exclude mention of Shakespeare from their marketing, particularly *Never Been Kissed* and *Get Over It*, it is a necessary corollary that those films for which marketers did elect to market their Shakespearian credentials were on the defensive and eager to position themselves as the natural popular culture successors to Shakespeare's stage. The interplay between the film marketers' ideal teen products, and what the teens are perceived to demand, indicates a malleable relationship between veneration and irreverence in the transmission of Shakespeare to the teen audience.

CHAPTER FIVE

Shakespeare in Love

THE MARKETING CAMPAIGN for *Shakespeare in Love* provides further evidence that the degree of success achieved when marketing Shakespeare on film resides in the simultaneous promotion of both high culture and popular elements in order to make filmed Shakespeare adaptations profitable commodities. If this hybrid, winning blend of high and low is not found, then the film will be a relative commercial failure. The marketing campaign for *Shakespeare in Love* provides an apposite means of determining how vital hybrid high/low marketing is in the process of promoting Shakespeare in contrast to other canonical figures. Analysis of the changing politics of representation in 1990s Hollywood film marketing, with particular reference to postmodernism, indicates that the marketing campaign for *Shakespeare in Love* exemplifies postmodern cultural transactions. The film *Shakespeare in Love* itself can be related to the symbiotic relationship between 'sacred' art and 'profane' commerce at the centre of this book, as the romantic comedy at one and the same time revolves around Shakespeare's struggle to express his genius, freed by love from the tedious commercial imperatives of Elizabethan theatre while manifestly benefiting from the competitive demands of the market, driving enterprise ever onwards and upwards. The message of the film and the message sought by the marketers would here seem to be in perfect harmony.

The campaign to market *Shakespeare in Love* also presents a more complex macro version of the interaction between finance and art. Hollywood film production in the late 1990s provided a site in which commerce and idealism were not so much contested as fused, as in the film. Both film and marketing demonstrate a delight in the witty way in which Shakespeare can be translated into visual images, and a diminishing sense of the need to make adaptation of Shakespeare's work look 'authentic', which formed a significant influence upon the marketing techniques of late 1990s teen filmed Shakespeare adaptations and Branagh's *Love's Labour's Lost*. *Shakespeare in Love* is the most significant single film associated with Shakespeare in the period under study, in terms of its financial performance, Oscar recognition and its impact on the Hollywood studio system and the manner in which filmed Shakespeare adaptations are marketed, and it therefore merits its own chapter. However, a special case has to be made for its inclusion, as it is evidently not an adaptation in the conventional sense. First, it stars Shakespeare as a biographical figure, which is unique in the films analysed in this study; second, it employs high/low hybridity particularly self-consciously throughout its marketing campaign and third, the film is also a very significant post-colonial export of 'Englishness', which in this study is taken to mean a marketable pastiche of English culture, literature and heritage.

Although postmodernism is the more evidently relevant cultural phenomenon to consider in relation to *Shakespeare in Love*, neo-Gramscian hegemony theory also plays a useful explanatory role. Postmodernism and neo-Gramscian hegemony within cultural studies share certain characteristics, which Douglas Kellner describes as 'no guarantees, no teleologies, no grand narrative of emancipation, no totalizing or reductive discourses or politics, no privileging of a class or social group, no home or solid basis from which to struggle'.[1] Following Kellner's concept of hegemony operating in a postmodern fashion, a concept shared by Stuart Hall and Lawrence Grossberg, Miramax's hegemony may be taken to consist of an attempted incorporation of the great majority of its audience into the same 'broadly based relations of cultural consumption [and] this required both the incorporation of culture into the sphere of market relations and the application of modern industrial techniques to cultural production'.[2] Study of film marketing in the late 1990s indicates the unstable and contested nature of cultural hegemony, as Hollywood's marketing machine could not guarantee the success and domination of its individual films despite highly developed, industrialised and self-conscious attempts to control cultural consumption. Whilst cinema has always prompted debates concerning the representation and 'effects' of violence, war, religion and sexuality, this book examines the more subtle but arguably more fundamental issue of the interface between art and commerce. Although a large body of critical literature on *Shakespeare in Love* rapidly developed after its cinematic release in 1998, very little of the research focuses in detail on the film's marketing campaign.[3] This chapter presents for the first time research in which such marketing is pivotal rather than incidental.

Miramax and Shakespeare in Love

The development of Miramax from 1989 to 2001 was partially responsible for the broad cultural transition from arthouse independent to the multiplex that Shakespeare made in Hollywood in the 1990s. Outlining the background to Miramax's successful production and promotion of *Shakespeare in Love* enables analysis of the conditions of the Hollywood marketplace in the mid-1990s. Miramax, a New York-based film company founded in 1981 by brothers Bob and Harvey Weinstein, played a significant role in increasing the commercial prosperity of American independent cinema in the 1990s. Louise Levison describes the status of Miramax as follows:

> Miramax is not a studio. Disney is. However, Miramax has its own fund for greenlighting films and distributes them itself. They are also the 800-LB gorilla in indie film so sure people resent them. Spending money on Oscar noms works, and they are the best in the business. I don't think the Weinsteins care what people think.[4]

Levison usefully recognises that Miramax has a very different status to smaller independent studios, partly because of its distribution capability.[5] These important points: the status of Miramax in relation to the established studio system, the independent sector, their Oscar spending and their iconoclasm, are all addressed in this chapter, but initially their place in the studio system will be considered. The leading film-industry publication *Variety* in the late 1990s had an editorial policy of terming Miramax 'Minimajor', thus placing it in a uniquely liminal position between profitable independent and full-grown multinational conglomerate.

The type of films that Miramax released in the 1990s can be divided in retrospect into four broad sub-genres: Oscar contender films, the closely related but generally less ambitious arthouse films, the successful commercial film, for example the *Scream* franchise, and the 'break-out' commercial film. *Shakespeare in Love* and *Pulp Fiction* are the most striking examples of the first category for Miramax in the 1990s. Miramax represents the most evident example of a Hollywood studio facilitating its corporate growth by adopting the hybrid notion of a venerable and irreverent product. Despite the release of commercial franchises such as *Scream*, Miramax's corporate growth and profitability in the first half of the period covered by this study was primarily attained by distributing a large number of 'arthouse' films that had sufficient crossover and mass-market appeal to justify broader distribution, including *Sex, Lies, and Videotape, Reservoir Dogs* and *The Piano*, and they paved the way for Miramax to back a Shakespeare project which exhibited similar, or greater, crossover potential. In April 1993 the Weinsteins, who had gained a powerful reputation in Hollywood founded on both their marketing and their management style, sold a majority share of Miramax to Disney for an estimated 60 million dollars, and in the late 1990s Miramax's successes at the box office enabled the company to diversify into music and publishing.

Miramax makes what may be termed a postmodern intervention in the Hollywood film industry, producing and distributing marginal films that lie outside the modernist cinematic canon, unlike, for example, Sony Classics, which distributes and re-releases 'classic films'. However, Miramax simultaneously pays homage to the highbrow and elitist canonisation of the 'arthouse' film, even though their production cannot be indisputably classified as high culture. By 2001 a developing backlash against the Miramax marketing-juggernaut approach was evident in both North American and British film journalism, exemplified by the hostility several critics expressed towards the Oscar nominations for *Chocolat*. For example, Rob Vaux's review observed:

> There's nothing like unwarranted praise to turn an otherwise mediocre piece of fluff into a hateful testament to Hollywood ego. The robber barons at Miramax Pictures have apparently decided that they should have a continuous lock on quality films, and have resolutely set out to claim Oscar glory from more deserving candidates. Every year, they launch a fearsome marketing campaign [...] In the process, they have championed some very questionable pieces of "art", films whose banality only becomes clear in the spotlight they shine on it. This year's specimen is *Chocolat*, a

forgettable bit of nothing whose greatest transgression is claiming to be more than it is.[6]

Miramax's incorporation into the Hollywood mainstream in the late 1990s follows a postmodern cultural trajectory; a celebration of films that possess controversial or intellectually difficult content entertaining mainstream audiences. Criticism of Miramax from 2000 onwards centres on the accusation that Miramax 'sold out' to produce films that would appeal to the lowest common denominator. Miramax took the bold step of emphasising the existence of high art credentials within films it was marketing for the multiplex.

However, it was partially Miramax's expensive marketing tactics, particularly their Oscar vote-seeking techniques, that ensured the company's profitability. Miramax promoted itself into a major distributor in part by employing market saturation, a mimetic process of commodification in the film industry that Martin Dale describes as a movement from 'prototype' to 'product':

> Although film development and production continues to have an artisan flavour, marketing and distribution are fully industrialized processes with comparable techniques to that of any other consumer product [...] The Majors' distribution arms do everything in their powers to guarantee the most effective release of their films. The Majors are aware that if they left film promotion to film critics, many of their most popular films would be killed at birth. They therefore spend millions in film advertising and only really pay attention to the critics for certain "quality" films which need a strong write-up.[7]

Dale's distinction between film-making as artisan and marketing and distribution as industrialised processes reiterates the key binary of this book. Film marketers have to employ Shakespearian content in their campaigns with even more sensitivity than writers and directors employing the content in their films, because it is the marketing side of the film business that is most likely to face criticism for crass commercialism and 'cashing in' on trends rather than producing 'art'. Dale also foregrounds an important tension between film reviewers and the studios and distributors, suggesting that once a film that is as critic-friendly as possible has been made, it falls to the marketing team to offset any poor reviews, promoting their product precisely by the type of means Miramax employs: saturation marketing, aggressive Oscar bidding, and many other devices that I will now analyse in the specific context of *Shakespeare in Love*.

When *Shakespeare in Love* was first pitched, six years before it became a feature film, Hugh Grant, Daniel Day-Lewis and Julia Roberts were early preferences for the leading roles of Will Shakespeare and Lady Viola De Lesseps, indicating that a British rather than an American male lead was targeted for Shakespeare's role from the outset. This set a precedent in terms of 'authenticity' and tradition that film marketers were unwilling to transgress. British actresses were not targeted for the role of Viola to the same degree, and Gwyneth Paltrow was eventually cast, ensuring that at least one American 'A-List' star was in one of the leading roles, and replicating Zeffirelli and Branagh's successful fusion of North American screen stars with British stage actors. Harvey Weinstein was the force behind both the casting of Paltrow and the development of Marc Norman's screenplay by Tom Stoppard. An article in the *Evening Standard* significantly suggests that the length of time from pitch to production might be partially ascribed to scepticism about the viability of Shakespeare in Hollywood: 'It was generally agreed among the powers-that-were that a film with the word Shakespeare in the title was dangerous box-office territory without sufficiently stellar names to guarantee widespread appeal'.[8] This article presents another version of the argument that it was difficult to make a film about Shakespeare in the early 1990s, also exemplified by Branagh and McKellen's contentions.[9]

Shakespeare's potential marketing liability, as perceived by Hollywood in the early 1990s, was offset by gaining the backing of a large studio, by ensuring the involvement of celebrities, and by employing a screen-writing duo who combined high cultural theatrical expertise (Tom Stoppard) with experience in the writing of Hollywood blockbusters (Marc Norman) in order to produce a relatively 'safe' script that effectively fused veneration and irreverence. Arguably Stoppard's 1966 play *Rosencrantz and Guildenstern Are Dead* represents the most celebrated (post)modern combination of veneration for Shakespeare with irreverent pastiche, and qualifies Stoppard as the ideal screenwriter for the *Shakespeare in Love* project. Whilst other studios, such as Fine Line Features, also aimed to bring films promoted as high culture into the mass market, Miramax uniquely accompanied their strategy with a heavily subsidised strategic Oscar campaign, ensuring their market dominance in the sector in the late 1990s.

Using Oscar to sell Shakespeare

Film marketing often mystifies the commercial processes behind film production, and the Oscars ceremony is perhaps the most obvious example of this mystification, in its global stature as the pinnacle of the movie year, and its suggestion that the decisions of the Academy rest upon aesthetic merit and some degree of the 'people's choice' rather than mere box-office success. However, operating concurrently is the alternative signification of the Oscars as corporate glamour and excess on parade, with the marketing in the case of, in particular, the action movie and epic genres actually promoting the budget involved. The late 1990s was marked by a much more explicit interplay between culture and commerce, exemplified by increased deployment of the film's budget as a marketing tool for films such as *Titanic* and *Pearl Harbor*. This trend may be interpreted as an essential consequence of the success of 'break-out' commercial films made and distributed on a relatively small budget by Miramax. Once it had been proven repeatedly that it was not necessary to spend vast sums of money to make money at the box office, epic and action films with huge financial outlays focused more intensely than ever before on the fruits of their budgets as marketing features, ensuring that spectacular special effects, stunts and huge sets and casts were constantly foregrounded in, for example, the films' trailers. Furthermore, cinema is, as Colin MacCabe persuasively argues, 'a cultural form permeated at every level by the practices and paradoxes of marketing – a post-modern practice which oscillates between the passive reproduction and the active remodelling of audiences'.[10] Passive reproduction was the strategy employed by action movie and epic marketers seeking to retain their core audience with the promise of ever more extravagant special effects. Miramax was engaged in an active remodelling of audiences in its efforts to heighten receptivity to traditionally arthouse subjects.

During the 1997 Oscar ceremony the Motion Picture Academy presented a ten-minute salute to filmed Shakespeare adaptations. Shakespeare provides an important source of cultural validation for an Academy aiming to balance commerce and art. *Shakespeare in Love* won three Golden Globes – Best Actress for Gwyneth Paltrow, Best Comedy and Best Comic Screenplay and, on 21 March 1999, *Shakespeare in Love* won seven of its thirteen Academy Award nominations, including Best Picture of the year. The seven Oscar awards for *Shakespeare in Love* were

Best Picture, Best Actress (Gwyneth Paltrow), Best Supporting Actress (Judi Dench), Original Screenplay (Marc Norman and Tom Stoppard), Art Direction, Original Musical or Comedy Score and Best Costume.

Shakespeare as high art legitimated not only the Oscar ceremony itself in 1998, but also the aggressive marketing tactics and non-Hollywood mainstream film-production methods employed by Miramax as well. The Oscar competition in 1998 involved four film companies, who collectively spent over 9 million dollars on Oscar campaigning in 1998, and were responsible for the five movies nominated for Best Picture: *Shakespeare in Love, Life is Beautiful, Saving Private Ryan, Elizabeth* and *The Thin Red Line*. Peter Bart describes the Oscar campaign from 1998 to 1999 as a 'contest between several marketing juggernauts'.[11] Academy members were invited to lavishly catered screenings of the films, where studio officials hoped to influence undecided voters, and members were offered souvenirs and soundtracks emblazoned with the films' logos. Oscar campaign expenditure was higher in 1998 than any time in the preceding decade, particularly more so than in 1997 when *Titanic* was by far the dominant contender from the outset. Miramax sources placed its Oscar campaign costs for *Shakespeare in Love* at about 2 million dollars and at about 1.3 million dollars for *Life is Beautiful*, with most of the money spent on trade ads, travel expenses and videos. Another 1.1 million dollars was spent on newspaper and television advertising for *Shakespeare in Love* in New York and Los Angeles, with the dual purpose of reaching both Academy voters and ticket buyers. To place these statistics in context, Gramercy Pictures and 20th Century Fox were believed to have spent less than 1 million dollars each on their respective campaigns for *Elizabeth* and *The Thin Red Line*, whilst studio sources estimated DreamWorks' spending at about 4 million dollars, including print ads, television commercials and copying and mailing special Academy cassettes of *Saving Private Ryan*.

Generally film marketers run television advertisements around the time of the launch, but they also did so post-Oscar nominations in both America and Britain for *Shakespeare in Love*. Interestingly, DreamWorks and Miramax were the highest spenders, and it was their marketing battle for the Oscars that received most press coverage during the 1998 Oscar contest, with Miramax's *Shakespeare in Love* and *Life is Beautiful* the contenders against DreamWorks' *Saving Private Ryan*. In a film-industry article, Terry Press, a studio official and marketing chief of DreamWorks, prompted to suggest campaign reform in the light of such high expenditure, and possibly because Miramax was winning the contest, insists that 'the Academy will take a look at this process and get involved in some kind of reform', and in the same article Harvey Weinstein suggests that he might reconsider the Miramax marketing strategy in 1999: 'Maybe we did go too far ... I hope not'. [12] This remark suggests an acknowledgement that the fiction of the Oscars as a celebration of Hollywood art rather than commerce must be carefully maintained, and that Harvey Weinstein is aware that his reputation rests on promoting films, rather than overly commercialising them, in order for Hollywood to prosper.

An Oscar nomination for Best Picture such as that received by *Shakespeare in Love* in 1998 may be demonstrated to have a large impact at the box office, and Oscar nominations are crucial to certain genres, such as arthouse films or foreign films breaking into the mainstream North American market, whilst largely irrelevant for action or comedy franchises such as *Terminator* and *Men in Black*, whose commercial success rests upon their status as pure popular entertainment. Oscar nominations provide marketing executives with a significant means of enhancing a film's all-important North American box-office receipts if it lacks pre-sold attributes such as a star cast or huge budget, and diminished audiences towards the end of a film's cinematic run can be increased by the profile Oscar nominations grant. For example, after the 1999 Oscar nominations were announced, having gained six Oscar nominations, *The Sixth Sense* earned an additional 6.5 million dollars, for a total of 288.5 million dollars. The Best Picture nomination for *The Green Mile* contributed to the additional 10 million dollars of the film's gross, increasing it to 134.4 million dollars. This is all part of the process whereby marketing executives determine and influence their 'return audiences': initially on repeat visits to the cinema and then on pay-per-view, DVD, video, and again later, when the film is broadcast on television. Academy Award spending formed part of an ever-increasing budget accorded to the marketing process in the 1990s, emphasising the distinctiveness of the 1990s as an era of unprecedented commercial investment in cinema. The Oscars form a significant component of trailers too, as Andy Medhurst observes: 'trailers seem to be the only cultural space where the laughable notion that Oscars mean real merit is actively, passionately believed in to the point where "Academy-Award winning" has become the most repeated phrase in the trailer lexicon'.[13] This practice represents not so much a cherished belief in the institution of Oscars as a marketing opportunity that is a crucial selling point for many film genres.

The growing commercial significance of Oscar success also arguably influenced the nature of films themselves in the 1990s, as David Gritten observes:

> Increasingly [their] financial and marketing importance to Hollywood is barely hidden [...] Because the whole world is watching, academy voters tend to prefer films eliciting universal emotions. *Shakespeare in Love* and *Life is Beautiful* were both in what might be termed the "you'll laugh, you'll cry" category. In contrast, *Saving Private Ryan* may be too stern and bloody for Hollywood to endorse with relish ... Gwyneth Paltrow's victory as Best Actress was no shock. She is a Hollywood favorite – talented, versatile, intelligent and beautiful. Why would that matter? Because Hollywood is obsessed with looking good. This self-aggrandisement may have tipped the scales in favor of *Shakespeare in Love*. It is classy and likeable anyway; but its clever spin doctors positioned it as a film about a creative community. Perhaps, wishfully, Hollywood saw something of itself.[14]

Employment of the term 'spin doctors' is very suggestive here, as it emphasises that apparently embedded political and cultural preferences may be altered by effective campaigning. The secrecy over marketing expenditure also has its political parallels, and is of relevance to this book as it emphasises the absolute centrality of marketing in advanced consumer capitalism. Ken Green, head of marketing at United International Pictures and the lead manager for the British *Shakespeare in Love* marketing campaign, indicated that Paltrow was marketed much more aggressively in North America than in the UK because 'they aimed at a specific market in the US – an older audience than in the UK campaign'.[15] In the US, where in 1999 her celebrity status was highest, Paltrow was focused upon in the marketing campaign and the run-up to the Oscars, whereas in the UK a wider range of actors including those familiar from British television were employed. Although United's publicity agency did arrange for Paltrow and Fiennes to do UK promotional interviews in terms of marketing, Martin Clunes and Tom Wilkinson also did interviews in the UK.[16] Thus the varying regional significations of celebrities were capitalised upon by the distribution company.

Shakespeare is an exemplary vessel for film marketers seeking the type of universal emotional appeal Gritten describes above. Elizabethan England is idealised as both an organic unity mixing Queen and commoners in a 'Globe' and as a site of high cultural production in *Shakespeare in Love*, a myth borrowed from the famous opening to Olivier's *Henry V* which then holds a mirror up to Hollywood as the twentieth-century equivalent. Miramax proved to be adept at ensuring that, regardless of whether their films had the requisite Oscar quality, their marketing would virtually guarantee Oscar nominations for certain films.

Shakespeare in Love *and press marketing*

Ken Green's observation on the *Shakespeare in Love* campaign, that 'the press was very important – they can be flexible and change quotes and awards on ads', offers a useful starting point. The press pack for *Shakespeare in Love* formed a significant means of providing tailored marketing material to the press during the film's release. The press pack emphasises both English heritage and history and the flexible nature of Shakespeare's known biography: 'the point about Shakespeare's life is that nobody knows anything. All we know is that (Shakespeare) paid 50 pounds to join the Chamberlain's Men and that in his will he left his second best bed to his wife – that's about the sum of it'.[17] According to Martin Dale, the press book is a 'very significant' marketing tool for most films and typically includes 'a one or two page synopsis, filmographies of the leading talent, production notes, and full cast and crew lists'.[18] The Miramax press pack for *Shakespeare in Love* contains a brief biography of Shakespeare which conforms to the film's sentimentality by interpreting Shakespeare's writing methods as inspired by his personal life, and implies that it has access to sufficient information to term its biographies of historical personages 'fact'. The focus on the Shakespeare myth of a mysterious and shadowy national hero and genius in the press kit biography demonstrate a broader point about Shakespearian adaptation, expressed by Daniel Fischlin and Mark Fortier in the following terms: that it 'shapes the way in which literary culture participates in the construction of a seemingly palatable (commodifiable) narrative that is also a form of sentimental, historical amnesia'.[19] As has been seen throughout this book, any irreverence towards Shakespeare is complemented by veneration and grounding in bedrock of assumed 'authenticity'. The marketing angle provided by the press pack is discernible in subsequent press coverage of the film.

For example, some of the principal North American film critics follow the lead of the press pack in praising the film's blend of cultural pedagogy and populism. Anxious to preserve the 'cultural commodity' of a venerable Shakespeare, the prominent critic Janet Maslin praised *Shakespeare in Love* as 'far richer and more deft than the other Elizabethan film in town ("Elizabeth")', and expressed particular admiration for 'a splendid, hearty cast of supporting players (the actors in both films, like Fiennes, do notably better work here)'.[20] Culturally situated in an urbane paradigm of US East Coast intellectual publication, this article elects to dwell insistently upon the Elizabethan context of the film, rather than its 'modern' or 'accessible' aspects.

In the US, the press and newspaper and television ads were able to incorporate the Oscar nominations quickly. Similarly in the UK, when the 1999 Oscar nominations came out, an *Evening Standard* headline claimed 'Oscars Fall in Love with Olde England: Cate's Elizabeth and Gwyneth's Shakespeare Win an Amazing Twenty Nominations for Hollywood Film Honours'. The headline makes Hollywood's appropriation of Shakespeare and early modern England very explicit. The article continues by stating that the film 'was today nominated for an extraordinary thirteen Academy Awards – one fewer than last year's record-equalling *Titanic* – to lead the year's impressive British charge for Oscar glory'.[21] In post-colonial terms it is significant that the British press commonly present the Oscars in terms of 'the British are coming'. *Shakespeare in Love* won the Best Picture and Best Actress Oscars, categories in which *Elizabeth* also received nominations, suggesting that Shakespeare may provide the marketing 'X factor', although the smaller Oscar campaign for *Elizabeth* and the small amount of publicity that Cate Blanchett did in comparison to Gwyneth Paltrow is also significant. *Shakespeare in Love* also considerably outperformed *Elizabeth* at the box office despite a similar cast and historical milieu: it made 21.3 million dollars at the US box office in the first six weeks after opening; *Elizabeth* only took 18.9 million dollars, behind by more than two million dollars even at that early stage of release.

Indeed, on a budget of 45 million dollars, *Shakespeare in Love* took 224,000 dollars at eight screens on its opening weekend, and in the first three weeks after opening that figure had risen to 9.41 million dollars, showing at 299 screens. As Peter Myers, former senior vice president of domestic distribution at Fox in Los Angeles indicates:

> Much can be learned from the daily tracking of receipts from the nation's theatres. The first figures to be analyzed are from the opening day and then the opening weekend. After the first weekend, the executives at Fox get a good impression of the strength of a picture; what we don't yet know is its staying power. Confirmation of word-of-mouth occurs on the second weekend. If the second weekend is as strong as the first, it's potentially a big-grossing picture; if it falls off by 20%, it can still be very big; if it falls off 40% or more, there's a real problem.[22]

The sustained box-office profits combined with the large number of screens it was released onto indicate that *Shakespeare in Love* was a hit. Ken Green notes that 150,000 pounds was spent on the London premiere and party for the UK release of *Shakespeare in Love*, an unusually large amount.[23] *Shakespeare in Love* then played for three months in UK cinemas, which is extremely unusual for a film that is not a self-styled blockbuster. Exhibitors must be persuaded by distributors to keep playing their films: the exhibitor has to believe in it, and international exhibitors watch what a film's reception is in the US market. In multiplexes, source of much of the American box-office business in the 1990s, films can be moved from bigger screens to smaller screens,[24] and this strategy was employed in the *Shakespeare in Love* campaign to maintain its availability.

Analysis of critical response to *Shakespeare in Love* provides substantial evidence that filmed Shakespeare adaptations are a vital site of cultural contest. It was crucial when marketing the commodity *Shakespeare in Love* to retain sufficient elements of high cultural value in order to maintain the balance of hybridity between veneration and irreverence. Film critics are often quick to recognise the blend of irreverence and veneration towards the fictionalised version of history and literature presented in *Shakespeare in Love*. As Mick LaSalle observes of McKellen's *Richard III*:

> Despite added scenes, the film only makes one addition to Shakespeare's text, a swing number, "Come Live with Me and Be My Love". Shakespeare didn't write it. The lyrics are a conflation of two poems: Marlowe's "Passionate Shepherd to his Lover" and Sir Walter Raleigh's "The Nymph's Reply to the Shepherd". It's a witty touch that makes people in the know feel smart.[25]

This critic focuses upon the educative power of Shakespeare, surpassing the goal of pure entertainment, and although the film is enjoyable for non-Shakespeare scholars, comprehensive knowledge of the historical background is posited as an enhancement of cinema-viewing pleasure. There are limited examples in Loncraine's *Richard III*, but *Shakespeare in Love* interrogates the authenticity and stability of Shakespearian quotation on multiple occasions, thus flattering both those viewers and reviewers 'in the know'. For film, and many other products, this constitutes the ideal marketing formula: appeal and affordability for all categories from A through to E. An implied universalism is also present, an attempted celebration of common humanity.

An article on *Shakespeare in Love* in *The Times* exhibits awareness of the fundamentally conservative nature of the film's postmodern adaptation of early modern history and drama, and situates the film generically as a romantic comedy:

> *Shakespeare in Love* is one of those films purpose-built for the "courting couple". Yet, as with so many of the bard's romantic comedies, there is an element of mistaken identities here. You think you're getting a light romantic pick-me-up. As a twenty- or early thirty-something with intellectual pretensions, you would not dream of putting bum on seat for the likes of *You've Got Mail*. But with *Shakespeare in Love* you can cite witty Stoppardian dialogue and the ironic use of anachronism as justification. The appearance of Gary from *Men Behaving Badly* wearing a baggy doublet is an added bonus for men of the *Loaded* generation. Oh, and there is lots of sex, some of it involving Gwyneth Paltrow.[26]

The reviewer here manifests a dialogic relationship between high and low culture, eager to foreground knowledge of Shakespeare as an essential prerequisite to commentary upon *Shakespeare in Love*. Low culture, represented by *Men Behaving Badly*, *Loaded* and *You've Got Mail*, is rejected in favour of the high-culture *Shakespeare in Love*, which then ironically exhibits low cultural attributes anyway, corresponding to the 'recurrent pattern' mapped by Stallybrass and White in which 'the "top" attempts to reject and eliminate the "bottom" for reasons of prestige and status, only to discover, not only that it is in some way frequently dependent upon that low-Other [...] but also that the top *includes* that low symbolically'.[27] This dependence is economic as well as symbolic and fantastic in the context of film marketing. An equally significant broader narrative is that the *idea* of the high/low distinction has formed a crucial cultural determinant in Western culture even though what actually constitutes high and low culture is unstable and constantly changing, particularly at a time of so-called 'identity crisis' in terms of class, race, nationhood and gender.

In a promotional interview to market *Shakespeare in Love*, Tom Stoppard emphasises that his mandate is to fictionalise Shakespeare rather than to attempt an 'authentic' portrayal of William Shakespeare's life. Stoppard states that 'I have no insecurity or doubt about working in this strange area between fact and fiction. There is a point, I tell myself, where accuracy becomes the last resort of the scoundrel, or, at least, the playwright'.[28] Whilst film marketers avoid overtly satirising Shakespeare, the philistine forces of commercialism that he has to pit his genius against are considered fair targets. Shakespeare is a Hollywood screenwriter as well as an Elizabethan playwright in both *Shakespeare in Love* and the secondary marketing of the film. He must contend with celebrity egos, the comparatively insignificant status of the writer and the unwanted interventions of 'the money' just as the makers of filmed Shakespeare adaptations have to in Hollywood. According to Richard Burt, the tension between art and the demands of commerce in *Shakespeare in Love* offers 'a critique of Hollywood film production [...] positioned as a low mass culture, from the vantage of "high" literary and theatrical culture'.[29] However, the process may be alternatively interpreted as a cunning exercise in reverse marketing psychology. By drawing attention to their own reputation for commodification of high culture, film marketers can reassure audiences that they are self-consciously avoiding 'cheapening' Shakespeare.

Examples abound of journalistic anxiety regarding the hybrid reverent/irreverent approach adopted towards Shakespeare's biography in *Shakespeare in Love*. The film magazine *Salon*, which positions itself at the esoteric end of the film-magazine market, contains an unfavourable review by Laura Miller regarding the elements of the film she describes as a 'corny, old-fashioned backstage farce', foregrounding the importance of genre in this debate:

> Madden clearly wants the movie to feel like one of Shakespeare's sunny, mature comedies – a bit of melodrama, a few clowns, some disguises, a touch of philosophy, some bawdy jokes, all wrapped around a romance – a grab bag of whimsies transformed by the bard's uncanny alchemy into something sublime. Of course, not even Stoppard is Shakespeare, and the

end result resembles one of Neil Simon's middlebrow romps more than it does *As You Like It*. Veins of Shakespeare's poetry run throughout the screenplay, and they deliver occasional jolts of genius, heady and rich, that tend to dull the surrounding prose.[30]

This review exhibits concern that comparison might be made between Tom Stoppard and the peerless William Shakespeare as literary figures. A 1998 interview with Tom Stoppard states 'even before it opens here on Friday, *Shakespeare in Love* is already being hailed as the film of the year. Sir Tom Stoppard, who crafted the final screenplay, insists he's a romantic. But when it comes to love … ' The word 'crafted' implies both an earthy artisanship and the screenplay as work of art. The article criticises Marc Norman, the co-author, arguing that the film 'was originally written by Marc Norman, author of *Waterworld*, and then reworked to dazzling advantage by Stoppard', and such privileging of the British high-culture playwright Stoppard over the American multiplex-fodder hack writer Norman is a common trope in the marketing. However, Shakespeare is invariably placed far above even Stoppard in these reviews:

> To take against it you'd have to believe that Stoppard was really comparing himself to Shakespeare. Unlike Stoppard, of course, the Bard would never have descended to penning a putative screen version of *Cats*. Or, there again, taking note of the analogies *Shakespeare in Love* draws between showbiz in the 1590s and the 1990s, maybe he would.[31]

Several telling points are made in this article, beginning with the unquestioned assumption that it would indicate unattractive hubris for Stoppard to compare himself to Shakespeare. Shakespeare's venerable status is then elevated still further, to the increased disadvantage of Stoppard. The final sentence allows a degree of irreverence to ostensibly enter into the description of Shakespeare, but on closer inspection it is Stoppard's version of Shakespeare that is being mocked. There is too much at stake in the cultural representation of Shakespeare for this reviewer to allow the parallels between the reigns of Elizabeth I and II to extend to an equating of Stoppard's talent with Shakespeare's, even a light-hearted one. Stoppard may aspire to be Will, but not the Bard, and there are dangers as well as rewards in appropriating Shakespeare.

A particularly significant passage of an article promoting the premiere of *Shakespeare in Love* focuses on the problem of generic representation of Shakespeare, and the decorum of Shakespeare's representation as cultural capital:

> A terrific romantic romp, *Shakespeare in Love*, which had its premiere in London last night, is a thoroughly British affair which looks set to be the hottest ticket in town. And is the film a romantic comedy, a comedic romance, or none of these? (John Madden, the film's director, replies) "It is, I hope, a film which has no label to sum it up. It takes the work seriously, but at the same time, it is mischievous … Go and see it because this is a portrait of Will Shakespeare as you have never thought about him before!" [32]

In this promotional piece, *Shakespeare in Love* is marketed as unpredictable generically and in its depiction of Shakespeare, a film that evades simple classification as high or low culture. The piece also suggests that one reason to see the film is that 'Kenneth Branagh has had nothing whatsoever to do with this film', and there is an insert in the article which nominates five 'high-culture' Shakespeare films as the best ever: *Chimes at Midnight, Throne of Blood*, Polanski's *Macbeth*, Olivier's *Henry V* and Kosintsev's *Hamlet*. The reviewer appears keen to emphasise that *Shakespeare in Love*, unlike Branagh, manages to retain high cultural credentials whilst also providing fun entertainment. According to Ken Green,[33] John Madden saw all the promotional material for *Shakespeare in Love* and approved most of it, making only minimal changes, suggesting that Madden was very involved with the marketing and that his statements to the press about the film are carefully considered components of that involvement. What is, however, undeniable according to the article is the Englishness of the project: the one aspect that is not open to interpretation. The marketing of *Shakespeare in Love* demonstrates that British cultural imperialism forms a powerful remaining vestige of British imperial and commercial power. Whilst Shakespeare was employed as a tool of cultural colonisation during the height of the British Empire, by the late twentieth century Hollywood Shakespeare was an appropriation of a powerful signifier, British in origin, by the now dominant global power. The poster, trailer, web site and press kit for *Shakespeare in Love* conform to this model of cultural consumption and exchange, as they exclude any of the film's references to the New World in favour of emphasising Shakespeare's specific Elizabethan English context.

Shakespeare in Love: *tag lines, posters, trailers and radio spots*

Alterations to the poster text during the poster campaign for *Shakespeare in Love* emphasise the importance of Oscar, Golden Globe and BAFTA nominations and awards in marketing. Before the film was nominated for any awards, the US poster used a close-up image of Fiennes and Paltrow embracing and the tag line, 'Love is the only inspiration'. A British variation on that poster used the alternative tag line, 'A comedy about the greatest love story almost never told', and includes pictures of not only the main stars but of many respected British actors with smaller roles such as Simon Callow and Anthony Sher. The same tag line is used on the poster which is headed '6 Golden Globe', and then in smaller font size, 'nominations', and the list of nominations, using the list to legitimate the marketing claim that it is 'the greatest love story'. The same image and tag line are reproduced in full-page newspaper advertisements, for example in the *Sunday Times Culture* supplement on 14 January 1999.

After the Oscar nominations, the US poster was altered again, with a header that read 'The year's biggest crowd-pleaser is now nominated for more Oscars than any other motion picture', and under this caption in larger font is the text '13 Academy Award nominations', and then 'Best Picture' in larger font still. The post-Oscars UK poster is captioned with 'Winner 7 Oscars Best Picture' in large font, accompanied by a picture of the Oscar statuette, and in the post-Golden Globe UK poster the tag line is replaced by a quote from the well-known British film critic Christopher Tookey. The Golden Globe award for Best Picture is printed in a very large font, whilst the indication that the film was only nominated in the Comedy/Musical category is printed in a much smaller font. The inclusion of award nominations on posters and newspaper advertisements confirms to their viewers that this is a quality picture as well as a popular favourite.

Colin Kennedy, deputy editor of *Empire* magazine at the time of my interview with him, confirms the importance of inclusion of text from film reviews on posters for the film-marketing campaigns:

> *Empire* and its ilk are useful to large marketing campaigns, up to a point. For smaller, independent distributors publicity is vital oxygen; for those studios with significant P&A [press and advertising] spend there are always alternative avenues. One of the most common phrases we hear when a publicity campaign is running into trouble is "we'll just buy it", which

Poster for John Madden's *Shakespeare in Love* (PHOTOFEST)

roughly translates into TV ads in heavy rotation, or saturation poster coverage. Our reviews are a useful commodity, and will always be pillaged for poster campaigns but it is not hard to find a favourable review, or a positive spin somewhere.[34]

The most important distinctions raised by Kennedy are the difference in approach between the campaigns for independent films and studio pictures, and the tension between the putative desire for impartiality on the part of film reviewers and their inevitable role in the film-marketing process. The makers of posters may be flexible when reproducing critical comment on films. The *Daily Telegraph* film critic James Delingpole indicates that, once published, film reviews are considered to be in the public domain, and the critic lacks the ability to control their subsequent meaning and uses:

> Film companies don't ring you up and ask for permission to use your quotes on posters and such like. They just go ahead and do it, editing as they feel necessary. Obviously, it's quite important for the marketing campaign to find at least some favourable quotes from the critics to put on posters etc, though I don't think Hollywood particularly cares where they come from.[35]

Delingpole's opinion usefully emphasises that critics do not necessarily present an impartial viewpoint, as they may be motivated by their desire for visibility if they work for small publications, and possibly by pressure from the studios if they have a high profile. It also emphasises the flexible approach to reviews adopted by film marketers seeking critical text for favourable poster endorsements. The three review quotes in the half-page advertisement placed in the *Guardian* the day before the British general release of *Shakespeare in Love* represent the opinions of three of the most respected British film critics: Barry Norman states 'I doubt if we'll see a better British film in the rest of this entire Millennium', Christopher Tookey terms it 'a classic romantic comedy, sparkling with wit and wonderful performances', and grants it five stars, and Cosmo Landesman focuses upon 'the brilliance of Gwyneth Paltrow. If you see a better performance in a film this year, I'll eat my codpiece'. The image of Paltrow and Fiennes embracing is placed next to the quotes, providing visual consistency which accompanies those consistent elements of the campaign drawn out by the text: the film's Britishness, its generic status as an intelligent, quality romantic comedy and as a momentous cinematic event, the celebrity power of Gwyneth Paltrow and a pun on the Elizabethan content.

The tag lines on the posters for *Shakespeare in Love* differ in Britain and North America. In North America the tag line emphasises the film's romance: 'Love is the only inspiration'. In Britain, comic and romantic elements are combined with a literary subtext for the *Shakespeare in Love* tag line: 'A comedy about the greatest love story almost never told'. In both instances, the quotations are not from Shakespeare but instead employ the generic conventions of tag lines for romantic comedies. Ken Green indicated that many other tag lines were also considered but rejected to market *Shakespeare in Love*. These tag lines focus upon Shakespeare's status both as a writer and as a lover: 'The greatest wit is about to woo', 'When it comes to romance ... he wrote the book', 'A love story for everyone who's fallen in love ... and been lost for words', 'It's all about reading between the lines and getting between the sheets', 'It's all about losing your heart without losing your head', 'Where there's a will there's a way', 'What love through yonder window breaks', 'Anything else would be a tragedy', 'An inspiration for anyone whose [*sic*] ever fallen in love ... and been lost for words' and 'The penis mightier than the sword'. The rejection of all these tag lines forms a crucial instance of careful maintenance of the hybrid balance between high and low. The tag lines eventually selected emphasise romance over sexual suggestiveness, and replace references to writer's block and Shakespeare's human shortcomings with the poetic, romantic tag line 'Love is the only inspiration'. The variety of tag lines that underwent serious consideration also indicates the complexity of the decision-making processes in marketing *Shakespeare in Love*.

The trailer as well as the tag lines for *Shakespeare in Love* accentuate romance. Indeed, emphasis upon romance is a consistent feature of the campaign as a whole, and highlighting Will Shakespeare as a romantic hero provides an important means of granting him humanity, a lover rather than an intellectual, and places the film in the romantic comedy genre. The film's trailer also references the heritage or costume film genre at many points, and expresses reverence in its visual references, which include the balcony scene, the Rose Theatre and a dance at the De Lesseps residence. The *Shakespeare in Love* trailer pays homage to previous filmed adaptations of Shakespeare, for example, as Desmet observes, 'in one of the film's cleverest scenes, Viola and Shakespeare meet at her balcony to parody not just the balcony scene from *Romeo and Juliet* but specifically Zeffirelli's staging of the scene'.[36] The appropriative and eclectic aspects of postmodernism are the salient ones in the posters and trailers, represented by David Harvey as a series of 'gestures towards historical legitimacy by extensive and often eclectic quotation of past styles'. Harvey goes on to add, 'through films, television, books, and the like, history and past experience are turned into a seemingly vast archive instantly retrievable and capable of being consumed over and over again at the push of a button'.[37] The parody of the balcony scene creates a multi-textual reference spanning several media, cleverly combining a wide range of educational fields, and offering multiple opportunities for high/low cultural crossover. The notion of hybridity is once again significant here.

Conformity of the majority of the images in the *Shakespeare in Love* poster and trailers to costume-drama conventions, such as Joseph Fiennes's appearance as Shakespeare and Judi Dench's appearance as Elizabeth, reassures the potential audience for the film that it displays a degree of reverence to the historical setting, but also highlights the irreverence of frame-breaking moments such as the comic play on the phrase 'the show must go on'. Judith Williamson's research on the varied use of another high/popular cultural icon in marketing, the *Mona Lisa*, indicates the complexity of the hybrid significations that cultural icons possess in the hands of professional marketers. After observing that the *Mona Lisa* 'is a familiar reference, a picture that even the "uneducated" have heard of', and that the use made of such icons varies according to the type of product they are being used to market, Williamson goes on to suggest that the use of such familiar cultural figures as the *Mona Lisa* or Picasso provides 'multiple values: snobbery, or reassurance. It depends how much you know about Art'.[38] These 'multiple values' are self-consciously employed in order to reach the broadest possible audience.

Such comprehensible parody is crucial in analysis of film marketing because posters and trailers rely on immediate accessibility by the target audience for their impact, whereas a film can develop themes gradually and invite audience comprehension over a period of time. Any stable binary between the products that reinforce high culture and those that subvert it breaks down in the context of *Shakespeare in Love*, however, because neither the film nor the marketing campaign can be easily categorised as high or low, which is what makes it so interesting.

Although 'pleasant incongruities' are exhibited in the film-marketing campaign, for example the shot in the trailer of Will falling off the balcony as he woos Viola, or the final trailer shot of Will drinking in a tavern, Shakespeare's status as a creative genius and lover is stressed even more strongly.

According to Ken Green, 'Radio was used as a sustaining medium – again, very quick turnaround and can be used tactically. It was of great importance in the UK because the distributor had less than a month with a full print to work with before the film was released'.[39] Radio spots are able to respond rapidly to new award nominations and to adapt the campaign accordingly. The three radio spots created prior to the BAFTA awards for UK radio emphasise that *Shakespeare in Love* had already won seven Oscars and list them, and focus upon the film's romantic-comedy credentials and its popularity with audiences and critics alike. They describe the film in two spots as 'the year's most celebrated movie', in the third spot as the film 'everyone's in love with', extending the romance of the film out to the audience, and drawing the audience into the concept of the film as an event in a manner that failed, as I have discussed, during the Branagh *Hamlet* campaign. The radio spots also allow the marketers to use the concept of theatre production to make a self-congratulatory statement about the film's array of awards – after listing the film's Oscar and BAFTA achievements, 'rapturous applause' is played on the radio soundtrack.

Will vs. William Shakespeare

My preceding analysis of many facets of the *Shakespeare in Love* campaign indicates the necessity of examining how an iconic Shakespeare is deployed as a multiple signifier more broadly in the film's marketing campaign. It is first helpful to make some points about what Shakespeare might reasonably be taken to signify to the audience for *Shakespeare in Love*. Will Shakespeare is both a historical Elizabethan playwright and the imagined precursor to the Hollywood screenwriter in *Shakespeare in Love*. The lack of available, reliable biographical information that has survived about Shakespeare enabled Tom Stoppard and Marc Norman to reconstitute Shakespeare's historical identity to appeal to a modern cinema audience. The postmodern concept of the simulacrum may be productively referred to in this context. Shakespeare's physical image, a familiar and iconic image on consumer objects from credit cards to souvenir mugs, does not have a single authentic original. Posthumous curiosity and speculation about the biographical Shakespeare's private life fuel the power of Shakespeare's celebrity as a marketing tool for *Shakespeare in Love*, just as the same fascinations prolong the afterlife of twentieth-century celebrities such as Elvis Presley and Marilyn Monroe. Shakespeare is both 'one of us' and a distant, mythical figure. The balancing act is how to maintain both when they push in opposite directions, but are both needed to maximise commercial exploitation. Hybrid marketing is a highly skilled and precarious operation. There is a Bard/Will binary too, in terms of celebrity packaging.

One means of accounting for the commercial success of *Shakespeare in Love* is that its marketing provides a simulacrum of an idealised, harmonious Elizabethan past. Jameson's reading of postmodern nostalgia is of a confrontation between past and present:

> Our social, historical and existential present, and the past as "referent" – the incompatibility of a postmodernist "nostalgia" art language with genuine historicity becomes dramatically apparent. The contradiction propels this mode, however, into complex and interesting new formal inventiveness; it being understood that the nostalgia film was never a matter of some old-fashioned "representation" of historical content, but instead approached the past through stylistic connotation, conveying "pastness" by the glossy qualities of the image.[40]

The marketing campaign for *Shakespeare in Love* conforms to Jameson's identification of postmodern historicity as a process of connotation rather than representation. However, as with so many postmodern tropes and processes, there are parallels in the Shakespeare texts' treatment of historical materials. Martin Harries's attack upon *Shakespeare in Love* as 'a mirror in which Hollywood ogles its own genius' relates to the film's connotation rather than representation of Shakespeare. He continues, 'Hollywood sees Shakespeare not as a playwright or a man, but as the enterprise of Elizabethan theatre, which turns emptiness into genius. Just like Hollywood. The film is an allegory of Hollywood's self-love'.[41] Significantly, Harries emphasises the breadth and complexity of meaning Shakespeare embodies for Hollywood, and his claim implicitly refers to a significant concept in postmodernist theory, that all art is simulacrum; a copy without an original. The version of Elizabethan England presented in the film's marketing campaign is also a simulacrum, enabling the marketers to repackage the realities of Elizabethan history and culture into a more appealing fantasy heritage package.

Such a preoccupation with postmodern playfulness and irreverence towards Elizabethan history forms a linchpin in the film's marketing campaign for several important reasons. Partially, in the wake of postmodernism, *Shakespeare in Love* demonstrates the increasing permeability of the perceived boundaries between elite and popular culture; as McRobbie comments, 'we live in a consumer culture predicated on forgetting or else on highly selective remembering, e.g. through nostalgia or the "heritage industry"'.[42] Embracing this ethos, Joseph Fiennes (Will Shakespeare in *Shakespeare in Love*) presents a highly collaborative version of Shakespeare steeped in the material conditions of cultural production, and in doing so indicates his awareness of the tension between high and low cultural representations of Shakespeare:

> I love Tom Stoppard's idea of him plagiarising. Copyright laws hadn't begun so it was a great idea to steal. But who doesn't? Consciously or subconsciously. I'm plagiarising, borrowing and manipulating information from all over. Nothing is holy. I see him like a leech, a reporter of human frailty of his time. Stoppard's script is a homage to Shakespeare, and to his methods. It uses some of his themes – cross-dressing and hidden identity for example. I thought, fuck it, he's a hustler. He's a gypsy, he's a wheeler-dealer … Above all, though, he's inky … I was covered with ink. He must have been! I said to the make-up people "Let's keep that in. He's a wordsmith – that's what he is!"[43]

Fiennes's concern with historical veracity is carefully couched in a colloquial tone that reassures the potential audience for the film that Shakespeare has been rewritten as an updated, accessible, contemporary artist. However, in a contradictory appraisal of Shakespeare, Fiennes also speaks of 'homage' and a 'wordsmith', ensuring that reverence to the author and the text is also paramount. The hybrid text can be both a homage and an irreverence at the same time, necessarily so in the neo-colonial, Anglo-American Shakespeare text.

The very beginning of the *Shakespeare in Love* trailer emphasises the same memorable image of Shakespeare as a wordsmith; after a shot of Fiennes pushing past London pedestrians comes a close-up shot of an ink-stained hand writing with a quill pen, followed by a shot of Fiennes lost in thought as he tries to write, and then a shot of him destroying manuscript papers. This is a very careful conflation of genius and fallibility. The handwriting itself is also of interest. It is unclear whether it is actual Elizabethan secretary hand or simply cod scribble comment on the iconic significance of 'authentic' handwriting. Stray signatures are very powerful in the sparse field of traditional Shakespeare biography, and Elizabethan writing or 'Shakespeare's hand' becomes a suggestive symbol that the film's trailer rehearses in a consciously excessive way, particularly by having ink everywhere on Will Shakespeare's person, clothing and study. In an even more potent expression of the marketing campaign's focus on Will Shakespeare's eternal genius as a writer, the interior of the VHS box for *Shakespeare in Love* is illustrated by a still in which Shakespeare faces the Rose audience, hands outstretched in a Christ-like pose whilst the crowd cheers and he is bathed in a celestial light. Examination of other marketing devices for the film will serve to illustrate this tension between quality and populism, the sacred and the profane, in more depth.

Marketing and merchandising tie-ins for Shakespeare in Love

The many other means by which Miramax marketed *Shakespeare in Love*, including the film's web site, product promotions, book tie-ins and two DVDs, are characterised by the same ethos governing the use of the Oscars as a marketing tool – they simultaneously raise the film's profile in the marketplace and consolidate its status as a 'quality' product. The official web site for *Shakespeare in Love* prominently advertised the video, the book of poetry and the DVD for the movie. It also ran a *Shakespeare in Love* Getaway Sweepstakes: which provided a chance 'to relive the romance of Miramax Home Entertainment's award-winning love story with a trip for two to London and a year's worth of cosmetics!' A Max Factor promotion run as another component of the *Shakespeare in Love* marketing campaign in North America offered free rental of the *Shakespeare in Love* video from the huge Blockbuster Video store chain if selected items from the Max Factor cosmetics range were purchased. Ken Green indicates that:

Marketing stunts start with product placement, for example, what car does Bond drive? That company commits to promoting a film at the time of release. But you are looking for *compatible* companies to tie in with, for example, Toys'R'Us and Burger King for the *ET* re-release. The promotions manager is in charge, and the licensing and consumer product group.[44]

The distributor for *Shakespeare in Love* strategically used consistent commercial tie-ins such as a trip to London, site of Shakespeare's cultural production, and a complimentary video of the film with the cosmetics range, seeking to maintain a dignified aura of high culture at all times. Exemplifying the failed attempt to blend high and popular culture that characterises the marketing campaign for the 1999 film *William Shakespeare's A Midsummer Night's Dream*, that film's marketing team appeared unsure to which audience to pitch their product tie-ins. A North American promotional tie-in offered free tickets when a 'Taste of Tuscany' pasta sauce was purchased, suggesting a desire to be perceived as a 'quality' picture, rooted in sophisticated European, old world culture. However, a Max Factor 'Midsummer Night's Dream collection of cosmetics' was also launched, to appeal to a younger audience. Created by Ronnie Specter, who did the make-up for the film, items were named for characters in the play, such as CobWeb nail varnish. Shakespearian subject matter enabled *Shakespeare in Love* to be marketed, not as an alienating exclusively high-culture product, but nevertheless as a 'quality' picture, and as a film that could be used in the educational market. The notion of hybridity is once again very important here, as the audience can both indulge and feel intellectual simultaneously.

A study guide was issued to accompany the film in the UK, suggesting that the film is sufficiently highbrow to be employed for educational purposes, but also an entertaining way to learn about history and literature. Produced by Film Education, a British film-industry-funded charity which encourages the use of film in school curricula, the study guide's front cover is illustrated with the picture of Fiennes and Paltrow embracing which forms the basis for virtually all the visuals in the *Shakespeare in Love* marketing campaign. The film title and the outlines of the couple are illustrated with ink swirls that combine the irreverence of graffiti writing with a reference to calligraphic Elizabethan writing and the ink blots of Shakespeare's literary endeavour. The study guide, which claims to be aimed at students of GCSE English and Drama and A Level

English and Theatre Studies, is divided into subsections which combine education with entertainment: 'Fact, Fiction and Fun', 'Shakespeare's London', 'Playhouses', 'Players and Playwrights', 'Love and Marriage in the Sixteenth Century', 'Writing for Stage and Screen' and, perhaps most tellingly, 'Should We Approach Shakespeare with a Sense of Fun?' The appendices combine a chronology of Shakespeare's life and work, a scene from *Romeo and Juliet* and the poems 'Silvia', Joshua Sylvester's 'Ubique' and Christopher Marlowe's 'The Passionate Shepherd to his Love' with an extract from the screenplay that adapts the extract from *Romeo and Juliet*. Some of the set study questions carefully lead the students towards a belief that appreciation of Shakespeare has no access limitations and must not be treated with fear and reverence, for example, 'Do you agree with Tom Stoppard's comments that entertainment values are not age-related?' The most important statement in the context of this book comes in the introductory section 'Fact, Fiction and Fun':

> Since he is probably the best-known playwright in the world and his plays have been performed more or less continually for over four hundred years, Shakespeare and his works have acquired a certain reverent distance that quite often makes us forget that, in his time his plays were enjoyed by all levels of society.

The synopsis also carefully maintains the hybrid veneration and irreverence balance: describing the film as 'a fast-moving romantic comedy' in which Will's writer's block is cured by 'the startlingly beautiful young Viola', and, 'inspired by love, his creative powers are unleashed as his great love story, *Romeo and Juliet*, is brought to life for the first time'.[45] Film Education also offered free preview screenings of *Shakespeare in Love* to school parties at a variety of cinemas nationwide, a pragmatic means of expanding the film's audience.

The DVD release of *Shakespeare in Love* is also a very significant marketing tool. *Shakespeare in Love* was released on DVD on 16 August 1999, on the same DVD release date as *10 Things I Hate About You* and *Never Been Kissed*. Columbia TriStar was responsible for the DVD distribution for *Shakespeare in Love* although Miramax and UIP handled the majority of the campaign. Prior to release Kerina Lee, the DVD distribution manager for *Shakespeare in Love* at Columbia, observed that 'I can't tell you what a big release this will be for UK!! Bigger than

Godzilla on DVD',[46] emphasising the significant place occupied by *Shakespeare in Love* in Columbia's distribution slate, and the increasing complexity and significance of the place of DVDs in the corporate American marketplace. The DVD disc charted at No. 1, and had special 'added value' features including a Behind-the-Scenes Documentary, Director's Commentary, Television Spots, Costume Design Featurette, Deleted Scenes and Theatrical Trailers. The promotional material on VHS and DVD boxes provides a lasting marketing tool, and a means of archiving other marketing such as trailers and television spots. Video and DVD also provide a source of long-term marketing for films once they have ceased to circulate in cinemas. DVD provides an unusual forum within film marketing in which a comprehensive attempt to position the films as 'quality' products, worthy of preservation, may be made.

On 7 December 1999, a pre-Christmas collectors' edition of *Shakespeare in Love* was released on DVD, which also contains special features in the form of director and cast commentary. *Empire*, with the caption 'The life of the A-Level syllabus stalwart revisited with japery, jokes and Gwyneth Paltrow', lists the DVD in its 'must buy' section and gives the DVD four out of five stars. The caption imitates the cornerstones of the marketing campaign: educational value, irreverence, humour and celebrity. The review praises the 'inventive, accessible screenplay' and focuses on other issues relevant to this study:

> "Broke, horny and starved for an idea", is screen scribe Marc Norman's encapsulation of his hero's predicament in *Shakespeare in Love*, and as the Bard struggles to craft the genius of Romeo and Juliet, this notion is played out to smart, funny, gloriously uplifting effect … John Madden … drives the whole affair at a cracking pace without ever sacrificing beautiful craft or the unique serio-comic tone […] Joyous. Special features: A Making of Featurette, a too brief glimpse into the creation of the costumes or some deleted scenes (including an elaborate dig at producer Harvey Weinstein). On the commentary front, there is a cast and crew option and a much more satisfying John Madden voice-over whose insights further deepens your appreciation. If you ever wondered why *SIL* bagged all those gongs, the answer lies in the 21 TV spots, designed to highlight the film's Academy-friendly strengths.[47]

The final sentence suggests that the marketing of the film is as pertinent to its Oscar success as its quality as a motion picture. Ken Green calculated that the *Shakespeare in Love* advertising spend was 2.2 million pounds, and remarks that this was a very high figure, comparable to the advertising spend for *Jurassic Park.* He indicated that the original budget was much lower, but they used television and press and kept spending money in order to keep changing the campaign and making it look different.[48] The 'elaborate dig' at Harvey Weinstein on the DVD is a typically clever self-deprecating ploy by the Miramax chairman, reinforcing his status as a money-orientated and irreverent, but also cultured and discerning, film distributor. The director is praised for achieving a commercially effective balance between veneration and irreverence, and Shakespeare is also presented in those tones, as both all-too-human and the immortal Bard simultaneously: immortal because he is so mortal. Such tight-rope walking between veneration and irreverence is necessary, as a tilt too far either way can lead to commercial failure.

Shakespeare in Charge, by Kenneth Adelman and Norman Augustine, is also tied in to *Shakespeare in Love*, as the book describes means by which Shakespeare can be used as a motivational tool in a business context, and is marketed in a trailer on the North American *Shakespeare in Love* video. For a period after the book's publication, *Talk Magazine* sponsored a book tour with a tie-in to MasterCard. If a Mastercard was used to purchase *Shakespeare in Charge*, the consumer was entitled to a free copy of the *Shakespeare in Love* soundtrack. Miramax Books/Hyperion in North America and Faber in Britain published the screenplay under the title *Shakespeare in Love: A Screenplay* by Marc Norman and Tom Stoppard. Another film tie-in book, *Shakespeare in Love: The Love Poetry of William Shakespeare*, a collection of Shakespeare's verse mixed in with snippets and photos from the movie, was also published. This book of sonnets published to accompany the film had the added value of suggesting that, in a reciprocal cultural movement, *Shakespeare in Love* could actually be used to promote Shakespeare, in much the same way that a volume of W. H. Auden's love poetry became a best-seller in the wake of its association with the film *Four Weddings and a Funeral.* The book of sonnets consolidates the film marketers' claims for the film's merit as a teaching aid. Hyperion/Miramax also released an attractively printed full screenplay with complete screen credits and eye-catching photographic illustrations.

Just as Hollywood film stars since cinema's inception have enhanced their credibility and American cultural hegemony by acting in Shakespearian productions, so Shakespeare's celebrity appeal is supported by contemporary celebrities. At the reopening ceremony for the remains of the Rose Theatre in 1999 an unusual marketing stunt was employed. Life-size figures of Gwyneth Paltrow and Joseph Fiennes in full Elizabethan costume were placed in view, smiling benignly upon the flood-lit remains of the Rose Theatre's foundations, in an engaging mixture of veneration and irreverence. These stills from the film had been 'kindly lent' by the *Shakespeare in Love* distributor Miramax, providing further exemplification of Miramax's adept marketing techniques. The film received free publicity and the Rose Theatre was granted some modern celebrity appeal, placing it on a more equal footing with its better-known neighbour, the Globe. In addition to considering the most advanced marketing devices, however, Miramax was trading on a brand image of Elizabethan heritage that had a 400-year pedigree. *Shakespeare in Love* venerates Elizabethan Englishness and haphazard, inspirational artistic creativity, but Miramax marketed the film with American corporate efficiency and celebrity. Thus a winning combination was created of self-conscious mapping of New World onto Old, a form of reverse cultural imperialism.

In the 1980s, celebrities from the British theatre world famously played a part in the campaign to preserve the archaeological remains of the Rose Theatre, although they were unsuccessful in stopping the site's development by a corporation. The Rose preservation appeal represented the sacrilegious demands of commerce as directly opposed to reverential enshrining of Shakespeare's sacred art. 1990s marketing of filmed Shakespeare adaptations adopts a more pragmatic 'third-way' of the two: exemplified by the cardboard cut-out character stills from *Shakespeare in Love* on display at the reopening of the remains of the Rose in 1999. Such a fusion of film marketing and historically portentous occasion produces a phenomenon in which high culture, heritage and Englishness are harnessed in order to place the triumphant resurrection of Elizabethan history by *Shakespeare in Love* on a par with the triumph of uncovering the Rose. As in the poster art which markets the film, the visual juxtaposition of the English theatre actor Joseph Fiennes as Will Shakespeare and the blonde American film star Gwyneth Paltrow as the pseudo-English, fictional Lady Viola De Lesseps imports a range of significations of the actors' celebrity to contribute to the complex messages communicated by the presence of the stills. The Rose's pre-eminent Elizabethan sister heritage site, the Globe, also represents an American, Sam Wanamaker's, project to 're-Shakespearise' Shakespeare, creating a popular space (although, as suggested by the modern entrance fees even for 'groundlings', not having as broad a social base as Shakespeare's Globe) in which a high cultural element of authenticity is nevertheless retained, resembling the cultural arena in which Hollywood filmed Shakespeare adaptations may be situated. The 'wooden O' is, after all, also central to *Shakespeare in Love*.

The complex interaction between celebrity signifiers at work in the Rose Theatre reopening may be related to P. David Marshall's helpful formulation of celebrity as ambiguous rather than coherent in its signification, a product constructed by both the media and the audience. He empowers the audience, making reference to the cultural politics of hegemony in the process, rather than the corporate myth-making machine, and emphasises that celebrity 'articulates the individual as commodity', and, Marshall continues, 'offers the reader of culture a privileged view of the representative forms of modern subjectivity that pass through the celebrity as discourses'.[49] Ascribing to Marshall's version of articulation, can Shakespeare retain his 'authenticity' in Benjamin's 'age of mechanical reproduction'? Robert C. Allen effectively reverses Walter Benjamin's argument in *The Work of Art in the Age of Mechanical Reproduction* by claiming that:

> The movies continue to possess a lingering residue of their connection with the cinema in their promise of the auratic elevation of products, people and experience above the level of the ordinary, the quotidian, the mere commodity. The movies continue to want to claim the ground of authenticity, as the originating site of experience in relation to which licenced products are souvenirs, as the prior body for which the "Happy Meal" figure is substituted as fetish part.[50]

This 'lingering residue' is debased by a loss of aura, and this extremely useful passage permits an imagining of cinema as (modernist) aura and the movies as (postmodernist) post-aura, placing the films on a sliding scale until there is no more 'lingering' and they reach full commodity status. Although Allen's model is by no means unassailable, the *idea* of difference between cinema and movies maps usefully onto the *idea* of high and low culture in the context of filmed Shakespeare adaptations. This difference is grounded in both chronology, in which the 1990s mark a post-aura era, and place, in which 'cinema' is envisaged as European whilst 'movies' are American.

Shakespeare in Love *and post-colonialism*

An assumption that the American post-colonial state is appropriating Shakespeare to 'write back'[51] to Britain forms another facet of the theory of Hollywood's hegemony over global cultural production. The manner in which this hegemonic ideology operates is extrapolated from the marketing of Shakespeare as a product to American cinema audiences. The post-colonial elements of *Shakespeare in Love* indicate that a reworked American paradigm of Shakespeare was created by Hollywood film marketers in the 1990s in order to create a cultural figure representative of American global cultural hegemony. In the context of the marketing campaign for *Shakespeare in Love* the difficult term 'post-colonialism' is rationalised in terms of Hollywood's position as a major neo-colonial cultural force. Hollywood's stronghold on the global film industry ensures that the equation of 'American' with 'global' may now be treated as almost a given in such an age of high American global imperialism.

Shakespeare's dual status as an icon of both British and American cultural imperialism consolidates his position as a figure of popular culture, a brand name to be employed for adaptation indefinitely. The concern of Miramax, Branagh and McKellen that Shakespeare would not sell in Hollywood appears to have underestimated the many potentially appealing connotations that the Elizabethan era holds for North American film-makers and cinema audiences. The early modern period allows safe displacement as a stable, organic setting, creating a space for potentially radical disjunction between form and content in much the same way as classical settings provided an ostensibly neutral space upon which Elizabethan dramatists might imprint their own political and cultural milieu. The Elizabethan era conventionally represents a Golden Age in literature and governance; viewed from a present state of decline for Britons, and denoting for Americans the beginning of a phase of their history.

Hollywood marketing is genre-dependent and 'Elizabethan' became an appealing shorthand for film marketers positioning *Shakespeare in Love* as, in part at least, a heritage movie. *Shakespeare in Love* appropriately ends with Viola's journey from Elizabethan England to the American New World, an exotic and malleable export that may be re-formed by America, completing the education of Viola that Shakespeare began. Furthermore, as Ken Green indicates, it is the British marketing campaign for *Shakespeare in Love* that formed the globally exported version, rather than Hollywood's vision alone. The version of Elizabethan England created is a post-colonial export from America to Britain and back again. The heritage movie genre enables literature and history to be repackaged into a format with more broad-based audience appeal. The success of the films produced by the Merchant Ivory collaborations in the 1980s and early 1990s provided an environment in Hollywood in which receptivity to literary adaptations was enhanced as belief in their commercial viability increased. *Shakespeare in Love*, in common with Merchant Ivory films, promoted and exported not only Shakespeare but an appealing heritage version of England.

Chronological and generic diversity form one means by which marketers sought to maximise the appeal of *Shakespeare in Love* to a broad range of audiences. Shakespeare's words, scribbled in manuscript in the closing scene of *Shakespeare in Love*, are verbally and visually inscribed upon the New World landscape Viola enters, where she may, it is implied, pass on Shakespeare's words to a new colonial population. The global cultural discourse of Hollywood continues this colonial project with its worldwide dissemination of filmed Shakespeare adaptations. Richard Burt's exploration of American attitudes to Shakespeare leads him to view 'the citation of Shakespeare as paradoxically cool and uncool [as] symptomatic of America's own doubts about its status as an imperial power' and 'of an unconscious and vestigial American post-colonial identification with British colonial culture'. This 'post-colonial identification' in Hollywood, particularly in *Shakespeare in Love*, is, however, neither 'unconscious' nor 'vestigial'. Burt's subsequent claim that 'Shakespeare appears in American kiddie culture not as unmarked, universal, but as marked, colonial, British'[52] can be extended by recognising that Shakespeare signifies in that manner for a much broader audience than he concedes.

The marketing of *Shakespeare in Love* indicates that the high/low or elite/popular binary is the key area of problematisation in postmodernism. It is vital to view this master binary in terms of creative interaction rather than the struggle for domination, as the high/low binary is provisional and constantly shifting. Both in the film and its marketing there is a deliberately jarring postmodern effect rather than an attempt to privilege one term above the other. Such a strategy neutralises attempts to set art above commerce or commerce over art, bypassing the seemingly outmoded mid-twentieth-century anxiety about cultural standards and canon formation. Stuart Hall also adopts this more positive view of the relationship between high and low culture, in celebrating what he calls 'aggressive resistance to difference':

> If the global postmodern represents an ambiguous opening to difference and to the margins and makes a certain kind of decentring of the western narrative a likely possibility, it is matched [by] the aggressive resistance to difference; the attempt to restore the canon of western civilization; the assault, direct and indirect, on multiculturalism; the return to grand narratives of history, language and literature (the three great supporting pillars of national identity and national culture).[53]

Thus postmodernism may reinforce high culture as often as it enfranchises low culture, and here crucially represents an assault on difference, with its implications of hierarchy, although Hall's formula applied to marketing reinforces the need for a postmodern component to successfully package *Shakespeare in Love* as an upmarket blockbuster.

As has often been observed, modernism shares many of the characteristics of postmodernism, such as pastiche, or the deliberately shocking or incongruous importation of traditional high cultural elements into a new work. However, postmodernism arguably draws attention to its own characteristics more self-consciously than modernism, which tends to be normalising in its representation of the canon. Postmodernism in part, according to Douglas Kellner, denotes a reactive attempt to debunk the elitist aura of the great modernist text,[54] although modernism had itself begun the task of desegregating high and low cultural classification, which postmodernism continues, intensifies and tends to welcome rather than view with anxiety.

Hall's approving quotation of Bakhtin's concept of 'carnivalesque' rests upon its status as '*not* simply a metaphor of inversion – setting the "low" in the place of the "high", while preserving the binary structure of the division between them'. Hall continues by noting that 'the low invades the high, blurring the hierarchical imposition of order; creating, not simply the triumph of one aesthetic over another, but those impure and hybrid forms of the "grotesque"; revealing the interdependency of the low on the high'.[55] Here Hall aptly illustrates the complexity of the cultural transactions that have taken place between high and low throughout history. It suggests a model of 'reversibility' in which the Bard can be reconfigured as low or grotesque, irrevocably dissolving the secure identity of the high with Shakespeare as its traditional cornerstone. However, in the marketing of filmed Hollywood adaptations there is nothing arbitrary about the calculated fusion of high and low cultural elements in order to secure the broadest possible audience for the films, although marketing may only influence rather than ensure. Hollywood film marketing provides one site in which the articulation between culture and power is particularly evident. The marketing campaign for *Shakespeare in Love* reveals itself as an intrinsically postmodern phenomenon as Shakespeare the (elusive) historical persona and cultural signifier is transformed into a fictional and marketable 'image' appropriate for mass-consumer consumption. The marketing of *Shakespeare in Love* indicates a process not of high cultural concealment but of high cultural translation and adaptation.

CHAPTER SIX

Selling Shakespeare to Hollywood: Into the new millennium

TWO FILMED SHAKESPEARE adaptations of the new millennium suggest that even the most fundamental elements of the Shakespeare myth, from his most famous plots to his very identity, are open to creative reinscriptions, although the space for more 'faithful' adaptations shows signs of diminishing. The 2002 film *Romeo and Juliet Revisited* has a plot outline suggesting: 'this is the story of what happens to the star-cross'd lovers after Shakespeare's famous play ends'. The first film to specifically address the authorship debate in depth is a documentary, *Much Ado about Something*, which was released in North America in February 2002. The increasingly irreverent and postmodern marketing of filmed Shakespeare adaptations from the early 1990s to the early 2000s provided an opportunity for film directors and distributors to continue to expand the boundaries of what constitutes both mainstream cinema and Shakespeare in American culture. Despite continued adherence to the idea of the high/low binary and anxiety about cultural disintegration amongst members of the Academy and film critics, Hollywood's appropriation of Shakespeare is driven by financial rather than ideological imperatives, and must therefore be viewed pragmatically rather than cynically. Filmed Shakespeare adaptations naturally display as much variation in their quality as any other film genre, but they do enable the stimulating dissemination of Shakespeare in a broad variety of forms to a wide audience.

Directed by Michael Radford and starring Al Pacino as Shylock, *William Shakespeare's The Merchant of Venice* was released in 2004. The marketing of the film suggests that tried and tested 1990s formulae were still being deployed halfway through the first decade of the new millennium. The sepia-tinted poster used in the UK marketing campaign grants the image a 'heritage' look. It is also a celebrity-driven image, featuring a very large head shot of a brooding Al Pacino, flanked on his right-hand side by smaller head shots of Jeremy Irons, Joseph Fiennes and Lynn Collins. To emphasise the picture's cultural credentials, 'Toronto Film Festival Official Selection' and 'Venice Film Festival Official Selection' are inscribed just below the title in the lower right-hand corner. A coin-shaped insert, perhaps reflecting the play text and film's preoccupation with money and commerce, advertises the 'Royal European Charity Premiere of *The Merchant of Venice* in the Presence of HRH The Prince of Wales', drawing upon the cultural *kudos* of the Prince much as Branagh had done with his consultation of Prince Charles for his stage version of *Henry V* at the RSC many years earlier. In contrast to his upbeat, casual demeanour in the posters for *Looking for Richard*, Pacino strikes a morose and pensive pose in the poster for *William Shakespeare's The Merchant of Venice*, his gaze, unlike that of the other featured actors, staring out from the poster at the spectator. Supporting the image created by Pacino, the most prominent of three quotes from film critics featured on the poster, taken from *Empire*, exclaims that 'Al Pacino delivers a nuanced, powerful performance. ... a sumptuous production'. The Region One DVD release of the film includes a web link to an on-line teachers' guide, indicating that a strong appeal to the educational market and use of the Internet as a marketing tool also remain cornerstones of the marketing of Shakespeare on film in the new millennium.

There are both points of continuity in the marketing of filmed Shakespeare adaptations in the 1990s, and discernible changes in strategy between the early 1990s through to the new millennium. A significant point of continuity is a shared appeal in all these films to generic diversity. The films in this study are careful to position themselves as more than just Shakespeare, in order to broaden their appeal. However, as Shakespeare on film became a more discernible genre, the appeal to generic diversity was heightened, until some campaigns either confused their potential audiences by mixing too many genres, particularly *Love's Labour's Lost*, or put emphasis on a multi-genre film and removed any emphasis on the film as a Shakespeare adaptation, such as *Never Been Kissed* and *Get Over It*.

Another discernible change in strategy is the balance between reverence and irreverence. As indicated in Chapter 3, in the early 1990s Branagh's adaptations of *Henry V* and *Much Ado about Nothing*, and Zeffirelli's adaptation of *Hamlet*, aimed to appeal to those seeking 'quality' entertainment, and although their campaigns placed some emphasis on more popular elements, the hybrid dynamic between veneration and irreverence was not yet fully evident. In the mid- to late 1990s, the campaigns for *William Shakespeare's Romeo + Juliet* and *Shakespeare in Love* foregrounded the interplay between high and low in their films much more adeptly. This change in strategy may be ascribed to a variety of causes. The polarity of the British heritage film genre, particularly Merchant Ivory films in Hollywood in the 1980s, was replaced, following Branagh's early successes, with a more hybrid product. The development in the 1990s of sub-genres such as the Branagh Shakespeare film or the teen filmed Shakespeare adaptation also enabled film marketers to play with the pioneering work of the campaigns for *Henry V* and *William Shakespeare's Romeo + Juliet* effectively, selecting the most successful elements of the campaigns and recycling them in modified forms.

It can be concluded that film marketing is neither simple nor static, neither stable nor predictable, neither top-down nor bottom-up, and 'truth to Shakespeare' can be marketed or abandoned based on the only criterion that matters – profitability of the merchandise. My analysis, for example of poster art, has indicated that when considering 1990s filmed Shakespeare adaptations, whilst their common features are significant, the variety of the sub-genres and the degrees and modes of adaptation make this a heterogeneous grouping. However, the filmed adaptations that display the most consistent marketing campaigns, in which the central love story forms a consistent emblem throughout and the blurring of the binary between high and low is a constant motif, *Shakespeare in Love* and *William Shakespeare's Romeo + Juliet*, proved more successful than campaigns in which the marketing oscillated inconsistently between an appeal to high and low, for example the campaigns for *William Shakespeare's A Midsummer Night's Dream* and *Love's Labour's Lost*. The marketing of 1990s filmed Shakespeare adaptations utilised Shakespeare's popular appeal and high-culture credentials simultaneously in order to maximise its audience. The most commercially successful filmed Shakespeare adaptations of this period, including *William Shakespeare's Romeo + Juliet*, Zeffirelli's *Hamlet*, *Much*

Ado about Nothing and *Shakespeare in Love*, all achieve this synthesis self-consciously in their promotion of the films.

The significant growth in the number of filmed Shakespeare adaptations in the 1990s enables more meaningful comparisons to be made in the late 1990s than in the early period. Providing a coherent, updated context, accompanied by drawing upon 'universal' themes and Shakespeare's 'universal' genius are the most salient common features of the marketing strategy in the early 1990s. Late 1990s films with outmoded and difficult-to-market heritage settings tended to under-perform, as with the nineteenth-century Tuscan setting of *William Shakespeare's A Midsummer Night's Dream* or Branagh's 1930s fantasy musical, *Love's Labour's Lost*. Although the marketing of *Shakespeare in Love* draws upon a heritage version of Britain, the setting often functions as postmodern pastiche, relying upon anachronism rather than authenticity for effect. For example, the first audible dialogue in the trailer for *Shakespeare in Love* is a verbal play on the modern phrase 'the show must go on' in an Elizabethan theatre setting. This is followed by Fiennes scrunching up a sheet of manuscript and throwing it at a skull atop a pile of books in a humorous reference to the iconic skull in *Hamlet*.

It can safely be concluded, then, that filmed Shakespeare adaptations in the 1990s might be commercially successful in terms of recouping negative costs but could not be box-office hits at the multiplex unless they blurred the distinction between arthouse and mainstream cinema, and exploited such blurring in the marketing, as seen in the marketing of, for example, Branagh's *Henry V* and *Much Ado about Nothing* and Radford's *The Merchant of Venice*. The distinctive broad movement that I have delineated from 1989 to 2005 is not a movement from Shakespeare as an unpopular to a popular source for filmed adaptations, but from arthouse filmed Shakespeare adaptations to box-office successes with a heightened commercial agenda. Branagh's, Luhrmann's and Madden's films marketed themselves as authentic and reverent interpretations of Shakespeare whilst also reconstructing and reinterpreting those texts to appeal to their audience.

Perhaps the most important conclusion to be drawn from investigation of how filmed Shakespeare adaptations were sold to late twentieth- and early twenty-first-century audiences, therefore, is that a hybrid form of high and low Shakespeare is consistently deployed in order to market the films. My research does not indicate the type of growing divide between high and low within film marketing which has been convincingly posited by Deborah Cartmell as existing in education. She claims that 'with the current backlash against media studies because of the so-called "dumbing down" of English, the divide between "high" and "low" culture widens; as does the manner in which filmic representation of Shakespeare is regarded'.[1]

Despite Cartmell's legitimate concerns, I would suggest that increasingly sophisticated and varied film-marketing techniques form a highly significant means of ensuring that filmed Shakespeare adaptations are commercially viable as both high and low, in the face of anxieties concerning the 'dumbing down' of Shakespeare through commercial exploitation, and opposing fears that Shakespeare is too highbrow for modern Hollywood. I have recognised the complexity of the interactions between film and audience and product and market, and examined film marketing's challenge to easy distinctions between product and market. The foregrounding of the interaction between art and commerce in contemporary cultural debate indicates the level of anxiety concerning the place of Shakespeare in contemporary culture, an anxiety heightened by the notable proliferation of filmed Shakespeare adaptations in 1990s Hollywood. As noted in my first chapter, this book's blurring of high and low supports Stuart Hall's rereading of Gramsci, in particular his key assertion that 'the important point is […] not an inventory of what is high versus what is low at any particular moment'.[2] The binary constructed between art and commerce in filmed Shakespeare adaptations is alternatively read in this study as symbiotic, an active exchange.

The notable proliferation of filmed Shakespeare in the 1990s provided film marketers with cultural credit that could be dispensed for cash. I consequently wish to avoid the hostility displayed by many academics to celebration of the fusion between art and commerce, in favour of the symbiotic relationship which John Drakakis describes as: 'the combination of universal culture and global capitalism locked in an arabesque of mutual validation'.[3] Ulrike Weissenborn's analysis of the 1992 Robert Altman film *The Player* demonstrates how deeply the art/commerce binary pervades both Hollywood's self-representation and academia's relation to Hollywood:

> The Hollywood of the film cares little about the needs of its audience. In the name of business "the movies are not really being made to satisfy

people, they're made to satisfy a checklist of pre-sale requirements." Once a veritable "dream factory", the new Hollywood of "the deal" has turned into a genuinely dreamless community, without ambition or inspiration beyond the fervid tone of the sales pitch.[4]

Both Altman and Weissenborn conflate 'business' with antipathy towards art and audience too readily, creating a static model that fails to recognise the complexity of the balancing act between 'art' and 'money' in Hollywood.

This book challenges both a reductive view of top-down cultural hegemony as operating throughout film marketing and the concept of bottom-up audience control, as, given the evidence, there is no doubt that film marketing can be used to mobilise audiences that would otherwise not have attended. The desire of Hollywood film marketers to find a wide audience cannot always translate into control over what audiences will watch, although there are means at their disposal to make a significant impact. The 'partipulation' debate is, as stated in my introductory chapter, a crucial issue here, as marketing itself is obsessed with passive versus active audience behaviour, but it is, of course, not an easily resolved problematic. Study of the marketing of 1990s filmed Shakespeare adaptations cannot conclusively indicate the degree to which Hollywood is able to control audience tastes. It does, however, indicate that a mystification of any attempt to control audience taste is a popular trope.

Given the shortcomings of ethnographic research, marketing is better viewed as a notoriously imprecise discipline, in which the relation between cause and effect can rarely be established with certainty, as encapsulated by the aphorism that nobody in Hollywood knows anything. Russell Jackson emphasises the need for caution when tracking the complex interplay between corporate output and control of audience tastes:

> Although the world of film finance is in most respects as difficult to fathom and as unpredictable as any branch of commerce, it appears to be true that at least moderate success on the part of one film – say, *Henry V* – can engender temporary enthusiasm on the part of "the money" for other mixtures with some or all of the same ingredients. Multinational finance brings with it responsibility to multinational market pressures, in which the demands of the cinema-going and video-viewing public of the USA carry the greatest weight.[5]

Study of film marketing indicates that the success of *Henry V* did encourage the marketers of future Kenneth Branagh films to use some of the same winning ingredients in their marketing. The success of *William Shakespeare's Romeo + Juliet* encouraged the marketers of subsequent teen filmed Shakespeare adaptations to sell their films on the same winning ticket of hybrid and high and low culture, although a similarly successful balance was not always achieved. My study supports Russell Jackson's more measured approach, which serves to counter the inflated claim of Jerry Bruckheimer that Hollywood producers '*dictate* what they [teen film audiences] want to see'.[6] Faced with these alternative models, I would conclude that Hollywood did not dictate what its audiences wanted to see but that film marketers did seek to recapture the most successful elements of previous campaigns for similar films.

I have charted a process of conservative reinforcement in Hollywood, using Shakespeare as its tool. The contained subversion of Hollywood's irreverent, light-hearted and postmodern filmed Shakespeare adaptations serves to perpetuate Shakespeare's role as universal educator and timeless high-culture symbol. Furthermore, small instances of irreverence may reinforce the audiences' desire for an 'authentic' text, a sacred original capable of imparting timeless knowledge in spite of what modern adaptations 'do' to the text. Although Hollywood's conservatism throughout the twentieth century in areas such as gender relations, race and homosexuality is not a site of much contestation, exploring the promotion of this conservatism in film marketing provides new ground, and helps to consolidate the assumption that a corollary of Hollywood's profit motive is a trend towards conservatism, tempered by instances of appealing irreverence. Film marketers are a vital part of a much broader cultural project of promoting Hollywood as a 'dream factory', and its actors and screenwriters, as well as Shakespeare, as the global stars or celebrities who inhabit that fantasy version of a commercial enterprise.

Notes

1 Introduction: Selling Shakespeare to Hollywood

1. The most significant research in the field of film marketing includes: Peter Bart, *The Gross: The Hits, the Flops – the Summer that Ate Hollywood* (New York: St Martin's Press, 1999), Barry R. Litman, *The Motion Picture Mega-Industry* (Boston, Mass. and London: Allyn & Bacon, 1998), Tiiu Lukk, *Movie Marketing: Opening the Picture and Giving it Legs* (Los Angeles, Calif.: Silman-James Press, 1997), Jason E. Squire, ed., *The Movie Business Book* (Bromley: Columbus Books, 1986), Thom Taylor, *The Big Deal: Hollywood's Million Dollar Spec Script Market* (New York: William Morrow, 1999), and Justin Wyatt, *High Concept: Movies and Marketing in Hollywood* (Austin, Tex.: University of Texas Press, 1994). On the Shakespeare industry, although not specifically focused on film marketing, notable publications include Barbara Hodgdon, ed., *The Shakespeare Trade* (London: Routledge, 1998), Graham Holderness, ed., *The Shakespeare Myth* (Manchester: Manchester University Press, 1988), and Graham Holderness, *Shakespeare Recycled: The Making of Historical Drama* (Hemel Hempstead: Harvester Wheatsheaf, 1992), and on the general process of marketing high culture, see Stephen Brown, *Postmodern Marketing* (London and New York: Routledge, 1995).
2. Fredric Jameson, *Postmodernism, or, The Cultural Logic of Late Capitalism* (London and New York: Verso, 1991), p. xxii.
3. Fredric Jameson, *Postmodernism*, pp. 17–18.
4. See filmography for the directors and dates of all films referred to in this book.
5. Useful recent research conducted upon the validity of the term 'globalisation' forms pertinent background to this section of my introduction. See Toby Miller, Geoffrey A. Lawrence, Jim McKay and David Rowe, eds, *Globalization and Sport: Playing the Field* (London: Sage, 2001).
6. Dick Hebdige, 'Postmodernism and the "Other Side"', in *Stuart Hall: Critical Dialogues*, ed. by David Morley and Kuan-Hsing Chen (London: Routledge, 1996), p. 182.
7. Graeme Turner, *British Cultural Studies: An Introduction*, 2nd edn (London:

Routledge, 1996), pp. 146–7.

8. Graeme Turner, *British Cultural Studies*, pp. 196–7. Turner nevertheless adheres to Pierre Bourdieu's concept of cultural competency, which might be termed elitist

9. Stuart Hall, 'What is this "Black" in Black Popular Culture?', in *Stuart Hall: Critical Dialogues*, p. 465.

10. David Forgacs and Geoffrey Nowell-Smith, eds, *Antonio Gramsci: Selections from Cultural Writings*, trans. by William Boelhower (London: Lawrence & Wishart, 1985), p. 55.

11. Alan Swingewood, *Cultural Theory and the Problem of Modernity* (London: Macmillan Press, 1998), pp. 20–1.

12. Fredric Jameson, *Postmodernism*, p. 67.

13. Imelda Whelehan and Deborah Cartmell, 'Introduction: Pulping Fictions, Consuming Culture Across the Literature/Media Divide', in *Pulping Fictions: Consuming Culture Across the Literature/Media Divide*, ed. by Deborah Cartmell, I.Q. Hunter, Heidi Kaye and Imelda Whelehan (London and Chicago, Ill.: Pluto Press, 1996), p. 2.

14. Jonathan Dollimore and Alan Sinfield, 'Foreword', in *Political Shakespeare, Essays in Cultural Materialism*, ed. by Jonathan Dollimore and Alan Sinfield, 2nd edn (Manchester: Manchester University Press, 1994), p. viii.

15. Alan Sinfield, 'Heritage and the Market, Regulation and Desublimation', in *Political Shakespeare*, p. 260.

16. Colin Kennedy, *Empire*, interview with author, 12 December 2001.

17. Louise Levison, *Filmmakers and Financing: Business Plans for Independents*, 3rd edn (Boston, Mass.: Focal Press, 2001), p. 112.

18. Louise Levison, *Filmmakers and Financing*, p. 111.

19. Peter Holland, 'Foreword', in *Shakespeare, Film, Fin de Siècle*, ed. by Mark Thornton Burnett and Ramona Wray (Basingstoke: Macmillan Press, 2000), p. xiii.

20. Duncan J. Petrie, *Creativity and Constraint in the British Film Industry* (Basingstoke: Macmillan Press, 1991), p. 109.

21. John Heminges and Henry Condell, 'To the Great Variety of Readers', *Comedies, Histories and Tragedies*, in *The Oxford Shakespeare: The Complete Works*, ed. by Stanley Wells and Gary Taylor (Oxford: Oxford University Press, 1998), p. xlv.

22. Colin MacCabe, *The Eloquence of the Vulgar: Language, Cinema and the Politics of Culture* (London: BFI Publishing, 1999), p. 29.

23. Throughout this book, standard film-industry discourse is adhered to as much as possible. Hence, my use of the term North America denotes the USA and Canada, plus territories such as Puerto Rico, which constitutes the domestic market for film distributors. The term also avoids the misleading implication that South or Central America is included in the domestic market. However, when discussing a broader cultural mindset American rather than North American is used, following standard academic discourse. Whenever a dollar money amount is referred to, it refers to the US dollar currency unless otherwise specified.

24. Dorothy Viljoen, *Art of the Deal: The Essential Guide to Business Affairs for Television and Film Producers*, 2nd edn (London: PACT, 1997), p. 217.

25. Louise Levison, *Filmmakers and Financing*, p. 171.

26. Richard Maltby, 'Introduction', in *Identifying Hollywood's Audiences: Cultural Identity and the Movies*, ed. by Melvyn Stokes and Richard Maltby (London: BFI Publishing, 1999), p. 1.

27. Duncan J. Petrie, *Creativity and Constraint*, p. 110.
28. Christy Desmet outlines a methodology for describing the popular cultural connotations of Shakespeare throughout her 'Introduction', in *Shakespeare and Appropriation* , ed. by Christy Desmet and Robert Sawyer (London and New York: Routledge, 1999), pp. 1–14.
29. Alan Sinfield, 'Heritage and the Market, Regulation and Desublimation', *Political Shakespeare*, pp. 269–70.
30. Robert Shaughnessy, ed., *Shakespeare on Film*, Casebooks (Basingstoke: Macmillan, 1998), p. 5.
31. Michael Bristol, *Big Time Shakespeare* (London: Routledge, 1996), p. 90.
32. Peter Holland, 'Foreword', *Shakespeare, Film, Fin de Siècle*, p. xiii.
33. Gary Taylor, 'Afterword: The Incredible Shrinking Bard', in *Shakespeare and Appropriation*, p. 198.
34. Stephen Brown, *Postmodern Marketing*, p. 134.
35. Louise Levison, *Filmmakers and Financing*, p. 174.
36. Mick LaSalle, *San Francisco Chronicle*, interview with author, 13 December 2001.
37. Harold Bloom, *Shakespeare: The Invention of the Human* (New York: Riverhead, 1998), p. 420.
38. Daniel Fischlin and Mark Fortier, 'General Introduction', in *Adaptations of Shakespeare: A Critical Anthology of Plays from the Seventeenth Century to the Present*, ed. by Daniel Fischlin and Mark Fortier (London and New York: Routledge, 2000), p. 14.
39. Deborah Cartmell, 'The Shakespeare on Screen Industry', in *Adaptations from Text to Screen, Screen to Text*, ed. by Deborah Cartmell and Imelda Whelehan (London and New York: Routledge, 1999), p. 37.
40. Deborah Cartmell, 'The Shakespeare on Screen Industry', pp. 31–2.
41. Bill Ashcroft, Gareth Griffiths and Helen Tiffin, *The Empire Writes Back: Theory and Practice in Post-Colonial Literatures* (London and New York: Routledge, 1989).
42. Angela Carter, *Wise Children* (London: Vintage, 1992), p. 133.
43. Many attempts have been made to create a comprehensive taxonomy of filmed Shakespeare adaptations, with varying degrees of success. Kenneth Rothwell's excellent *Shakespeare on Screen: An International Filmography and Videography* (New York: Neal-Schuman, 1990) nevertheless indicates how rapidly outdated such taxonomies become, and Eddie Sammons, *Shakespeare: A Hundred Years on Film* (London: Shepheard-Walwyn, 2000) is comprehensive but inevitably excludes some films that only reference Shakespeare very freely or incidentally.
44. Alan C. Dessen, *Elizabethan Stage Conventions and Modern Interpreters* (Cambridge: Cambridge University Press, 1984), p. 161.
45. Richard Burt, *Shakespeare after Mass Media* (New York: Palgrave Macmillan, 2002), p. 12.
46. Alison Light, 'The Importance of Being Ordinary', *Sight and Sound*, 3: 9 (1993), 18.

2 The use of posters and trailers to sell Shakespeare

1. Richard Burt, *Unspeakable ShaXXXspeares: Queer Theory and American Kiddie Culture* (Basingstoke: Macmillan Press, 1998), p. 11.
2. The body of secondary literature on the use of posters and trailers in film marketing is limited, but increased from the late 1990s onwards. The most influential full-length work is Duncan J. Petrie, *Creativity and Constraint*, and research into posters employing semiotic forms of analysis forms useful background to this chapter, especially Jonathan Bignell, *Media Semiotics: An Introduction* (Manchester and New York: Manchester University Press, 1997), Victoria Bonnell, *Iconography of Power: Soviet Political Posters under Lenin and Stalin* (Berkeley, Calif.: University of California Press, 1997), P. David Marshall, *Celebrity and Power: Fame in Contemporary Culture* (London and Minneapolis, Minn.: University of Minnesota Press, 1997) and Judith Williamson, *Consuming Passions: The Dynamics of Popular Culture* (London and New York: Marion Boyars, 1986). The most useful journal articles on the topic are: Brant Drewery, 'Trailer for Sale or Rent', Creation, 12/1999, 28–31, David Geffner, 'Clip Art. The Art of Trailer Production', *Filmmaker*, 5: 3 (1997), 31–4, Dade Hayes, 'The Preshow Must Go On . . . and On', Variety, 8 November 1999, 9–10 and Andy Medhurst, 'The Big Tease', *Sight and Sound*, 8: 7 (1998), 24–6.
3. Martin Dale, *The Movie Game: The Film Business in Britain, Europe and America* (London: Cassell, 1997), p. 325.
4. Fred Goldberg, *Motion Picture Marketing and Distribution: Getting Movies into a Theatre Near You* (Boston, Mass. and London: Focal Press, 1991), p. 42.
5. Michael Barlin, film director, interview with author, 10 February 2000.
6. Paul Watson, 'There's No Accounting for Taste: Exploitation Cinema and the Limits of Film Theory', in *Trash Aesthetics: Popular Culture and its Audience*, ed. by Deborah Cartmell, I.Q. Hunter, Heidi Kaye and Imelda Whelehan (Chicago, Ill. and London: Pluto Press, 1997), p. 79.
7. Wheeler Winston Dixon, *The Transparency of Spectacle: Meditations on the Moving Image* (Albany, NY: State University of New York Press, 1998), p. 6. A similar argument concerning the quality of trailers, particularly their editing, is provided in abbreviated form by Andy Medhurst, 'The Big Tease', p. 24. Medhurst also supports the contention that trailers are a discrete form of entertainment in this piece.
8. Russell Jackson, 'Introduction', *The Cambridge Companion to Shakespeare on Film*, p. 8.
9. Fred Goldberg, *Motion Picture Marketing and Distribution*, p. 44.
10. Dorothy Viljoen, *Art of the Deal*, pp. 192–3.
11. Information about the factors determining which trailers run before cinema screenings and video and DVD releases from my interview with Sara Bird, Manager, DVD Distribution at Columbia TriStar, London, 30 September 2001.
12. Jane Hamsher, *Killer Instinct: How Two Young Producers Took on Hollywood and Made the Most Controversial Film of the Decade* (London: Orion Media, 1997), p. 192.
13. Andy Medhurst, 'The Big Tease', p. 24.
14. For a shot-by-shot breakdown of the *William Shakespeare's Romeo + Juliet* theatrical trailer and video trailer, see Appendix.
15. Baz Luhrmann and Craig Pearce, *William Shakespeare's Romeo + Juliet: The Contemporary Film, The Classic Play: The Screenplay by Craig Pearce and Baz Luhrmann and the Text of Shakespeare's Original Play Together in One Volume* (London: Hodder Children's Books, 1997), p. 1.

16. Box-office information from the Internet Movie Database, <http://www.imdb.com>. All subsequent box-office figures in this book, unless otherwise specified, are also taken from the Internet Movie Database and verified where possible by figures from the Motion Picture Association of America web site, <http://www.mpaa.com>.

17. Roger Ebert, 'Looking for Richard', *Chicago Sun-Times*, 25 October 1996, <http://www.suntimes.com/ebert/ebert_reviews/1996/10/102507.html>.

18. Jerry Brotton, ' "This Tunis, sir, was Carthage": Contesting Colonialism in The Tempest', in *Post-Colonial Shakespeares*, ed. by Ania Loomba and Martin Orkin (London: Routledge, 1998), p. 27.

19. Branagh's *Hamlet, William Shakespeare's Romeo + Juliet* and *Looking for Richard* shared release dates within a few months of each other. *Looking for Richard* was released on 11 October 1996 in North America and 31 January 1997 in the UK. *William Shakespeare's Romeo + Juliet* was released before Branagh's *Hamlet* in North America, on 1 November 1996, just a day after Branagh's *Hamlet* on 26 December 1996 in the director's home territory of Australia, but after Branagh's film in the UK, on 28 March 1997. Branagh's *Hamlet* was released on Christmas Day 1996 in North America and on Valentine's Day 1997 in the UK. The proximity of release dates encourages juxtaposed analysis of the marketing campaigns for the three films.

20. Bastard, *King John*, I.1.96, Stanley Wells and Gary Taylor, eds, *The Oxford Shakespeare*.

21. Lorne M. Buchman, *Still in Movement: Shakespeare on Screen* (Oxford: Oxford University Press, 1991), p. 68.

22. Bela Balazs, *Theory of the Film: Character and Growth of a New Art*, trans. by Edith Bone (New York: Dover Publications, 1970), p. 60.

23. Desson Howe, 'Titus, A Modern Tragedy', *Washington Post*, 11 February 2000, <http://www.washingtonpost.com/wp-srv/entertainment/movies/reviews/titushowe.htm>. The rhetoric of this review insistently recalls that of Gary Taylor, also critiqued in this chapter.

24. Christopher Dunne, interview with author, 17 June 2001.

25. Christopher Dunne, interview with author, 26 June 2001.

26. Kenneth Branagh, quoted in John F. Andrews, 'Kenneth Branagh's *Hamlet*', *Shakespeare Newsletter* 46: 3 (1996), p. 62.

27. Martha Frankel, 'Sex Pointers from Women Men Love', *Glamour*, May 1999, p. 23.

28. Miles Thompson and Imelda Whelehan, 'Shakespeare and the Homoerotic', in *Talking Shakespeare: Shakespeare Into the Millennium*, ed. by Deborah Cartmell and Michael Scott (Basingstoke: Palgrave, 2001), pp. 136–7.

29. Fred Goldberg, *Motion Picture Marketing and Distribution*, pp. 42–3.

30. Angie Errico, 'William Shakespeare's *A Midsummer Night's Dream*', *Empire*, October 1999, p. 18.

31. Anon., 'Videos to Rent: *A Midsummer Night's Dream*', *Empire*, April 2000, p. 110. The film was released on DVD in January 2000.

32. Stephen Applebaum, '*A Midsummer Night's Dream*', *Flicks*, September 2000, p. 92.

33. Information from Ken Green, Head of Marketing at United Pictures, London, interview with author, 20 March 2002.

34. Jeff Smith, *The Sounds of Commerce: Marketing Popular Film Music* (New York: Columbia University Press, 1998), p. 200.

35. Jeff Smith, *The Sounds of Commerce*, p. 205.

36. Michael Almereyda, *William Shakespeare's Hamlet: Adapted by Michael Almereyda* (London and New York: Faber & Faber, 2000), p. 143.

37. Michael Almereyda, *William Shakespeare's Hamlet*, p. 135.
38. Michael Wiese, *Film and Video Marketing* (Studio City, Calif.: Michael Wiese Productions, 1989), p. 348.
39. Richard of Gloucester, 'Why, I can smile, and murder whiles I smile', *Henry VI*, III.2.182 and 'I am determined to prove a villain, and hate the idle pleasures of these days', Richard of Gloucester, *Richard III*, I.4.30–1, Stanley Wells and Gary Taylor, eds, *The Oxford Shakespeare*.
40. Helena, 'Love looks not with the eyes, but with the mind; and therefore is winged Cupid painted blind', *A Midsummer Night's Dream*, I.1.234–5, Stanley Wells and Gary Taylor, eds, *The Oxford Shakespeare*.
41. Samuel Crowl, '*A Midsummer Night's Dream*', *Shakespeare Bulletin*, 17: 3 (1999), pp. 41–2.
42. Titus, 'O sweet Revenge, now do I come to thee', V.2.68, Titus, 'I know thou dost; and, sweet Revenge, farewell', V.2.148, *Titus Andronicus*, Stanley Wells and Gary Taylor, eds, *The Oxford Shakespeare*.
43. 'O Romeo, Romeo, Wherefore art thou Romeo. Deny thy father and refuse thy name', Juliet, *Romeo and Juliet*, II.1.75–6 and Lucentio, 'Tranio, I burn, I pine, I perish, Tranio', *The Taming of the Shrew*, I.1.153, Stanley Wells and Gary Taylor, eds, *The Oxford Shakespeare*.
44. Edmond, *King Lear*, folio text, 'the wheel is come full circle: I am here', V.3.165, Stanley Wells and Gary Taylor, eds, *The Oxford Shakespeare*.

3 Kenneth Branagh's filmed Shakespeare adaptations

1. Alison Light, 'The Importance of Being Ordinary', p. 18.
2. Branagh's filmed Shakespeare adaptations began to attract a mini-industry in Branagh scholarship from the early 1990s onwards. Mark Thornton Burnett maintains a substantial Branagh archive at Queen's University, Belfast. The most significant full-length studies on Branagh are Sarah Hatchuel, *A Companion to the Shakespearean Films of Kenneth Branagh* (Winnipeg: Blizzard Publishing, 2000) and Tanja Weiss, *Shakespeare on the Screen: Kenneth Branagh's Adaptations of Henry V, Much Ado about Nothing and Hamlet* (Frankfurt: Peter Lang, 1999). Significant periodical articles on Branagh's filmed Shakespeare adaptations include: John F. Andrews, 'Kenneth Branagh's *Hamlet*', *Shakespeare Newsletter* 46, 3 (1996), Kenneth Branagh, 'Henry V', in *Players of Shakespeare 2*, ed. by Russell Jackson and Robert Smallwood (Cambridge: Cambridge University Press, 1988), Curtis Breight 'Branagh and the Prince, or a "Royal Fellowship of Death"', *Critical Quarterly*, 33: 4 (1991), 95–111, Stephen M. Buhler, 'Double Takes: Branagh gets to Hamlet', *Post Script*, 17: 1 (1997), 43–52, Deborah Cartmell, 'The Henry V Flashback: Kenneth Branagh's Shakespeare', in *Pulping Fictions*, pp. 73–84, Susanne Collier, 'Post-Falklands, Post-Colonial: Contextualising Branagh as Henry V on Stage and on Film', *Essays in Theatre*, 10: 2 (May 1992), H. R. Coursen, 'The Critical Reception of Branagh's Complete Hamlet in the U.S. Popular Press', *Shakespeare and the Classroom*, 5: 2 (Fall 1997), 29–39, Samuel Crowl, 'Flamboyant Realist: Kenneth Branagh', pp. 222–40, *The Cambridge Companion to Shakespeare on Film*, Chris Fitter, 'A Tale of Two Branaghs: Henry V, Ideology and the Mekong Agincourt', in *Shakespeare Left and Right*, ed. by Ivo Kamps (London and New York: Routledge, 1991), Russell Jackson, 'Kenneth

Branagh's Film of *Hamlet*: the Textual Choices', *Shakespeare Bulletin* (Spring 1997), 37–8, Bernice W. Kliman, 'The Unkindest Cuts: Flashcut Excess in Kenneth Branagh's *Hamlet*', in *Talking Shakespeare*, ed. by Deborah Cartmell and Michael Scott, pp. 151–67, Courtney Lehmann, '*Much Ado about Nothing?* Shakespeare, Branagh and the "National-Popular" in the Age of Multinational Capital', *Textual Practice*, 12: 1 (1998), 1–22, Courtney Lehmann, 'Making Mother Matter: Repression, Revision, and the Stakes of "Reading Psychoanalysis Into" Kenneth Branagh's *Hamlet*', *Early Modern Literary Studies*, 6: 1 (May 2000), 2–24, Nina da Vinci Nichols, 'Branagh's Hamlet Redux', *Shakespeare Bulletin*, 15: 3 (Summer 1997), 38–41, Michael Skovmand, 'Introduction, with a Discussion on Branagh and *Much Ado*', in *Screen Shakespeare*, ed. by Michael Skovmand (Aarhus: Aarhus University Press, 1994), pp. 7–11, Lisa S. Starks, 'The Displaced Body of Desire: Sexuality in Kenneth Branagh's Hamlet', in *Shakespeare and Appropriation* , pp. 160–78, Mark Thornton Burnett, 'The "Very Cunning of the Scene": Kenneth Branagh's *Hamlet*', *Literature/Film Quarterly* 25: 2 (1997), 78–82, Anny Crunelle Vanrigh, 'All the World's a Screen: Transcoding in Branagh's *Hamlet*', *Shakespeare Yearbook*, 8 (1997), 349–69, Michael Williams, 'Shakespeare, Branagh, and Popular Culture', in Bill Corcoran, Mike Hayhoe and Gordon M. Pradl, eds, *Knowledge in the Making: Challenging the Text in the Classroom* (Portsmouth: Heinemann, 1994) and Ramona Wray and Mark Thornton Burnett, 'From the Horse's Mouth: Branagh on the Bard', in *Shakespeare, Film, Fin de Siècle*, pp. 165–78.

3. Kenneth Branagh, *Much Ado about Nothing by William Shakespeare: Screenplay, Introduction, and Notes on the Making of the Film by Kenneth Branagh* (London: Chatto & Windus, 1993), p. 2.

4. Suzanna Thomas, *An Analysis of how the Study of Film Contributes to our Understanding of the Production and Consumption of Cultural Commodities* (Worcester: Worcester College of Higher Education, 1988), p 37.

5. J. G. Ballard, *Super-Cannes* (London: Flamingo, 2001), p. 16, p. 15.

6. Kenneth Branagh, *Hamlet: Screenplay, Introduction and Film Diary* (London: Chatto & Windus, 1996), p. iv.

7. Kenneth Branagh, *Hamlet*, p. viii.

8. Russell Jackson, 'Introduction', in *The Cambridge Companion to Shakespeare on Film*, p. 4. The term 'negative costs' includes production costs, studio overhead and capitalised interest (abandoned project costs are no longer included in studio overhead, and as such are no longer a part total of negative costs). 'Negative costs' relates to the profits made from global cinema admission receipts, not just the proceeds from the North American box office.

9. Michael Posner, *Canadian Dreams: The Making and Marketing of Independent Films* (Vancouver: Douglas & McIntyre, 1993), p. 47.

10. Terry Ilott, *Budgets and Markets: A Study of the Budgeting of European Film* (London: Routledge, 1996), p. 125.

11. Michael Billington, 'A "New Olivier" Is Taking on Henry V', *New York Times*, 8 January 1989, <http://www.branaghcompendium.com/artic-nyt89–1.htm>.

12. Fred Goldberg, *Motion Picture Marketing and Distribution*, p. 179.

13. Deborah Cartmell, *Pulping Fictions*, p. 79.

14. Graham Holderness, 'Radical Potentiality and Institutional Closure', in *Political Shakespeare*, pp. 223–4.

15. This identification occurs throughout the Holderness critique of *Henry V* in *Shakespeare Recycled*.

16. Michael Skovmand, 'Introduction', *Screen Shakespeare*, p. 10.
17. Articles that exhibit notable hostility to the patriotism/jingoism of Branagh's *Henry V* film include Curtis Breight, 'Branagh and the Prince', *Critical Quarterly* 33: 4 (1991), 95–111, and Michael Pursell, 'Playing the Game: Branagh's Henry V', *Literature/Film Quarterly*, 20: 4 (1992), 268–75. Branagh is accused of blandness in his *Henry V* and *Much Ado about Nothing* by Alison Light, 'The Importance of Being Ordinary'.
18. Roger Ebert, 'Much Ado about Nothing', *Chicago Sun-Times*, 21 May 1993, <http://www.suntimes.com/ebert/ebert_reviews/1993/05/858482.html>.
19. Peter Drexler, 'Laurence Olivier's *Henry V* and Veit Harlan's *Der Grosse Konig*: Two Versions of the National Hero on Film', in *Negotiations with Hal: Multi-Media Perceptions of (Shakespeare's) Henry the Fifth*, ed. by Peter Drexler and Lawrence Guntner (Braunschweig: Technische Universitat Braunschweig, 1995), p. 127.
20. Deborah Cartmell, *Pulping Fictions*, p. 80.
21. Fredric Jameson, *Postmodernism*, p. 19.
22. Alan Sinfield, 'Heritage and the Market: Regulation and Desublimation', *Political Shakespeare*, p. 271.
23. Tino Balio, 'The Art Film Market in the New Hollywood' in *Hollywood and Europe, Economics, Culture, National Identity 1945–95*, ed. by Geoffrey Nowell-Smith and Steven Ricci (London: BFI Publishing, 1998), p. 69.
24. Peter Wollen, 'Tinsel and Realism', in *Hollywood and Europe*, p. 129.
25. Michael Skovmand, 'Introduction', *Screen Shakespeare*, p. 10.
26. Kenneth Branagh, *Hamlet*, pp. vii-viii.
27. Hal Hinson, 'Much Ado about Nothing', *Washington Post*, 21 May 1993, <http://www.washingtonpost.com/wp-srv// muchadoaboutnothingpg13hinson_a0a81a.html>.
28. Kenneth Branagh, *Much Ado about Nothing*, pp. ix-x.
29. Trinh T. Minh-Ha, *When the Moon Waxes Red: Representation, Gender and Cultural Politics* (London and New York: Routledge, 1991), p. 116.
30. Roger Ebert, 'Much Ado about Nothing', *Chicago Sun-Times*.
31. Sarah Keene, interview with author, 22 April 2002.
32. Neil Taylor, 'National and Racial Stereotypes in Shakespeare Films', *The Cambridge Companion to Shakespeare on Film*, p. 264.
33. Kenneth Branagh, *Chat* interview, 15 February 2001, <http://www.homeworkhigh.com>.
34. Kenneth Branagh, *In the Bleak Midwinter* (London: Nick Hern Books, 1995).
35. Tino Balio, 'The Art Film Market in the New Hollywood', in *Hollywood and Europe*, p. 72.
36. Kenneth Branagh, *Hamlet*, p. vii.
37. Ian McKellen and Richard Loncraine, *William Shakespeare's Richard III* (London: Doubleday, 1996), p. 24.
38. Ian McKellen, 'McKellen Shakespeare Film, Production Notes', *Richard III Mayfair Entertainment International Press Kit*, p. 4.
39. Mick LaSalle, 'Right Time for "Richard III": The Lowdown on Ian McKellen's "30s Melodrama"', *San Francisco Chronicle*, 19 January 1996, <http://www.sfgate.com/cgi-bin/article.cgi?f=/c/a/1996/01/19/DD62199.DTL>.
40. Eddie Dyja, ed., *BFI Film and Television Handbook 1999* (London: BFI Publishing, 1998), p. 41.
41. Richard B. Woodward, 'Tragic Kingdom', *The Village Voice*, 31 December 1996,

<http://www.geocities.com/Athens/Parthenon/6261/Articles/village.html>.
42. Russell Jackson, 'Introduction', in *The Cambridge Companion to Shakespeare on Film*, p. 5.
43. Kenneth Branagh, *Hamlet*, p. v.
44. Sarah Keene, interview with author.
45. Bernice W. Kliman, 'The Unkindest Cuts: Flashcut Excess in Kenneth Branagh's *Hamlet*', *Talking Shakespeare*, p. 239, n. 1.
46. Ian McKellen and Richard Loncraine, *William Shakespeare's Richard III*, pp. 25–6.
47. Peter Brooker and Will Brooker, *Postmodern After-Images: A Reader in Film, Television and Video* (London: Arnold, 1997), p. 55.
48. John Drakakis, 'Shakespeare in Quotations', in *Studying British Cultures: An Introduction*, ed. by Susan Bassnett (London: Routledge, 1997), p. 166.
49. Kenneth Branagh, *Love's Labour's Lost Official Web Site*, <http://www.guildpathe.co.uk/LLL/docs/cont2.html>.
50. Sarah Keene, interview with author.
51. Carol Hemming, 'Studio Production Notes for Love's Labour's Lost', *Love's Labour's Lost Official Web Site*, <http://members.tripod.com/dailytelegiraffe/loveslaboursloststudionotes.html>.
52. John Drakakis, 'Shakespeare in Quotations', in *Studying British Cultures: An Introduction*, p. 161.
53. Christine Battersby, *Gender and Genius: Towards a Feminist Aesthetics* (London: The Women's Press, 1994), p. 211.
54. Sarah Gristwood, 'What is this thing called "Love's Labour's Lost"?', *Guardian*, 27 March 2000, <http://film.guardian.co.uk/Feature_Story/feature_story/0,4120,152536,00.html>.
55. Portia, *The Merchant of Venice*, IV.1.205, Stanley Wells and Gary Taylor, eds, *The Oxford Shakespeare*.
56. Yahlin Chang, 'Bloom the Bardolator', *Newsweek*, 33: 7, 15 February 1999, p. 64.
57. Anon., 'Parting from Bard is Such Sweet Sorrow for Branagh', *The Belfast Telegraph Online*, 1 February 2001, <http://www.belfasttelegraph.com/today/feb01/News/kenn.ncml>.
58. Statistics from the MPAA 2000 *US Economic Review: Box Office*.
59. Kenneth Branagh, *Chat* interview.
60. Leo Braudy and Marshall Cohen, eds, *Film Theory and Criticism: Introductory Readings*, 5th edn (New York and Oxford: Oxford University Press, 1999), p. 540.
61. Ramona Wray and Mark Thornton Burnett, 'From the Horse's Mouth: Branagh on the Bard', in *Shakespeare, Film, Fin de Siècle*, p. 177.
62. Roberta E. Pearson and William Uricchio, 'How Many Times shall Caesar Bleed in Sport: Shakespeare and the Cultural Debate about Moving Pictures', *Screen*, 31 (1990), 257.
63. Allan Bloom with Harry V. Jaffa, *Shakespeare's Politics* (Chicago, Ill.: University of Chicago Press, 1964), p. 10.

4 Hollywood teen Shakespeare movies

1. Deborah Cartmell, 'Introduction', in *Adaptations from Text to Screen, Screen to Text*, p. 25.

2. Although there are no published book-length studies on the specific subject of the marketing of filmed Shakespeare adaptations to a teen audience, there is an extensive literature employed as a research tool upon both youth and the media and upon film marketing. Jon Lewis, *The Road to Romance and Ruin: Teen Films and Youth Culture* (London and New York: Routledge, 1992) and the research of Martin Barker and Angela McRobbie were particularly influential in the formation of my position on the degree to which hegemony operates in the consumption of film by the teen audience. Kathryn H. Fuller, Rick Altman and Martin Dale have all written upon film audiences in a manner that was particularly pertinent to the teen movie audience. Baz Luhrmann's self-reflexive discussions of marketing in his screenplays and in press and journal interviews, such as Eric Bauer, 'Re-Revealing Shakespeare: An Interview with Baz Luhrmann', *Creative Screenwriting*, 5 (1998), were influential. Richard Burt's research on teen filmed Shakespeare adaptations was also influential, in particular my private correspondence with him, his chapter, 'T(e)en Things I Hate About Girlene Shakesploitation Flicks in the Late 1990s, or, Not So Fast Times at Shakespeare High', in *Screening the Bard: Shakespearean Spectacle, Critical Theory, Film Practice*, ed. by Lisa S. Starks and Courtney Lehmann (New Jersey: American University Presses, 2001), pp. 205–32, and his book, *Unspeakable ShaXXXspeares*. Although it considers the adaptation of Austen rather than Shakespeare for a teen audience, another useful study is Esther Sonnet, 'From *Emma* to *Clueless:* Taste, Pleasure and the Scene of History', in *Adaptations from Text to Screen, Screen to Text*, pp. 51–62.

3. Important research has also been published on the influence of Hollywood films, particularly Disney animated features, on a younger audience, notably Annalee R. Ward, *Mouse Morality: The Rhetoric of Disney Animated Film* (Austin, University of Texas Press, 2002) and Richard Finkelstein, 'Disney Cites Shakespeare', in *Shakespeare and Appropriation*, pp. 179–96.

4. Charles Fleming, *High Concept: Don Simpson and the Hollywood Culture of Excess* (London: Bloomsbury, 1998), p. 72.

5. Jon Lewis, *The Road to Romance and Ruin: Teen Films and Youth Culture*, p. 2.

6. This argument is advanced particularly forcefully throughout Richard Burt's article 'Shakespeare in Love and the End of the Shakespearean: Academic and Mass Culture Constructions of Literary Authorship', in *Shakespeare, Film, Fin de Siècle*, pp. 203–31.

7. Louise Levison, *Filmmakers and Financing*, p. 88. According to the '2000 Motion Picture Attendance Survey', in 2000, the age group of twelve to seventeen years old accounted for 14 per cent of total yearly cinema admissions, compared to 17 per cent in 1990, 1998 and 1999, 16 per cent in 1996 and 14 per cent in 1997. Among the total US population over twelve years of age, a higher percentage classified themselves as frequent or occasional moviegoers in 2000 than in 1999, compared to those who classified themselves as infrequent or never moviegoers. At the beginning of the 1990s, twelve- to twenty-four-year olds accounted for 48 per cent of total frequent moviegoers. In contrast they accounted for just 39 per cent of total frequent moviegoers in 2000. However, about half of the teen (twelve to seventeen) population attended at least once a month compared to just 27 per cent of the adult population in 2000. Figures from the '2000 Motion Picture Attendance Survey' conducted by the Motion Picture Association of America, <http://www.mpaa.org/useconomicreview/2000attendancestudy>.

8. Lucy Rollin, *Twentieth-Century Teen Culture by the Decades: A Reference Guide* (Westport, Conn., London: Greenwood Press, 1999), p. ix.

9. Angela McRobbie, *Postmodernism*, p. 178.
10. Angela McRobbie, *Postmodernism*, p. 172.
11. These ideas find their most cogent expression in David Buckingham, ed., *Reading Audiences*, David Morley, *Television, Audiences and Cultural Studies* (London: Routledge, 1992), David Morley, *The Nationwide Audience: Structure and Decoding* (London: BFI Publishing, 1980) and Paul Willis, *Moving Culture: An Enquiry into the Cultural Activities of Young People* (London: Calouste Gulbenkian Foundation, 1990).
12. Baz Luhrmann and Craig Pearce, *William Shakespeare's Romeo + Juliet*, p. 1.
13. Richard Burt, *Unspeakable ShaXXXspeares*, pp. 3–4.
14. *William Shakespeare's Romeo + Juliet*, Official Site, <http://www.romeoandjuliet.com>.
15. Jeffrey Zeldman, Creative Director, SenseNet Inc., interview with author, 19 August 1999.
16. The phenomenon of web-site marketing prompted a spate of journal and newspaper articles on the subject, with particular reference to the astonishing success of *The Blair Witch Project* Internet and word-of-mouth campaign. Relevant articles include: Marc Graser and Chris Petrikin, 'Geek Gab Freaks Film Biz', *Variety*, 18 October 1999, pp. 1, 57, David Geffner, 'Cars, Soap and Celluloid', *Filmmaker*, 7: 4 (summer 1999), 18–22, 68–9, 92, and Raphael Simon, 'Don't Believe the Anti-Hype', *Premiere*, 13 December 1999, pp. 39–40.
17. 'William Shakespeare's Romeo + Juliet', *Official Site*, <http://www.romeoandjuliet.com>.
18. Deborah Cartmell, 'The Shakespeare on Screen Industry', pp. 29–30.
19. *William Shakespeare's Romeo + Juliet*, Official Site, <http://www.romeoandjuliet.com>.
20. Desson Howe, 'This "Romeo" is Bleeding', *Washington Post*, 1 November 1996, <http://www.washingtonpost.com/wp-srv/style/longterm/movies/review97/romeoandjuliethowe.htm>, Stephanie Zacharek, 'Saved by the Belle', *Salon.com*, 1 November 1996, <http://www.salon.com/oct96/rome0961104.html>, Mick LaSalle, 'This "Romeo" is a True Tragedy, DiCaprio, Danes Weak in Shakespeare Update', *San Francisco Chronicle*, 1 November 1996, <http://www.sfgate.com/cgi-bin/article.cgi?f=/c/a/1996/11/01/dd15503.dtl>. More general expressions of concern at the vogue for teen literary adaptations include: Bruce Newman, 'Can't Read the Classic? See the Teen Movie', *New York Times*, 28 February 1999, pp. 13, 22, and two articles by Jessica Shaw, 'Hey Kids! Teensploitation!: Inside Hollywood's Box Office Boom', *Entertainment Weekly*, 476, 12 March 1999, pp. 22–4 and 'Good Will Hunting', *Entertainment Weekly*, 471, 12 February 1999, p. 9.
21. Richard Burt, *Unspeakable ShaXXXspeares*, p. 201.
22. Yahlin Chang, 'Bloom the Bardolator', p. 64.
23. Anon., 'Bard Burn Out', *Premiere: Oscar Edition*, April 1999, p. 26.
24. Emma Cochrane, *Empire*, interview with author, 13 December 2001.
25. P. David Marshall, *Celebrity and Power*, p. 60.
26. Buena Vista official site, *10 Things I Hate About You*, <http://movies.go.com/10things/990410/index.html>.
27. Stephen Holden, '*10 Things I Hate About You*: It's Like, You Know, Sonnets and Stuff', *New York Times*, 31 March 1999, <http://www.nytimes.com/library/film/033199things-film-review.html>.

28. Thomas Schatz, *Hollywood Genres: Formulas, Filmmaking and the Studio System* (New York: Random House, 1981), p. 29.

29. Stephen Holden, '10 Things I Hate About You', *New York Times*.

30. Mary Elizabeth Williams, 'One Shrew Thing', *Salon.com*, 1 April 1999, <http://www.salon.com/ent/movies/reviews/1999/04/01review.html?cp=sal&dn=110>.

31. Sharon Waxman, 'Studio Keeps a Lid on "O" After School Shootings', *Washington Post*, 9 March 2001, p. C01.

32. Ian McKellen and Richard Loncraine, *William Shakespeare's Richard III*, p. 25.

33. 'Greg's Preview Thoughts', 'Upcoming Movies', 27 April 2001, <http://www.upcomingmovies.com>.

34. Bill Thompson, 'Phifer: Modern-Day Othello', *New York Post and Courier*, 18 March 1999, p. 7.

35. Anon., 'Bard Burn Out', *Premiere*, p. 26.

36. Stephen Brown, *Postmodern Marketing*, p. 116.

37. James White, 'Get Over It', *Total Film*, May 2001, p. 97.

38. Angie Errico, 'William Shakespeare's A Midsummer Night's Dream', *Empire*, October 1999, p. 18.

39. Anon, 'Parting from Bard is Such Sweet Sorrow for Branagh', *The Belfast Telegraph*.

40. Emma Cochrane, *Empire*, interview with author.

41. Tony Howard, 'Shakespeare's Cinematic Offshoots', in *The Cambridge Companion to Shakespeare on Film*, p. 309.

42. Gary Taylor, *Shakespeare and Appropriation*, p. 201.

43. Richard Burt, despite concerns about the infantilising effect of American popular culture, has done perhaps more than any other scholar to celebrate even the most marginal, pornographic or loosely filmed adaptations of Shakespeare. His earlier work *Unspeakable ShaXXXspeares* displays a less ambivalent celebration of Shakespearian appropriation than his more recent pieces, which are tempered by a concern that Shakespeare in popular culture is often 'Shakespeare without Shakespeare', for example, 'Shakespeare in Love and the End of the Shakespearean: Academic and Mass Culture Constructions of Literary Authorship', in *Shakespeare, Film, Fin de Siècle*, pp. 203–31, and 'T(e)en Things I Hate About Girlene Shakesploitation Flicks in the Late 1990s, or, Not So Fast Times at Shakespeare High', in *Screening the Bard*, pp. 205–32. Deborah Cartmell and Imelda Whelehan celebrate the efflorescence of Shakespeare on film, but express a mixed perspective on the vexed question of fidelity in their volume *Adaptations from Text to Screen*. Even relatively recent scholarship, however, at times exhibits extreme anxiety regarding Shakespeare's appropriation on film, for example: throughout Douglas Brode, *Shakespeare in the Movies: From the Silent Era to Shakespeare in Love* (New York: Oxford University Press, 2000).

5 Shakespeare in Love

1. Douglas Kellner, *Media Culture: Cultural Studies, Identity and Politics between the Modern and the Postmodern* (London and New York: Routledge, 1996), p. 45.

2. Lawrence Grossberg, 'History, Politics and Postmodernism', in *Stuart Hall: Critical Dialogues*, ed. by David Morley and Kuan-Hsing Chen (London: Routledge, 1996), p. 161.

3. The journal articles on *Shakespeare in Love* of most relevance to this book are: Sujata Iyengar, 'Shakespeare in Love', *Literature/Film Quarterly* 29: 2 (2001), 122–7, Russell Jackson, 'Working with Shakespeare: Confessions of an Advisor', *Cineaste*, 24: 1 (1999), 42–4 and Kenneth Rothwell, '*Elizabeth* and *Shakespeare in Love*', *Cineaste*, 24 (1999), 78–80. In relation to the significant use of Shakespeare's celebrity as a marketing tool for *Shakespeare in Love*, research by P. David Marshall, Joshua Gamson, Richard Dyer and Richard De Cordova in the field of celebrity and popular culture is helpful. Influential film-marketing analysis in this chapter includes Peter Bart, *The Gross* and Justin Wyatt, *High Concept.*

4. Louise Levison, interview with author, 12 December 2001.

5. According to the British Film Institute in 2000, the recognised Hollywood majors were 'the US studios MGM/United Artists, Paramount, Sony (Columbia TriStar), 20th Century Fox, Disney and Warner Bros. The newcomer Dreamworks SKG is now often added to this list', <http://www.bfi.org.uk/nationallibrary/collections>.

6. Rob Vaux, 'Chocolat', Flipsidemovies.com, 3 January 2001, <http://www.flipsidemovies.com/chocolat.html>.

7. Martin Dale, *The Movie Game*, pp. 31–2.

8. Pete Clark, 'The Divine Gwyneth and Shakespeare in Love', *Evening Standard*, 20 January 1999, p. 20.

9. See Chapter 3 for Branagh and McKellen's descriptions of Hollywood studios' apparent reluctance to make filmed Shakespeare adaptations.

10. Colin MacCabe, *The Eloquence of the Vulgar*, p. 123.

11. Peter Bart, 'The Bard's Big Night', *Variety*, 26 March 1999, pp. 4, 86.

12. Michael Fleeman, 'More on the '99 Oscars: Studios spend $$$ in race for Oscar', *Associated Press*, <http://www.canoe.ca/jamoscar1999/mar17_bestpic_ap.html>. Exact figures for studio spending in 1998 are unverifiable, because studios were under no obligation to report spending and the line between Oscar marketing and larger marketing efforts is ill defined.

13. Andy Medhurst, 'The Big Tease', p. 25.

14. David Gritten, 'How to Win an Oscar or Seven', *The Age*, 24 March 1999, p. 12.

15. Ken Green, interview with author.

16. Ken Green, interview with author.

17. 'Shakespeare in Love', *Miramax Press Kit* (Los Angeles, Calif.: Miramax, 1998).

18. Martin Dale, *The Movie Game*, p. 325.

19. Daniel Fischlin and Mark Fortier, 'General Introduction', *Adaptations of Shakespeare*, p. 15.

20. Janet Maslin, 'Shakespeare in Love: Shakespeare Saw a Therapist?', *New York Times*, 11 December 1998, <http://www.nytimes.com/library/film/121198shakespeare-film-review.html>. The significance of a positive review in this publication is emphasised by Fred Goldberg, who observes of *New York Times* and *The Los Angeles Times* that: 'Stories in these newspapers are probably the most effective way to give the film an early name recognition', in *Motion Picture Marketing and Distribution*, p. 22.

21. Robin Stringer and Tim Cooper, 'Where There's a Will, There's an Oscar (or 13)', *Evening Standard*, 9 February 1999, p. 5.

22. Peter S. Myers, 'The Studio as Distributor', in *The Movie Business Book*, ed. by Jason E. Squire, p. 281.

23. Ken Green, interview with author.

24. Information on exhibitor behaviour provided by Ken Green, interview with author.

25. Mick LaSalle, 'Right Time for "Richard III"', *San Francisco Chronicle*.

26. Grace Bradberry, 'Love Turns Bard', *The Times*, 5 February 1999, p. 21.

27. Peter Stallybrass and Allon White, *The Politics and Poetics of Transgression* (London: Methuen, 1986), p. 5.

28. Tom Stoppard, *Evening Standard*, 27 January 1999, p. 27.

29. Richard Burt, '*Shakespeare in Love* and the End of Shakespeare', in *Shakespeare, Film, Fin de Siècle*, p. 206.

30. Laura Miller, 'Star-Cross'd Lovers', *Salon.com*, 11 December 1998, <http://archive.salon.com/ent/movies/reviews/1998/12/11reviewa.html>.

31. Andrew Billen, 'Sir Tom, the Ageless Time Lord', *Evening Standard*, 28 January 1999, <http://www.thisislondon.co.uk/entertainment/films/articles/ 567701?version=1&null>.

32. Pete Clark, 'The Divine Gwyneth and Shakespeare in Love', *Evening Standard*, p. 20.

33. Ken Green, interview with author.

34. Colin Kennedy, interview with author.

35. James Delingpole, interview with author, 14 December 2001.

36. Christy Desmet, 'Introduction', in *Shakespeare and Appropriation*, p. 12.

37. David Harvey, *The Condition of Postmodernity: An Enquiry into the Origins of Cultural Change* (Oxford: Basil Blackwell, 1989), p. 85.

38. Judith Williamson, *Consuming Passions*, pp. 73–4.

39. Ken Green, interview with author.

40. Fredric Jameson, *Postmodernism*, p. 19.

41. Martin Harries, *Los Angeles Chronicle*, 16 April 1999, p. B9.

42. Angela McRobbie, *Postmodernism*, p. 117.

43. Brian Case, 'Fiennes Romance', *Time Out*, 27 January 1999, pp. 14–15.

44. Ken Green, interview with author.

45. Teresa O'Connor, *Shakespeare in Love Study Guide* (London: Film Education, 1999), p. 9, p. i.

46. Kerina Lee, personal email correspondence with author, 21 May 1999.

47. Ian Freer, 'Shakespeare in Love: Must Buy', *Empire*, October 1999, p. 154.

48. Ken Green, interview with author.

49. P. David Marshall, *Celebrity and Power*, p. xi.

50. Robert C. Allen, 'Home Alone Together: Hollywood and the "Family Film"', in *Identifying Hollywood's Audiences: Cultural Identity and the Movies*, ed. by Melvyn Stokes and Richard Maltby, p. 122.

51. Bill Ashcroft, Gareth Griffiths and Helen Tiffin, *The Empire Writes Back*.

52. Richard Burt, *Unspeakable ShaXXXspeares*, p. 11.

53. Stuart Hall, 'What is this "Black" in Black Popular Culture?', in *Stuart Hall: Critical Dialogues*, p. 468.

54. Douglas Kellner, *Media Culture*, p. 235.

55. Stuart Hall, 'For Allon White: Metaphors of Transformation', in *Stuart Hall: Critical Dialogues*, p. 292.

6 Selling Shakespeare to Hollywood: Into the new millennium

1. Deborah Cartmell, 'The Shakespeare on Screen Industry', in *Adaptations from Text to Screen, Screen to Text*, ed. by Deborah Cartmell and Imelda Whelehan, p. 34.

2. Stuart Hall, 'What is this "Black" in Black Popular Culture?', in *Stuart Hall: Critical Dialogues*, p. 469.
3. John Drakakis, 'Shakespeare in Quotations', in *Studying British Cultures: An Introduction*, p. 162.
4. Ulrike Weissenborn, *"Just Making Pictures": Hollywood Writers, The Frankfurt School, and Film Theory* (Tubingen: Narr, 1998), p. 141.
5. Russell Jackson, 'Shakespeare and the Cinema', in *The Cambridge Companion to Shakespeare*, ed. by Margreta de Grazia and Stanley Wells (Cambridge: Cambridge University Press, 2001), p. 230.
6. Charles Fleming, *High Concept*, p. 72.

Appendix

Shot-by-Shot Breakdown of William Shakespeare's Romeo + Juliet *Theatrical Trailer*

Green screen. 'The following preview has been approved for all audiences by the MPAA'

20th Century Fox logo, menacing music begins

Shot of: ext. day. Close-up of Leonardo DiCaprio (Romeo) walking on Verona Beach in his tuxedo

Black screen. '20th Century Fox presents' text

Shot of: ext. day. John Leguizamo (Tybalt) and Dash Mihok (Benvolio) holding guns aloft in a car park

Shot of: ext. day. Leguizamo and Mihok pointing guns at each other

Black screen. 'The greatest love story' text

Shot of: int. night. Pete Postlethwaite (The Friar) officiating at wedding service

Shot of: int. day. Clare Danes (Juliet) raising her bridal veil

Black screen. 'The world has ever known' text

Shot of: int. night. Close-up of DiCaprio viewed through a large fish tank, DiCaprio: 'did my heart love till now?'

Shot of: int. night. Close-up of Danes viewed through a large fish tank, voice-over of DiCaprio: 'forswear it sight'

Shot of: int. night. Danes in angel costume dancing with Paul Rudd (Paris) at the ball, looking at DiCaprio

Shot of: int. night. Close-up of DiCaprio in costume of suit of armour, DiCaprio: 'for I never saw true beauty till this night'

Shot of: int. night. Danes in angel costume dancing with Rudd at the ball, laughing, love theme begins to play

Shot of: int. night. Close-up of DiCaprio in costume of armour, smiling

Black screen. 'William Shakespeare's Romeo + Juliet' text appears, with the '+' represented by a stylised red crucifix

Shot of: ext. day. Mihok screaming

Shot of: ext. day. Leguizamo tumbling over a car

Shot of: ext. day. Danes looking startled
Shot of: ext. day. Danes gazing through the large fish tank
Shot of: ext. day. Leguizamo jumping and firing his gun
Shot of: Black screen
Shot of: ext. day. Helicopter flying above Verona Beach
Shot of: ext. day. Rioters running through Verona Beach
Shot of: ext. day. Verona Beach patrol car
Shot of: ext. day. Riot police
Shot of: ext. day. Skyscrapers, voice-over: 'in fair Verona where we lay our scene'
Shot of: ext. day. Harold Perrineau (Mercutio) with a gun
Shot of: ext. day. Mihok at Verona Beach wearing a Hawaiian shirt
Shot of: ext. day. Leguizamo walking on Verona Beach, voice-over: 'two households'
Shot of: ext. night. The Montague parents, voice-over: 'both alike'
Shot of: ext. night. The Capulet parents, voice-over: 'in dignity'
Shot of: ext. day. Helicopter flying above Verona Beach
Shot of: ext. day. Vondie Curtis-Hall (Captain Prince) shouting into a CB radio
Shot of: ext. day. Man rolling on the ground with a gun
Shot of: ext. day. Mihok with a gun
Shot of: ext. day. Leguizamo in a gun battle
Shot of: ext. day. Perrineau threatening Leguizamo
Shot of: ext. day. Leguizamo grimacing
Shot of: ext. day. Perrineau holding a gun
Shot of: ext. day. A gun lying in the sand, the sound of gunfire
Shot of: ext. day. DiCaprio and Mihok on Verona Beach mourning Mercutio, voice-over:
    'from forth the fair loins of these two foes'
Shot of: ext. day. Verona Beach, voice-over: 'must civil blood make civil hands unclean'
Shot of: int. night. Danes in angel costume
Shot of: int. night. DiCaprio, captivated, looking at Danes, voice-over: 'a pair of star-
    crossed lovers take their life'
Shot of: int. night. DiCaprio and Danes embrace before a large window
Shot of: int. night. DiCaprio and Danes embrace
Shot of: int. day. Mihok and DiCaprio, Mihok: 'who is it that you love?'
Shot of: ext. night. Fireworks display
Shot of: ext. night. DiCaprio watches fireworks display
Shot of: ext. night. DiCaprio and Danes in a pool
Shot of: ext. night. Fireworks display
Shot of: ext. night. Danes watches fireworks display
Shot of: int. day. DiCaprio to Postlethwaite: 'my heart's dear love is set'
Shot of: int. day. Close-up of Postlethwaite's face looking startled, DiCaprio voice-over:
    'on the fair daughter of rich Capulet'
Black screen. Two revolvers pictured, 'ancient grudge' text appears
Shot of: ext. day. DiCaprio on Verona Beach, Leguizamo shouts: 'Romeo'
Shot of: ext. day. Leguizamo and his cohorts on Verona Beach, DiCaprio and Mercutio
    walking away from them, Leguizamo shouts: 'thou art a villain!'
Shot of: ext. day. Leguizamo shouting and attacking DiCaprio on Verona Beach
Shot of: ext. day. Leguizamo shouting and attacking DiCaprio on Verona Beach
Shot of: ext. day. Leguizamo shouting and kicking DiCaprio to the sand on Verona Beach
Shot of: ext. night. DiCaprio looks up startled at sound of gunshot

Shot of: ext. night. Montagues and Capulets gathered in the rain, Diana Venora (Lady Montague) shouts: 'Romeo slew Tybalt. Romeo must not live'.

Shot of: ext. night. DiCaprio turning around to face camera on dark rainy night

Shot of: int. night. Postlethwaite officiating at wedding service

Shot of: int. night. Danes at the costume party, Danes: 'my only love'

Shot of: ext. night. DiCaprio on a fairground ride retreating backwards, Danes voice-over: 'sprung from my only hate'

Shot of: ext. night. Curtis-Hall shouts: 'Romeo is banished'

Shot of: ext. day. Car driving through the desert

Black screen. Flaming heart pictured, 'star-crossed lovers' text appears

Shot of: int. night. Religious statuary, statue of Virgin Mary most prominent

Shot of: int. night. Danes in a chapel in front of statue of Virgin Mary

Shot of: int. night. DiCaprio entering Danes's room

Shot ext. night. DiCaprio and Danes in a pool

Shot ext. night. DiCaprio and Danes in a pool

Shot of: int. day. DiCaprio diving under white bed covers

Shot of: int. day. Danes smiling under white bed covers

Shot of: int. day. Danes and DiCaprio laughing in bed together, DiCaprio wears a Hawaiian shirt

Black screen. Crucifix pictured, 'violent ends' text appears

Shot of: ext. day. Car accelerating, hard rock soundtrack begins playing

Shot of: ext. day. Perrineau turning, shouting: 'a plague on'

Shot of: ext. day. DiCaprio and Danes kissing, Perrineau voice-over: 'both your houses'

Shot of: ext. day. Close-up of ring, the words 'love thee' visibly inscribed on it

Shot of: ext. night. DiCaprio and Danes kissing in a pool

Shot of: ext. day. Close-up of Danes's face

Shot of: ext. day. Leguizamo throws his gun in the air

Shot of: ext. day. Close-up of Danes's face

Shot of: ext. day. Leguizamo catches his gun in the air

Shot of: ext. day. Poster advertising 'Montague vs Capulet' in flames

Shot of: ext. day. Leguizamo throws his gun in the air

Shot of: ext. day. Leguizamo tears off his jacket in front of a police car

Shot of: ext. day. Zak Orth (Gregory) turns back and laughs in a speeding convertible

Shot of: ext. day. Leguizamo with a smoking gun, kissing it

Shot of: int. night. Danes with the phial of sleeping potion

Shot of: ext. night. Romeo screaming up at the night sky: 'I am fortune's fool!'

Shot of: ext. day. Close-up of DiCaprio, voice-over: 'Leonardo DiCaprio'

Shot of: ext. day. Close-up of Danes, voice-over: 'Clare Danes'

Shot of: int. night. Back view of DiCaprio walking down a crucifix-lined tomb

Shot of: int. night. Front view of DiCaprio walking down a crucifix-lined tomb, in tears

Black screen. 'William Shakespeare's Romeo + Juliet' text appears, voice-over: 'William Shakespeare's Romeo + Juliet'

Shot of: ext. night. Danes at her balcony, Danes: 'goodnight, goodnight'

Shot of: ext. night. DiCaprio smiles back at Danes on the balcony

Shot of: ext. night. DiCaprio and Danes embracing underwater, 'At theaters November 1' superimposed on the image, choral music

Shot-by-Shot Breakdown of William Shakespeare's Romeo + Juliet *Video Trailer*

Fox Video logo, film's love theme, 'Kissing You' by Des'Ree, begins to play

Shot of: int. night. Close-up of Leonardo DiCaprio (Romeo) viewed through a large fish tank

Shot of: int. night. DiCaprio in costume suit of armour

Shot of: int. night. Close-up of Clare Danes (Juliet) viewed through a large fish tank

Shot of: int. night. Close-up of DiCaprio viewed through a large fish tank

Shot of: int. night. Close-up of a hand under a sheet

Shot of: ext. night. DiCaprio and Danes embracing underwater

Shot of: ext. night. DiCaprio and Danes embracing underwater

Shot of: int. night. Close-up of DiCaprio, 'William Shakespeare's Romeo + Juliet' text superimposed

Shot of: ext. day. DiCaprio kneeling with his back to the camera in the desert, screaming 'Juliet'

Shot of: ext. day. Speeding car. Love theme changes to rock soundtrack

Shot of: ext. day. Close-up of John Leguizamo (Tybalt)

Shot of: ext. day. Close-up of Danes

Shot of: ext. day. Leguizamo holding a gun aloft

Shot of: int. night. DiCaprio and Danes embracing at the costume party

Shot of: ext. day. Speeding car.

Shot of: ext. day. DiCaprio at Verona Beach wearing a tuxedo

Shot of: int. night. DiCaprio and Danes embracing at the costume party

Shot of: ext. day. Helicopter flying over the city

Shot of: ext. night. Close-up shot of Danes's face underwater

Shot of: ext. night. Speeding car, the sound of screaming

Shot of: int. night. DiCaprio cradling Danes in the tomb

Black Screen. 'Leonardo DiCaprio' text appears, love theme begins to play again

Black Screen. 'Clare Danes' text appears

Shot of: int. day. Danes lying in bed smiling

Black Screen. 'William Shakespeare's' text appears

Black Screen. 'Romeo + Juliet' text appears

Shot of: ext. day. Close-up of DiCaprio in a Hawaiian shirt

Black Screen. 'William Shakespeare's Romeo + Juliet' text appears

Shot of: ext. day. Close-up of DiCaprio in a Hawaiian shirt, DiCaprio voice-over: 'know, Juliet, I will lie with you tonight', as the shot fades out

Chronological filmography

The Private Lives of Henry VIII, Korda, Alexander (1934)
David Copperfield, Cukor, George (1935)
A Midsummer Night's Dream, Reinhardt, Max and Dieterle, William (1935)
A Tale of Two Cities, Conway, Jack and Leonard, Robert Z. (1935)
Romeo and Juliet, Cukor, George (1936)
Henry V, Olivier, Laurence and Beck, Reginald (1944)
Hamlet, Olivier, Laurence (1948)
Throne of Blood, Kurosawa, Akira (1957)
The Magnificent Seven, Sturges, John (1960)
West Side Story, Robbins, Jerome and Wise, Robert (1961)
Hamlet, Kosintsev, Grigori (1964)
Doctor Zhivago, Lean, David (1965)
Chimes at Midnight, Welles, Orson (1966)
Romeo and Juliet, Zeffirelli, Franco (1968)
Macbeth, Polanski, Roman (1971)
Rocky, Avildsen, John G. (1976)
The Tempest, Jarman, Derek (1979)
Arthur, Gordon, Steve (1981)
ET, the Extra-Terrestrial, Spielberg, Steven (1982)
Tempest, Mazursky, Paul (1982)
Sixteen Candles, Hughes, John (1984)
This is Spinal Tap, Reiner, Rob (1984)
The Breakfast Club, Hughes, John (1985)
Ran, Kosintsev, Grigori (1985)
Crocodile Dundee, Faiman, Peter (1986)
Pretty in Pink, Deutch, Howard (1986)
Top Gun, Scott, Tony (1986)
Lear, Godard, Jean Luc (1987)
Dangerous Liaisons, Frears, Stephen (1988)
Batman, Burton, Tim (1989)

Bill and Ted's Excellent Adventure, Herek, Stephen (1989)
Henry V, Branagh, Kenneth (1989)
Sex, Lies, and Videotape, Soderbergh, Stephen (1989)
Hamlet, Zeffirelli, Franco (1990)
Prospero's Books, Greenaway, Peter (1990)
My Own Private Idaho, Van Sant, Gus (1991)
The Silence of the Lambs, Demme, Jonathan (1991)
Terminator II: Judgment Day, Cameron, James (1991)
Peter's Friends, Branagh, Kenneth (1992)
Reservoir Dogs, Tarantino, Quentin (1992)
Strictly Ballroom, Luhrmann, Baz (1992)
Jurassic Park, Spielberg, Steven (1993)
The Last Action Hero, McTiernan, John (1993)
Much Ado about Nothing, Branagh, Kenneth (1993)
The Piano, Campion, Jane (1993)
True Romance, Tarantino, Quentin (1993)
The Crow, Proyas, Alex (1994)
Mary Shelley's Frankenstein, Branagh, Kenneth (1994)
Natural Born Killers, Stone, Oliver (1994)
Pulp Fiction, Tarantino, Quentin (1994)
The Baby-Sitters Club, Mayron, Melanie (1995)
Batman Forever, Schumacher, Joel (1995)
Clueless, Heckerling, Amy (1995)
Cutthroat Island, Harlin, Renny (1995)
In the Bleak Midwinter/A Midwinter's Tale, Branagh, Kenneth (1995)
Othello, Parker, Oliver (1995)
Waterworld, Reynolds, Kevin and Costner, Kevin (1995)
Hamlet, Branagh, Kenneth (1996)
Looking for Richard, Pacino, Al (1996)
Richard III, Loncraine, Richard (1996)
Scream, Craven, Wes (1996)
Twelfth Night: Or, What You Will, Nunn, Trevor (1996)
William Shakespeare's Romeo + Juliet, Luhrmann, Baz (1996)
The Fifth Element, Besson, Luc (1997)
Titanic, Cameron, James (1997)
Titus Andronicus, Dunne, Christopher (1997)
A Thousand Acres, Moorhouse, Jocelyn (1997)
You've Got Mail, Ephron, Nora (1998)
Elizabeth, Kapur, Shekhar (1998)
The Faculty, Rodriguez, Robert (1998)
The Gingerbread Man, Altman, Robert (1998)
Halloween: H20, Miner, Steve (1998)
Life is Beautiful, Benigni, Roberto (1998)
Saving Private Ryan, Spielberg, Steven (1998)
Shakespeare in Love, Madden, John (1998)
There's Something about Mary, Farrelly, Bobby and Peter (1998)
The Thin Red Line, Malick, Terrence (1998)
Wicked, Steinberg, Michael (1998)

Wide Awake, Shyamalan, M. Night (1998)
American Beauty, Mendes, Sam (1999)
American Pie, Weitz, Paul (1999)
The Blair Witch Project, Myrick, Daniel and Sánchez, Eduardo II (1999)
Bowfinger, Martin, Steve (1999)
Cruel Intentions, Kumble, Roger (1999)
The Insider, Mann, Michael (1999)
Love's Labour's Lost, Branagh, Kenneth (1999)
Never Been Kissed, Gosnell, Raja (1999)
Romeo Must Die, Bartkowiak, Andrzej (1999)
She's All That, Iscove, Robert (1999)
Star Wars: Episode One – The Phantom Menace, Lucas, George (1999)
10 Things I Hate About You, Junger, Gil (1999)
Titus, Taymor, Julie (1999)
William Shakespeare's A Midsummer Night's Dream, Hoffman, Michael (1999)
Chocolat, Hallstrom, Lasse (2000)
Gladiator, Scott, Ridley (2000)
Hamlet, Almereyda, Michael (2000)
O, Nelson, Tim Blake (2000)
The Patriot, Emmerich, Roland (2000)
Get Over It, O'Haver, Tommy (2001)
Moulin Rouge, Luhrmann, Baz (2001)
Much Ado about Something, Rubbo, Michael (2001)
Pearl Harbor, Bay, Michael (2001)
Save the Last Dance, Carter, Thomas II (2001)
K-19: The Widowmaker, Bigelow, Kathryn (2002)
Romeo and Juliet Revisited, Carver, N. Barry (2002)
William Shakespeare's The Merchant of Venice, Radford, Michael (2004)

Bibliography

Adamek, Pauline, 'Baz Luhrmann's Romeo + Juliet', *Cinema Papers* (February 1997).

Adelman, Kenneth and Norman Augustine, *Shakespeare in Charge* (Los Angeles: Hearst/Talk Magazine/Miramax, 1999).

Ades, Dawn, ed., *The 20th-Century Poster: Design of the Avant-Garde* (New York: Abbeville Press, 1984).

Aebischer, Pascale, Edward J. Esche and Nigel Wheale, *Remaking Shakespeare: Performance across Media, Genres and Cultures* (Houndmills: Palgrave, 2003).

Aebischer, Pascale, *Shakespeare's Violated Bodies: Stage and Screen Performance* (Cambridge: Cambridge University Press, 2004).

Alexander, Peter, ed., *William Shakespeare, the Complete Works* (London and Glasgow: Collins, 1962).

Almereyda, Michael, *William Shakespeare's Hamlet: Adapted by Michael Almereyda* (London and New York: Faber and Faber, 2000).

Altman, Rick, *Film/Genre* (London: BFI Publishing, 1999).

Anderegg, Michael A., *Cinematic Shakespeare* (Lanham, Md.: Rowman & Littlefield, 2003).

Anderegg, Michael A., *Orson Welles, Shakespeare, and Popular Culture* (New York: Columbia University Press, 1999).

Andrews, John F., 'Kenneth Branagh's *Hamlet*', *Shakespeare Newsletter* 46: 3 (Fall 1996).

Arroyo, José, 'Kiss Kiss Bang Bang', *Sight and Sound*, 7: 3 (March 1997), 6–9.

Ashby, Justine and Andrew Higson, *British Cinema Past and Present* (London: Routledge, 2000).

Ashcroft, Bill, Gareth Griffiths and Helen Tiffin, eds, *The Empire Writes Back: Theory and Practice in Post-Colonial Literatures* (London and New York: Routledge, 1989).

Austin, Bruce A., *The Film Audience: An International Bibliography of Research* (NJ and London: The Scarecrow Press, Methuen, 1983).

Avis, Tim, 'Unceremonious About Shakespeare', *Moving Pictures International*, 15 (01/1996), 71–6.

Balazs, Bela, *Theory of the Film: Character and Growth of a New Art*, trans. by Edith Bone (New York: Dover Publications, 1970).

Ballard, J.G., *Super-Cannes* (London: Flamingo, 2001).

Barkan, Leonard, 'Making Pictures Speak: Renaissance Art, Elizabethan Literature, Modern Scholarship', *Renaissance Quarterly* (Summer 1995).

Barker, Deborah and Ivo Kamps, eds, *Shakespeare and Gender: A History* (London: Verso, 1995).

Barker, Martin and Kate Brooks, *Judge Dredd: Its Friends, Fans and Foes* (Luton: University of Luton Press, 1998).

Barker, Martin and Julian Petley, eds, *Ill Effects: The Media/Violence Debate* (London and New York: Routledge, 1997).

Barker, Martin, ed., *The Video Nasties: Freedom and Censorship in the Media* (London and Sydney: Pluto Press, 1984).

Bart, Peter, *The Gross: The Hits, the Flops – the Summer that Ate Hollywood* (New York: St Martin's Press, 1999).

Bassnett, Susan, ed., *Studying British Cultures: An Introduction* (London: Routledge, 1997).

Bate, Jonathan, *Shakespearean Constitutions: Politics, Theatre, Criticism, 1730–1830* (Oxford: Oxford University Press, 1989).

Bath, Michael, *Speaking Pictures: English Emblem Books and Renaissance Culture* (London and New York: Longman, 1994).

Battersby, Christine, *Gender and Genius: Towards a Feminist Aesthetics* (London: The Women's Press, 1994).

Baudrillard, Jean, *The Consumer Society: Myths and Structures (Theory, Culture and Society)* (London: Sage Publications, 1997).

Bauer, Eric, 'Re-Revealing Shakespeare: An Interview with Baz Luhrmann', *Creative Screenwriting*, 5 (1998), 33.

Bechervaise, Neil E, *Shakespeare on Celluloid* (Rozelle, New South Wales: St. Clair Press, 1999).

Bellamy, Richard, ed., *Antonio Gramsci: Pre-Prison Writings*, trans. by Virginia Cox (Cambridge: Cambridge University Press, 1994).

Benshoff, Harry M., *Monsters in the Closet: Homosexuality and the Horror Film* (Manchester and New York: Manchester University Press, 1997).

Berry, Cicely, *The Actor and the Text* (London: Virgin Publishing, 2000).

Bignell, Jonathan, *Media Semiotics: An Introduction* (Manchester and New York: Manchester University Press, 1997).

Bloom, Allan with Harry V. Jaffa, *Shakespeare's Politics* (Chicago, Ill.: University of Chicago Press, 1964).

Bloom, Harold, *Shakespeare: The Invention of the Human* (New York: Riverhead Books, 1998).

Bloom, Harold, *The Anxiety of Influence: A Theory of Poetry*, 2nd edn (New York and Oxford: Oxford University Press, 1997).

Bonnell, Victoria, *Iconography of Power: Soviet Political Posters under Lenin and Stalin* (Berkeley, Calif.: University of California Press, 1997).

Boose, Lynda and Richard Burt, eds, *Shakespeare, the Movie: Popularizing the Plays on Film, TV, and Video* (London: Routledge, 1997).

Bordwell, David and Kristin Thompson, *Film Art: An Introduction*, 4th edn (McGraw-Hill: New York, 1993).

Bordwell, David, *On the History of Film Style* (Cambridge, Mass. and London, Harvard University Press: 1997).

Bourdieu, Pierre, Alain Darbel and Dominique Schnapper, *The Love of Art: European Art*

Museums and their Public, trans. by Caroline Beattie and Nick Merriman (Cambridge: Polity Press, 1991).

Bourdieu, Pierre, *Distinction: A Social Critique of the Judgement of Taste*, trans. by R. Nice (Cambridge, Mass: Harvard University Press, 1984).

Bradshaw, Graham, *Misrepresentations: Shakespeare and the Materialists* (Ithaca, NY: Cornell University Press, 1993).

Brake, Michael, *Comparative Youth Culture: The Sociology of Youth Cultures and Youth Subcultures in America, Britain and Canada* (London: Routledge & Kegan Paul, 1985).

Branagh, Kenneth, *A Midwinter's Tale: The Shooting Script* (New York: Newmarket Press, 1996).

Branagh, Kenneth, *Beginning* (London: Chatto & Windus, 1989).

Branagh, Kenneth, *Hamlet: Screenplay, Introduction and Film Diary* (London: Chatto & Windus, 1996).

Branagh, Kenneth, *Henry V by William Shakespeare: A Screen Adaptation by Kenneth Branagh* (London: Chatto & Windus, 1989).

Branagh, Kenneth, *In the Bleak Midwinter* (London: Nick Hern Books, 1995).

Branagh, Kenneth, '*Much Ado about Nothing' by William Shakespeare: Screenplay, Introduction, and Notes on the Making of the Film by Kenneth Branagh* (London: Chatto & Windus, 1993).

Branagh, Kenneth, '*Henry V*', in *Players of Shakespeare 2*, ed. by Russell Jackson and Robert Smallwood, (Cambridge: Cambridge University Press, 1988).

Braudy, Leo and Marshall Cohen, *Film Theory and Criticism: Introductory Reading*, 5th edn (Oxford: Oxford University Press, 1999).

Breight, Curtis, 'Branagh and the Prince, or a "Royal Fellowship of Death"', *Critical Quarterly*, 33: 4 (1991), 95–111.

Brennan, Anthony, *Onstage and Offstage Worlds in Shakespeare's Plays* (London and New York: Routledge, 1989).

Bristol, Michael, *Big Time Shakespeare* (London: Routledge, 1996).

Bristol, Michael, *Carnival and Theatre, Plebeian Culture and the Structure of Authority in Renaissance England* (London and New York: Routledge, 1989).

Brode, Douglas, *Shakespeare in the Movies: From the Silent Era to Shakespeare in Love* (New York: Oxford University Press, 2000).

Bromley, Roger, Macdonald Daly, Jim McGuigan, Morag Shiach and Jeff Wallace, eds, *Keywords: A Journal of Cultural Materialism*, Issue 1 (1998).

Brooker, Peter and Will Brooker, *Postmodern After-Images: A Reader in Film, Television and Video* (London: Arnold, 1997).

Brown, Stephen, *Postmodern Marketing* (London and New York: Routledge, 1995).

Brunsdon, Charlotte, *Screen Tastes: Soap Opera to Satellite Dishes* (London: Routledge, 1997).

Buchman, Lorne M., *Still in Movement: Shakespeare on Screen* (New York and Oxford: Oxford University Press, 1991).

Buckingham, David, ed., *Reading Audiences: Young People and the Media* (Manchester and New York: Manchester University Press, 1993).

Buhler, Stephen M., 'Double takes: Branagh gets to Hamlet', *Post Script*, 17 (1997) 43–52.

Buhler, Stephen M., *Shakespeare in the Cinema: Ocular Proof* (Albany, NY: State University of New York Press, 2002).

Bulman, J.C. and H.R. Coursen, eds, *Shakespeare on Television: an Anthology of Essays and Reviews* (Hanover, NH and London: University Press of New England, 1988).

Burt, Richard, *Shakespeare after Mass Media* (New York: Palgrave, Macmillan, 2002).

Burt, Richard, *Unspeakable ShaXXXspeares: Queer Theory and American Kiddie Culture* (Basingstoke and London: Macmillan Press, 1998).

Burton, Alan and Steve Chibnall, 'Promotional Activities and Showmanship in British Film Exhibition', *Journal of Popular British Cinema*, 2 (1999), 83–99.

Cartelli, Thomas, *Repositioning Shakespeare: National Formations, Postcolonial Appropriations* (London: Routledge, 1999).

Carter, Angela, *Wise Children* (London: Vintage, 1992).

Cartmell, Deborah and Michael Scott, eds, *Talking Shakespeare: Shakespeare into the Millennium* (Basingstoke: Palgrave, 2001).

Cartmell, Deborah and Imelda Whelehan, eds, *Adaptations from Text to Screen, Screen to Text* (London and New York: Routledge, 1999).

Cartmell, Deborah, I.Q. Hunter Heidi Kaye and Imelda Whelehan, eds, *Pulping Fictions: Consuming Culture Across the Literature/Media Divide* (London and Chicago, Ill.: Pluto Press, 1996).

Cartmell, Deborah, I.Q. Hunter and Imelda Whelehan, *Reinventing the Past in Film and Fiction* (London and Sterling, Va.: Pluto Press, 2001).

Castiglia, Christopher, 'Rebel without a Closet: Homosexuality and Hollywood', *Critical Texts 5:* 1 (1988), 31–5.

Caws, Mary Ann, *The Art of Interference: Stressed Readings in Verbal and Visual Arts* (Cambridge: Polity, 1989).

Charney, Maurice, 'Shakespearean Anglophilia: the BBC-TV Series and American Audiences', *Shakespeare Quarterly*, 31 (1980), 287–92.

Chedgzoy, Kate, *Shakespeare's Queer Children: Sexual Politics and Contemporary Culture* (Manchester and New York: Manchester University Press, 1995).

Collick, John, *Shakespeare, Cinema and Society* (Manchester and New York, Manchester University Press, 1989).

Collier, Susanne, 'Post-Falklands, Post-Colonial: Contextualising Branagh as "Henry V" on Stage and on Film', *Essays in Theatre*, 10: 2 (1992).

Cook, Guy, *The Discourse of Advertising*, 2nd edn (London: Routledge, 2001).

Corcoran, Bill, Mike Hayhoe and Gordon M. Pradl, eds, *Knowledge in the Making: Challenging the Text in the Classroom* (Portsmouth: Heinemann, 1994).

Coursen, H. R., 'Words, Words, Words: Searching for Hamlet', *Shakespeare Yearbook*, 8 (1997), 306–24.

Coursen, H.R, *Watching Shakespeare on Television* (Rutherford, NJ: Fairleigh Dickinson University Press, 1993).

Coursen, H.R., 'The Critical Reception of Branagh's Complete Hamlet in the U.S. Popular Press', *Shakespeare and the Classroom*, 5: 2 (Fall 1997), 29–39.

Cox, James D. and David Scott Kastan, eds, *A New History of Early Modern Drama* (New York: Columbia University Press, 1997).

Crowdus, Gary, 'Words, Words, Words: Recent Shakespearean Films', *Cineaste* 23: 4 (1998), 13–19.

Crowdus, Gary, 'Shakespeare is Up to Date: an Interview with Sir Ian McKellen', *Cineaste*, 24: 1 (1999), 46–7.

Crowdus, Gary, 'Sharing an Enthusiasm for Shakespeare: an Interview with Kenneth Branagh', *Cineaste*, 24: 1 (1999), 34–41.

Crowl, Samuel, 'Hamlet "Most Royal": An Interview with Kenneth Branagh', *Shakespeare Bulletin*, 12: 4 (1994), 5–8.

Crowl, Samuel, '*A Midsummer Night's Dream:* A Michael Hoffmann Film', *Shakespeare Bulletin*, 17: 3 (Easton, Pa.: Lafayette College, 1999).

Crowl, Samuel, *Shakespeare at the Cineplex: The Kenneth Branagh Era* (Athens, Ohio: Ohio University Press, 2003).

Crowl, Samuel, *Shakespeare Observed: Studies in Performance on Stage and Screen* (Athens, Ohio: Ohio University Press, 1992).

Crowl, Samuel, 'Zeffirelli's Hamlet: The Golden Girl and Fistful of Dust', *Cineaste*, 24: 1 (1998), 56–61.

Dale, Martin, *The Movie Game: The Film Business in Britain, Europe and America* (London: Cassell, 1997).

Danesi, Marcel, *Interpreting Advertisements: A Semiotic Guide* (New York: Legas, 1995).

Danna, Sammy R. ed., *Advertising and Popular Culture: Studies in Variety and Versatility* (Bowling Green, Ohio: Bowling Green State University Popular Press, 1992).

Davies, Anthony and Stanley Wells, eds, *Shakespeare and the Moving Image: The Plays on Film and Television* (Cambridge: Cambridge University Press, 1994).

Davies, Jude, and Carol Smith, *Gender, Ethnicity and Sexuality in Contemporary American Film* (Edinburgh: Keele University Press, 1997).

Dawson, Anthony B., *Shakespeare in Performance – Hamlet* (Manchester: Manchester University Press, 1995).

Desmet, Christy and Robert Sawyer, eds, *Shakespeare and Appropriation* (London and New York: Routledge, 1999).

Dessen, Alan C., *Elizabethan Stage Conventions and Modern Interpreters* (Cambridge: Cambridge University Press, 1984).

Dixon, Wheeler Winston, *The Transparency of Spectacle: Meditations on the Moving Image* (Albany, NY: State University of New York Press, 1998).

Docherty, David, David Morrison and Michael Tracey, *The Last Picture Show? Britain's Changing Film Audience* (London: BFI Publishing, 1987).

Dodsworth, Martin, *Hamlet Closely Observed* (London: Athlone Press, 1985).

Dollimore, Jonathan and Alan Sinfield, eds, *Political Shakespeare, Essays in Cultural Materialism*, 2nd edn (Manchester: Manchester University Press, 1994).

Donaldson, Peter S., *Shakespearean Films/Shakespearean Directors* (Boston, Mass.: Unwin Hyman, 1990).

Drewery, Brant, 'Trailer for Sale or Rent', *Creation*, December (1999), 28–31.

Drexler, Peter and Lawrence Guntner, eds, *Negotiations with Hal: Multi-Media Perceptions of (Shakespeare's) Henry the Fifth* (Braunschweig: Technische Universitat Braunschweig, 1995).

Durie, John, ed., *The Film Marketing Handbook: A Practical Guide to Marketing Strategies for Independent Films* (Madrid: Media Business School, 1993).

Dyer, Richard, ed., *Bad Object Choices, How Do I Look? Queer Films and Video* (Seattle, Wash.: Bay Press, 1991).

Dyer, Richard, ed., *Gays and Film* (London: BFI Publishing, 1977).

Dyer, Richard, *Now You See It: Studies on Gay and Lesbian Film* (London: Routledge, 1990).

Dyja, Eddie, ed., *BFI Film and Television Handbook 1999* (London: BFI Publishing, 1998).

Eckert, Charles, ed., *Focus on Shakespearean Films* (Englewood Cliffs, NJ: Prentice-Hall, 1972).

Edwards, Gregory J. and Robin Cross, *Worst Movie Posters of All Time: A Treasury of Trash* (London: Sphere, 1984).

Edwards, Gregory J., *The International Film Poster* (London: Columbus, 1985).

Elias, Norbert, *The Civilising Process: The History of Manners and State Formation and Civilisation*, trans. by Edmund Jephcott (Oxford: Blackwell Publishers, 1994).

Falk, Quentin, 'Shakespeare on Love', *Exposure*, Spring 1999, 10–13.

Farmer, Norman K. Jr., *Poets and the Visual Arts in Renaissance England* (Austin, Tex.: University of Texas Press, 1984).

Feist, Andrew and Robert Hutchison, eds, *Cultural Trends* Issue 6 (London: Policy Studies Institute, August 1990).

Fern, Alan, *The Fifth Hanes Lecture: Off The Wall, Research into the Art of the Poster* (Chapel Hill, NC: Hanes Foundation, 1985).

Fischlin, Daniel and Mark Fortier, eds, *Adaptations of Shakespeare: A Critical Anthology of Plays from the Seventeenth Century to the Present* (London and New York: Routledge, 2000).

Fiske, John, *Reading the Popular* (London and New York: Routledge, 1989).

Fiske, John, *Understanding Popular Culture* (London and New York: Routledge, 1989).

Fleming, Charles, *High Concept: Don Simpson and the Hollywood Culture of Excess* (London: Bloomsbury, 1998).

Ford, John R., 'Translating Audiences and Their Bottoms: Filming A Midsummer Night's Dream', *Publications of the Mississippi Philological Association* (2000), 1–9.

Forgacs, David and Geoffrey Nowell-Smith, eds, *Antonio Gramsci: Selections from Cultural Writings*, trans. by William Boelhower (London: Lawrence & Wishart, 1985).

Fornas, Johan and Goran Bolin, eds, *Youth Culture of Late Modernity* (London and Thousand Oaks, Calif.: Sage Publications, 1995).

Franssen, Paul, 'Shakespeare: The Lover and the Poet', *Folio 6.1* (The Shakespeare Society of the Low Countries, 1999).

Frith, Simon and Andrew Goodwin, eds, *On Record: Rock, Pop and the Written Word* (London: Routledge, 1990).

Fuller, Kathryn H., *At the Picture Show: Small-Town Audiences and the Creation of Movie Fan Culture* (London and Washington, DC: Smithsonian Institute Press, 1996).

Gallo, Max, *The Poster in History*, trans. by Alfred and Bruni Mayor (Feltham: Hamlyn, 1974).

Gamson, Joshua, *Claims to Fame, Celebrity in Contemporary America* (Berkeley, Calif. and London: University of California Press, 1994).

Garber, Marjorie, Jann Matlock and Rebecca L. Walcowitz, eds, *Media Spectacles* (London and New York: Routledge, 1993).

Geffner, David, 'Cars, Soap and Celluloid: Marketing Independent Film in a Studio Film Age', *Filmmaker*, 7: 4 (1999), 18–22, 68–9, 92.

Geffner, David, 'Clip Art: The Art of Trailer Production', *Filmmaker*, 5: 3 (1997), 31–4.

Giroux, Henry A. and Peter McLaren, eds, *Between Borders: Pedagogy and the Politics of Cultural Studies* (London and New York: Routledge, 1994).

Goldberg, Fred, *Motion Picture Marketing and Distribution: Getting Movies into a Theatre Near You* (Boston, Mass. and London: Focal Press, 1991).

Gombrich, E. H., *Art and Illusion: A Study in the Psychology of Pictorial Representation* (London: Phaidon, 1977).

Grainge, Paul, 'Branding Hollywood: Studio Logos and the Aesthetics of Memory and Hype', *Screen* 45 (4) (2004), 344–62.

Grazia, Margreta de and Stanley Wells, eds, *The Cambridge Companion to Shakespeare* (Cambridge: Cambridge University Press, 2001).

Greenberg, Bradley S., Jane D. Brown and Nancy L. Buerkel-Rothfuss, eds, *Media, Sex and the Adolescent* (Cresskill, NJ: Hampton Press, 1993).

Halio, Jay L. and Hugh Richmond, eds, *Shakespearean Illuminations: Essays in Honor of Marvin Rosenberg* (London and Newark, Del.: Associated University Press and University of Delaware Press, 1998).

Hall, Stuart, ed., *Representation: Cultural Representations and Signifying Practices* (London: Sage Publications, 1997).

Hamilton Ball, Robert, 'On Shakespeare Filmography', *Literature/Film Quarterly* 1: 4 (1973), 299.

Hamsher, Jane, *Killer Instinct: How Two Young Producers Took on Hollywood and Made the Most Controversial Film of the Decade* (London: Orion Media, 1997).

Hapgood, Robert, ed., *Hamlet: Shakespeare in Production Series* (Cambridge: Cambridge University Press, 1999).

Hardison, O. B., 'Shakespeare on Film: The Developing Canon', *PCLS*, 12 (1981), 131–45.

Harvey, David, *The Condition of Postmodernity: An Enquiry into the Origins of Cultural Change* (Oxford: Basil Blackwell, 1989).

Hatchuel, Sarah, *A Companion to the Shakespearean Films of Kenneth Branagh* (Winnipeg: Blizzard Publishing, 2000).

Hatchuel, Sarah, 'Leading the Gaze: From Showing to Telling in Kenneth Branagh's Henry V and Hamlet', 6: 1 (May 2000) *Early Modern Literary Studies*, Shakespeare on Screen, available online at <http://purl.oclc.org/emls/emlshome.html>.

Hatchuel, Sarah, *Shakespeare, from Stage to Screen* (Cambridge: Cambridge University Press, 2004).

Haug, Wolfgang Fritz, *Critique of Commodity Aesthetics: Appearance, Sexuality and Advertising in Capitalist Society*, trans. by Robert Bock (Cambridge: Polity, 1986).

Hazelton, John, 'For a Few Dollars More', *Screen International*, 1067 (1996).

Hazelton, John, 'Multiplicity', *Screen International*, 1067 (1996).

Hebdige, Dick, *Hiding in the Light* (London: Routledge, 1988).

Hedrick, Don and Bryan Reynolds, eds, *Shakespeare Without Class* (New York: St Martin's Press, 2000).

Hemming, Carol, *Studio Production Notes for Love's Labour's Lost*, <http://members.tripod.com/dailytelegiraffe/loveslaboursloststudionotes.html>.

Hibbard, G.R., ed., *Hamlet* (Oxford: Oxford University Press, 1987).

Hoffman, Michael and Kevin Kline, 'A Midsummer Night's Dream', *Shakespeare: A Magazine for Shakespeare Teachers and Enthusiasts*, 3: 2 (Summer 1999).

Hodgdon, Barbara, *The Shakespeare Trade* (London: Routledge, 1998).

Holderness, Graham, *Cultural Shakespeare: Essays in the Shakespeare Myth* (Hatfield: University of Hertfordshire Press, 2001).

Holderness, Graham, ed., *The Shakespeare Myth* (Manchester: Manchester University Press, 1988).

Holderness, Graham, *Visual Shakespeare: Essays in Film and Television* (Hatfield: University of Hertfordshire Press, 2002).

Holderness, Graham, *Shakespeare Recycled: The Making of Historical Drama* (Hemel Hempstead: Harvester Wheatsheaf, 1992).

Holstun, James, 'Ranting at the New Historicism', *English Literary Renaissance 19* (1989), 189–225.

Holtgen, K.J., *Word and Visual Imagination: Studies in the Interaction of English Literature and the Visual Arts* (Nurnberg: University Bibliothek Erlangen, 1988).

Howard, Jean and Scott Cutler Shershow, eds, *Marxist Shakespeares* (London: Routledge, 2001).

Howlett, Kathy M., *Framing Shakespeare on Film* (Athens, Ohio: Ohio University Press, 2000).

Ilott, Terry, *Budgets and Markets: A Study of the Budgeting of European Film* (London: Routledge, 1996).

Ioppolo, Grace, ed., *Shakespeare Performed: Essays in Honor of R.A. Foakes* (London and Newark, Del.: Associated University Press and University of Delaware Press, 2000).

Irace, Kathleen O., ed., *The New Cambridge First Quarto of Hamlet* (Cambridge: Cambridge University Press, 1998).

Iyengar, Sujata, 'Shakespeare in HeteroLove', *Literature/Film Quarterly* 29: 2 (2001), 122–7.

Jackson, Russell, 'Kenneth Branagh's Film of *Hamlet*: the Textual Choices', *Shakespeare Bulletin* (1997), 37–8.

Jackson, Russell, ed., *The Cambridge Companion to Shakespeare on Film* (Cambridge: Cambridge University Press, 2000).

Jackson, Russell, 'Working with Shakespeare: Confessions of an Advisor', *Cineaste*, 24: 1 (1999), 42–4.

Jameson, Fredric, *Postmodernism, or, The Cultural Logic of Late Capitalism* (London and New York: Verso, 1991).

Jarvie, Ian, *Hollywood's Overseas Campaign, the North Atlantic Movie Trade, 1920–1950* (Cambridge: Cambridge University Press, 1992).

Jenkins, Harold, ed., *Hamlet: The New Arden Shakespeare*, 2nd edn (London: Thomas Nelson & Sons, 1997).

Jensen, Michael P., 'Fragments of a Dream: Photos of Three Scenes Missing from the Reinhardt-Dieterle-Dream', *Shakespeare Bulletin*, 18: 4 (2000), 37–8.

Jhally, Sut, *The Codes of Advertising, Fetishism and the Political Economy of Meaning in the Consumer Society* (London: Pinter, 1989).

Johnson, Lemuel A., *Shakespeare in Africa (and Other Venues), Import and the Appropriation of Culture* (Trenton, NJ: Africa World Press, 1998).

Joughin, John, ed., *Shakespeare and National Culture* (New York: Manchester University Press, 1997).

Jorgens, Jack, *Shakespeare on Film* (Bloomington, Ind.: Indiana University Press, 1977).

Kamps, Ivo, ed., *Shakespeare Left and Right* (London and New York: Routledge, 1991).

Kastan, David Scott, *A Companion to Shakespeare* (Oxford and Malden, Mass.: Blackwell, 1999).

Keller, James R. and Leslie Stratyner, eds, *Almost Shakespeare: Reinventing his Works for Cinema and Television* (Jefferson, NC: McFarland & Co, 2004).

Kellner, Douglas, *Media Culture: Cultural Studies, Identity and Politics between the Modern and the Postmodern* (London and New York: Routledge, 1996).

Kliman, Bernice W., *Hamlet: Film, Television and Audio Performance* (Rutherford, NJ: Fairleigh Dickinson, 1988).

Kurosawa, Akira, *Seven Samurai and Other Screenplays: Ikiru, Seven Samurai, Throne of Blood* (London: Faber and Faber, 1992).

Lanier, Douglas, 'Now: The Presence of History in Looking for Richard', *Post Script*, 17: 2 (1998), 39–55.

Lehmann, Courtney, '*Much Ado about Nothing?* Shakespeare, Branagh and the "National-Popular" in the Age of Multinational Capital', *Textual Practice*, 12: 1 (1998), 1–22.

Lehmann, Courtney, 'Making Mother Matter: Repression, Revision, and the Stakes of

"Reading Psychoanalysis into" Kenneth Branagh's *Hamlet*, *Early Modern Literary Studies*, 6: 1 (2000), 2–24.

Lehmann, Courtney, *Shakespeare Remains: Theater to Film, Early Modern to Postmodern* (Ithaca, NY: Cornell University Press, 2002).

Levine, Lawrence W, *Highbrow/Lowbrow: The Emergence of Cultural Hierarchy in America* (London and Cambridge, Mass.: Harvard University Press, 1988).

Levison, Louise, *Filmmakers and Financing: Business Plans for Independents*, 3rd edn (Boston, Mass.: Focal Press, 2001).

Lewis, Jon, *The Road to Romance and Ruin: Teen Films and Youth Culture* (London and New York: Routledge, 1992).

Light, Alison, 'The Importance of Being Ordinary', *Sight and Sound*, 3: 9 (1993), 16–19.

Litman, Barry R., *The Motion Picture Mega-Industry* (Boston, Mass. and London: Allyn & Bacon, 1998).

Loehlin, James, *Shakespeare in Performance: Henry V* (Manchester: Manchester University Press, 1996).

Loomba, Ania and Martin Orkin, *Post-Colonial Shakespeares* (London: Routledge, 1998).

Luhrmann, Baz and Craig Pearce, *William Shakespeare's Romeo + Juliet: The Contemporary Film, The Classic Play: The Screenplay by Craig Pearce and Baz Luhrmann and the Text of Shakespeare's Original Play Together in One Volume* (London: Hodder Children's Books, 1997).

Lukk, Tiiu, *Movie Marketing: Opening the Picture and Giving it Legs* (Los Angeles, Calif.: Silman-James Press, 1997).

Lumbry, Catherine, *Gotcha: Life in a Tabloid World* (St Leonards: Allen & Unwin, 1999).

Lyons, Donald, 'Lights, Camera, Shakespeare', *Commentary*, 103: 2 (1997), 57–60.

Lyotard, Jean-François, *Postmodern Fables*, trans. by Georges Van Den Abbeele (Minneapolis, Minn.: University of Minnesota Press, 1997).

MacCabe, Colin, *The Eloquence of the Vulgar: Language, Cinema and the Politics of Culture* (London: BFI Publishing, 1999).

Macdonald, Andrew and Gina Macdonald, '(Re)Writing Shakespeare for film: Devore/Zeffirelli's vs. Branagh's *Hamlet*', *Creative Screenwriting*, 5: 2 (1998), 42–53.

Manvell, Roger, *Shakespeare and the Film* (South Brunswick, NJ: A. S. Barnes, 1979).

Manvell, Roger, *Theatre and Film* (London: Associated University Presses, 1979).

Marshall, P. David, *Celebrity and Power: Fame in Contemporary Culture* (London and Minneapolis, Minn: University of Minnesota Press, 1997).

Mayne, Judith, *Cinema and Spectatorship* (London and New York: Routledge, 1993).

McCracken, Scott, *Pulp: Reading Popular Fiction* (Manchester and New York: Manchester University Press, 1998).

McFarlane, Brian, 'Shakespeare for Everyone: Othello, Macbeth and Much Ado about Nothing', *Cinema Papers*, 96 (1993), 39–41.

McGee, Mark Thomas, *Beyond Ballyhoo, Motion Picture Promotion and Gimmicks* (Jefferson, NC and London: McFarland, 1989).

McGuigan, Jim, *Cultural Populism* (London: Routledge, 1992).

McKellen, Ian and Richard Loncraine, *William Shakespeare's Richard III* (London: Doubleday, 1996).

McRobbie, Angela, *In the Culture Society: Art, Fashion and Popular Music* (London and New York: Routledge, 1999).

McRobbie, Angela, *Postmodernism and Popular Culture* (London: Routledge, 1994).

Medhurst, Andy, 'Coming Attractions', *Sight and Sound*, 8: 7 (1998), 24–6.

Medhurst, Andy, 'The Big Tease', *Sight and Sound*, 8: 7 (1998), 24–6.
Meirer, Paul, 'Kenneth Branagh – with Utter Clarity', *The Drama Review* (1997), 82–9.
Mercer, Colin, Janet Woollacott and Tony Bennett, eds, *Popular Culture and Social Relations* (London: Open University Press, 1986).
Millard, Barbara C., 'Shakespeare on Film: Towards an Audience Perceived and Perceiving', *Literature/Film Quarterly* 5: 4 (1977), 352.
Miller, David Lee, Sharon O'Dair and Harold Weber, eds, *The Production of English Renaissance Culture* (Ithaca, NY and London: Cornell University Press, 1994).
Miller, Toby, Geoffrey A. Lawrence, Jim McKay and David Rowe, *Globalization and Sport: Playing the Field* (London: Sage Publications, 2001).
Minh-Ha, Trinh T., *When the Moon Waxes Red: Representation, Gender and Cultural Politics* (London and New York: Routledge 1991).
Montgomery, Michael V., *Carnivals and Commonplaces: Bakhtin's Chronotope, Cultural Studies, and Film* (New York: Peter Lang, 1993).
Morley, David and Kuan-Hsing Chen, *Stuart Hall: Critical Dialogues in Cultural Studies* (London: Routledge, 1996).
Morley, David, *Television, Audiences and Cultural Studies* (London: Routledge, 1992).
Morley, David, *The Nationwide Audience: Structure and Decoding* (London: BFI Publishing, 1980).
Mukerji, Chandra and Michael Schudson (Berkeley, Calif.: University of California Press, 1991).
Murphy, Robert, *British Cinema of the 90s* (London: BFI Publishing, 2000).
Murray, Timothy, *Like a Film, Ideological Fantasy on Screen, Camera and Canvas* (London, Routledge: 1993).
Natoli, Joseph, *Speeding to the Millennium: Film and Culture 1993–1995* (Albany, NY: State University of New York Press, 1998).
Neubauer, John, *The Fin-de-Siécle Culture of Adolescence* (New Haven, Conn. and London: Yale University Press, 1992).
Nichols, Nina da Vinci, 'Branagh's Hamlet Redux', *Shakespeare Bulletin*, 15: 3 (1997), 38–41.
Norman, Marc and Tom Stoppard, *Shakespeare in Love: A Screenplay* (New York: Hyperion, 1998).
Nowell-Smith, Geoffrey and Stephen Ricci, eds, *Britain vs. America: Hollywood and Europe, Economics, Culture, National Identity, 1945–95* (London: BFI Publishing, 1998).
Nunn, Trevor, *Twelfth Night, or What You Will: A Screenplay* (London: Methuen, 1996).
O'Connor, Teresa, *Shakespeare in Love Study Guide* (London: Film Education, 1999).
O'Sullivan, Maurice J., ed., *Shakespeare's Other Lives: An Anthology of Fictional Depictions of the Bard* (Jefferson, NC, London: McFarland, 1997).
Page, Nick, *The Tabloid Shakespeare* (London: Harper Collins, 1999).
Panofsky, Erwin, *Meaning in the Visual Arts* (London: Penguin, 1993).
Parmar, Pratibha, Martha Gever and John Greyson, eds, *Queer Looks: Perspectives on Lesbian and Gay Film and Video* (London and New York: Routledge, 1993).
Pearson, Roberta E. and William Uricchio, 'How Many Times Shall Caesar Bleed in Sport: Shakespeare and the Cultural Debate about Moving Pictures', *Screen*, 31 (1990), 243–61.
Pendleton, Thomas A., 'What (?) Price (?) Shakespeare (?)', *Literature/Film Quarterly*, 29: 2 (2001), 135–46.
Pequigney, Joseph, *Such is my Love, A Study of Shakespeare's Sonnets* (Chicago, Ill. and

London: University of Chicago Press, 1985).

Perrine, Toni A., *Film and the Nuclear Age: Representing Cultural Anxiety* (London and New York: Garland Publishing, 1998).

Petrie, Duncan J., *Creativity and Constraint in the British Film Industry* (London: Macmillan Press, 1991).

Philippian, Mardy, 'Welles, Shakespeare and Popular Culture', *Film Literature Quarterly*, 27: 4 (Westminster, Md.: Opera House Printing, 1999), 310–11.

Pilkington, Ace G., *Screening Shakespeare: From Richard II to Henry V* (Newark, Del. and London: University of Delaware Press, 1991).

Polanski, Roman, *Roman* (London and New York: Heinemann and William Morrow, 1984).

Poole, Edwin E. and Susan T. Poole, *Collecting Movie Posters, an Illustrated Reference Guide to Movie Art Posters, Press Kits and Lobby Cards* (Jefferson, NC: McFarland & Co., 1996).

Posner, Michael, *Canadian Dreams: The Making and Marketing of Independent Films* (Vancouver: Douglas & McIntyre, 1993).

Powers, Stephen, Stanley Rothman and David J. Rothman, eds, *Hollywood's America: Social and Political Themes in Motion Pictures* (Oxford: Westview, 1996).

Pursell, Michael, 'Playing the Game: Branagh's Henry V', *Literature/Film Quarterly*, 20: 4 (1992), 268–75.

Radway, Janice, 'Reception Study: Ethnography and the Problems of Dispersed Audiences and Nomadic Subjects', *Cultural Studies* 2: 3, 359–76.

Ray, Suranjan, *Macbeth on Celluloid: The Mirror and the Image*, trans. by Pranatik Dattagupta (Calcutta: CinEd, 1997).

Raymond, Ilene, 'An Interview with Kenneth Branagh, *Creative Screenwriting*, 5: 2 (1998), 20–3.

Raskin, Richard, *The Functional Analysis of Art: An Approach to the Social and Psychological Functions and Literature, Painting and Film* (Aarhus: Arkona, 1982).

Reid, Mary Anne, *Long Shots to Favourites: Australian Cinema Successes in the 90s* (Australian Film Commission, 1993).

Roddick, Nick, 'Shotguns and Weddings', *Sight and Sound, Mediawatch 99*, 9 (1999), 10–13.

Rollin, Lucy, *Twentieth-Century Teen Culture by the Decades: A Reference Guide* (London and Westport, Conn.: Greenwood Press, 1999).

Rosen, David and Peter Hamilton, *Off-Hollywood: The Making and Marketing of Independent Films* (New York: Grove Weidenfeld, 1990).

Rosenthal, Daniel, *Shakespeare on Screen* (London: Hamlyn, 2000).

Rothwell, Kenneth S., *A History of Shakespeare on Screen: A Century of Film and Television* (Cambridge: Cambridge University Press, 1999).

Rothwell, Kenneth S., 'Elizabeth and Shakespeare in Love', *Cineaste*, 24: 2–3 (1999), 78–80.

Rothwell, Kenneth S., 'Filmed Shakespeare: Scholarship and Criticism at the Millennium', *Shakespeare Bulletin*, 18: 4 (2000), 44–7.

Rothwell, Kenneth S., *Shakespeare on Screen: An International Filmography and Videography* (New York: Neal-Schuman, 1990).

Rowe, David, *Popular Cultures: Rock Music, Sport and the Politics of Pleasure* (London: Sage Publications, 1995).

Russo, Vito, *The Celluloid Closet: Homosexuality in the Movies* (New York: Harper & Row, 1981).

Rutter, Carol Chillington, *Enter the Body: Women and Representation on Shakespeare's*

Stage (London and New York: Routledge, 2001).

Sammons, Eddie, *Shakespeare: A Hundred Years on Film* (London: Shepheard-Walwyn, 2000).

Saunders, Michael William, *Imps of the Perverse, Gay Monsters in Film* (London and Westport, Conn.: Praeger, 1998).

Schatz, Thomas, *Hollywood Genres: Formulas, Filmmaking and the Studio System* (New York: Random House, 1981).

Schickel, Richard, *Common Fame, the Culture of Celebrity* (London: Pavilion, 1985).

Schickel, Richard, *Douglas Fairbanks, the First Celebrity* (London: Elm Tree Books, 1976).

Schmitt, Bernd, *Marketing Aesthetics: The Strategic Management of Brands, Identity and Image* (London and New York: Free Press, 1997).

Schwenger, Peter, 'Prospero's Books and the Visionary Page', *Textual Practice*, 8: 2 (1994), 268–78.

Shaughnessy, Robert, ed., *Shakespeare on Film* (Basingstoke: Macmillan Press, 1998).

Shuttleworth, Ian, *Ken and Em: A Biography of Kenneth Branagh and Emma Thompson* (London: Headline Press, 1994).

Skovmand, Michael, *Screen Shakespeare* (Aarhus: Aarhus University Press, 1994).

Smith, Bruce, *Homosexual Desire in Shakespeare's England: A Cultural Poetics* (Chicago, Ill.: Chicago University Press, 1991).

Smith, Jeff, *The Sounds of Commerce: Marketing Popular Film Music* (New York: Columbia University Press, 1998).

Sontag, Susan, 'Notes on Camp' (1964), *Against Interpretation* (London: Vintage, 1994).

Squire, Jason E., ed., *The Movie Business Book* (Bromley: Columbus, 1986).

Staiger, Janet, 'Announcing Wares, Winning Patrons, Voicing Ideals: Thinking about the History and Theory of Film Advertising', *Cinema Journal*, 29: 3 (1990), 3–31.

Stallybrass, Peter and Allon White, *The Politics and Poetics of Transgression* (London: Methuen, 1986).

Starks, Lisa S. and Courtney Lehmann, eds, *Screening the Bard: Shakespearean Spectacle, Critical Theory, Film Practice* (Madison, NJ: American University Presses, 2001).

Starks, Lisa S. and Courtney Lehmann, eds, *The Reel Shakespeare: Alternative Cinema and Theory* (London: Associated University Press, 2002).

Steinberg, Shirley R. and Joe L. Kincheloe, eds, *Kinder-Culture: The Corporate Construction of Childhood* (New York: Westview Press, 1997).

Stokes, Melvyn and Richard Maltby, eds, *Identifying Hollywood's Audiences: Cultural Identity and the Movies* (London: BFI Publishing, 1999).

Stokes, Melvyn and Richard Maltby, eds, *Hollywood Spectatorship: Changing Perceptions of Cinema Audiences* (London: BFI Publishing, 2001).

Stoppard, Tom, *Rosencrantz and Guildenstern Are Dead: The Film* (Boston, Mass. and London: Faber & Faber, 1991).

Storey, John, *An Introduction to Cultural Theory and Popular Culture*, 2nd edn (London: Prentice Hall, 1997).

Straayer, Chris, *Deviant Eyes, Deviant Bodies, Sexual Re-Orientations in Film and Video* (New York: Columbia University Press, 1996).

Strinati, Dominic, *An Introduction to Theories of Popular Culture* (London: Routledge, 1995).

Styan, J.L., *Perspectives on Shakespeare in Performance* (New York: P. Lang, 1999).

Swingewood, Alan, *Cultural Theory and the Problem of Modernity* (Basingstoke and London: Macmillan Press, 1998).

Taylor, Thom, *The Big Deal: Hollywood's Million Dollar Spec Script Market* (New York: William Morrow, 1999).

Taymor, Julie, *Titus: The Illustrated Screenplay* (New York: Newmarket Press, 2000).

Terris, Olwen and Luke McKernan, eds, *Walking Shadows: Shakespeare in the National Film and Television Archive* (London: National Film Theatre Press, 1994).

Thomas, Suzanna, *An Analysis of how the Study of Film Contributes to our Understanding of the Production and Consumption of Cultural Commodities* (Worcester: Worcester College of Higher Education, 1988).

Thompson, Ann, ed., *William Shakespeare, The Taming of the Shrew* (Cambridge: Cambridge University Press, 1984).

Thornton Burnett, Mark, 'The "Very Cunning of the Scene"': Kenneth Branagh's Hamlet', *Literature/Film Quarterly* 25: 2 (1997), 78–82.

Thornton Burnett, Mark and Ramona Wray, eds, *Shakespeare, Film, Fin de Siècle* (Basingstoke: Macmillan Press, 2000).

Tibbetts, John C., 'Backstage with the Bard: or, Building a Better Mousetrap', *Literature/Film Quarterly*, 29: 2 (2001), 147–64.

Traube, Elizabeth G., *Dreaming Identities: Class, Gender, and Generation in 1980s Hollywood Movies* (Boulder, Col. and Oxford: Westview Press, 1992).

Turner, Graeme, *British Cultural Studies: An Introduction*, 2nd edn (London: Routledge, 1996).

Tutty, Emma, 'Renaissance Player', *Screen International*, 1049 (1996), 12–14.

Tutty, Emma, 'The Great Dane', *Screen International*, 1049 (1996), 16.

Vanrigh, Anny Crunelle, 'All the World's a Screen: Transcoding in Branagh's *Hamlet*' *Shakespeare Yearbook*, 8 (1997), 349–69.

Various, *Proceedings of the Shakespeare on Screen Conference, Malaga* (Malaga: University of Malaga, 1999).

Vaughan, Alden T. and Virginia Mason, *Shakespeare's Caliban: A Cultural History* (Cambridge: Cambridge University Press, 1991).

Viano, Maurizio, *A Certain Realism: Making Use of Pasolini's Film Theory and Practice* (Berkeley, Calif. and London: University of California Press, 1993).

Viljoen, Dorothy, *Art of the Deal: The Essential Guide to Business Affairs for Television and Film Producers*, 2nd edn (London: PACT, 1997).

Vincendeau, Ginette, ed., *Film/Literature/Heritage: Contents: A Sight and Sound Reader* (London: BFI Publishing, 2001).

Ward, Annalee R., *Mouse Morality: The Rhetoric of Disney Animated Film* (Austin, Tex.: University of Texas Press, 2002).

Weissenborn, Ulrike, *"Just Making Pictures": Hollywood Writers, The Frankfurt School, and Film Theory* (Tubingen: Narr, 1998).

Weiss, Tanja, *Shakespeare on the Screen: Kenneth Branagh's adaptations of Henry V, Much Ado about Nothing and Hamlet* (Frankfurt: Peter Lang, 1999).

Wells, Stanley, 'Television Shakespeare', *Shakespeare Quarterly*, 33 (1983), 261–77.

Wells, Stanley and Gary Taylor, *The Oxford Shakespeare: The Complete Works* (Oxford: Oxford University Press, 1998).

Wernick, Andrew, *Promotional Culture, Advertising, Ideology and Symbolic Expression* (London, Newbury Park, New Delhi: Sage Publications, 1991).

Whittock, Trevor, *Metaphor and Film* (Cambridge: Cambridge University Press, 1990).

Wiese, Michael, *Film and Video Marketing* (Studio City, Calif.: Michael Wiese Productions, 1989).

Willemen, Paul, *Looks and Frictions: Essays in Cultural Studies and Film Theory* (Bloomington, Ind.. Indiana University Press, 1994).

Williamson, Judith, *Consuming Passions: The Dynamics of Popular Culture* (London and New York: Marion Boyars, 1986).

Willis, Paul, *Moving Culture: An Enquiry into the Cultural Activities of Young People* (London: Calouste Gulbenkian Foundation, 1990).

Willis, Susan, *The BBC Shakespeare Plays: Making the Televised Canon* (Chapel Hill, NC: University of North Carolina Press, 1991).

Willson, Robert F. Jr, 'Recontextualizing Shakespeare on Film: My Own Private Idaho, Men of Respect and Prospero's Books', *Shakespeare Bulletin*, 10 (3) (1992), 34–7.

Worthen, William B., *Shakespeare and the Force of Modern Performance* (Cambridge: Cambridge University Press, 2003).

Wulff, Helena and Vered Amit-Talai, eds, *Youth Cultures: A Cross-Cultural Perspective* (London and New York: Routledge, 1995).

Wyatt, Justin, *High Concept: Movies and Marketing in Hollywood* (Austin, Tex.: University of Texas Press, 1994).

Wyatt, Justin, 'Marketing', *Sight and Sound*, 7: 6 (1997), 38–41.

Wyke, Maria, *Projecting the Past* (London: Routledge, 1997).

Press articles and reviews

In order to maximise ease of access to the full article or review, a World Wide Web page address is provided instead of a page number when an article is available only on the Internet or is less readily available in print, as this provides the best means of retrieving the full piece. This list comprises only those articles which have been directly referenced or have been very influential as background reading for this book, and does not represent a comprehensive attempt to archive the huge body of press articles on filmed Shakespeare adaptations from 1989 onwards.

Anon., 'Parting from Bard is such Sweet Sorrow for Branagh', *Belfast Telegraph*, 1 February 2001, <http://www.belfasttelegraph.com/today/feb01/News/kenn.ncml>.

Applebaum, Stephen, 'A Midsummer Night's Dream: Video Review', *Flicks*, September 2000, p. 92.

Bart, Peter, 'The Bard's Big Night', *Variety*, 26 March 1999, p. 4, p. 86.

Bateman, Louise, 'Marketing Movies Matters', *Pact Magazine*, 8 September 1999, pp. 12–14.

Berardinelli, James, '*Chocolat* (2000)', <http://www.movie-reviews.colossus.net>.

Billen, Andrew, 'Sir Tom, the Ageless Time Lord', *Evening Standard*, 28 January 1999, <http://www.thisislondon.co.uk/entertainment/films/articles/567701?version=1&null>.

Billington, Michael, 'A "New Olivier" Is Taking on Henry V', *New York Times*, 8 January 1989, <http://www.branaghcompendium.com/artic-nyt89-1.htm>.

Billington, Michael, 'Bill's Big Screen Adventure', *Guardian*, Section 2, 3 January 1996, pp. 6–7.

Bradberry, Grace, 'Love Turns Bard', *The Times*, 2 May 1999, p. 21.

Burgi, Michael, 'Net results. Baby-boomer hits draw the biggest movie ad dollars, but the MTV generation is moving in', *Hollywood Reporter*, 347, 27 May 1997, pp. 18–20.

Case, Brian, 'Fiennes Romance', *Time Out*, 27 January 1999, pp. 14–15.

Clark, Pete, 'The Divine Gwyneth and Shakespeare in Love', *Evening Standard*, 20 January 1999, p. 20.

Chang, Yahlin, 'Bloom the Bardolator', *Newsweek*, 33: 7, 15 February 1999, p. 64.

Curtis, Nick, 'Luvvies face a full house to plead case for RSC', *Evening Standard*, 8 January 2002, p. 9.

Ebert, Roger, 'Much Ado about Nothing', *Chicago Sun-Times*, 21 May 1993, <http://www.suntimes.com/ebert/ebert_reviews/1993/05/858482.html>.

Ebert, Roger, 'Looking for Richard', *Chicago Sun-Times*, 25 October 1996, <http://www.suntimes.com/ebert/ebert_reviews/1996/10/102507.html>.

Errico, Angie, 'William Shakespeare's A Midsummer Night's Dream', *Empire*, October 1999, p. 18.

Farino, Julian, 'That Can't Be my Film They are Talking About', *Observer*, Screen Section, 28 November 1999, pp. 8–9.

Fleeman, Michael, 'Oscars Studios spend $$$ in race for Oscar', *Associated Press*, 17 March 1999, <http://www.canoe.ca/JamOscar1999/mar17_bestpic_ap.html>.

Frankel, Martha, 'Sex Pointers from Women Men Love', *Glamour*, May 1999, p. 23.

Freer, Ian, 'Shakespeare in Love: Must Buy', *Empire*, October 1999, p. 154.

Graser, Marc and Chris Petrikin, 'Geek Gab Freaks Film Biz: Sprouting Webs Heighten Din of Disinformation', *Variety*, 18 October 1999, p. 1, p. 57.

Gray, Marianne, 'Guy Hawke', *Evening Standard*, Hot Tickets, pp. 2–3.

Gristwood, Sarah, 'What is this thing called "Love's Labour's Lost"?', *Guardian*, 27 March 2000, <http://film.guardian.co.uk/Feature_Story/feature_story/0,4120,152536,00.html>.

Gritten, David, 'How to Win an Oscar or Seven', *The Age*, 24 March 1999, p. 12.

Hayes, Dade, 'The Preshow Must Go On … and On', *Variety*, 8 November 1999, pp. 9–10.

Hinson, Hal, 'Much Ado about Nothing', *Washington Post*, 21 May 1993, <http://www.washingtonpost.com/wp-srv/s …/muchadoaboutnothingpg13hinson_a0a81a.html>.

Hobson, Louis B., 'Gaining Insight into Richard', *Calgary Sun*, 1 November 1996, <http://www.canoe.ca/JamMovieReviewsL/lookingforrichard.html>.

Holden, Stephen, '"10 Things I Hate About You": It's Like, You Know, Sonnets and Stuff', *New York Times*, 31 March 1999, <http://www.nytimes.com/library/film/033199things-film-review.html>.

Howe, Desson, 'Titus, a Modern Tragedy', *Washington Post*, 11 February 2000, <http://www.washingtonpost.com/wp-srv/entertainment/movies/reviews/titushowe.htm>.

Howe, Desson, 'This "Romeo" is Bleeding', *Washington Post*, 1 November 1996, <http://www.washingtonpost.com/wp-srv/style/longterm/movies/review97/romeoandjuliethowe.html>.

Kennedy, Colin, 'Soundtracks: Hamlet', *Empire*, February 2001, p. 124.

LaSalle, Mick, 'Right Time for "Richard III": The Lowdown on Ian McKellen's "30s Melodrama"' *San Francisco Chronicle*, 19 January 1996, <http://www.sfgate.com/cgi-bin/article.cgi?f=/c/a/1996/01/19/dd62199.DTL>.

LaSalle, Mick, 'This "Romeo" is a True Tragedy, DiCaprio, Danes Weak in Shakespeare Update', *San Francisco Chronicle*, 1 November 1996, <http://www.sfgate.com/cgi-bin/article.cgi?f=/c/a/1996/11/01/dd15503.dtl>.

Maslin, Janet, 'Shakespeare in Love: Shakespeare Saw a Therapist?', *New York Times*, 11 December 1998, <http://www.nytimes.com/library/film/121198shakespeare-film-review.html>.

Maslin, Janet, 'More Things in "Hamlet" Than Are Dreamt of in Other Adaptations', *New York Times*, 25 December 1996, <http://query.nytimes.com/gst/full-

page?res=9B0CE5D91E31F936A15751C1A960958260>.

Miller, Laura, 'Star-Cross'd Lovers', *Salon.com*, 11 December 1998,
    <http://archive.salon.com/ent/movies/reviews/1998/12/11reviewa.html>.

Bruce Newman, 'Can't Read the Classic? See the Teen Movie', *New York Times*, 28 February
    1999, pp. 13, 22.

O'Toole, Lesley, 'Everyone's Wild about Harry', *Times*, 9 August 1999, p. 43.

Pearce, Garth, 'Will Shakespeare: Star Crossed Lover', *Sunday Times*, Section 2, 29
    November 1998, pp. 8–9.

Pendreigh, Brian, 'To the Max', *Guardian*, Section 2, 9 April 1999, pp. 2–3.

Schickel, Richard, 'The Infirmities of Our Age: Shakespeare's *Lear* Gets Updated in *A
    Thousand Acres*', *Time Magazine*, 22 September 1997, <http://www.time.com/time
    /archive/preview/from_redirect/0,10987,1101970922–138336,00.html>.

Shaw, Jessica, 'Good Will Hunting', *Entertainment Weekly*, 471, 12 February 1999, p. 9.

Shaw, Jessica, 'Hey Kids! Teensploitation!: Inside Hollywood's Box Office Boom',
    Entertainment Weekly, 476, 12 March 1999, pp. 22–4.

Sikov, Ed, 'Brush up your Shakespeare', *Premiere*, 4, 3 March 1996, pp. 70–4.

Simon, Raphael, 'Don't Believe the Anti-Hype', *Premiere*, 13, December 1999, pp. 39–40.

Sweet, Matthew, 'May Your Release be Merciful: Who Decides What Comes Out When –
    and Why?', *Independent on Sunday*, Culture Section, 26 December 1999, p.7.

Vaux, Rob, 'Chocolat', *Flipsidemovies.com*, 3 January 2001,
    <http://www.flipsidemovies.com/chocolat.html>.

Waxman, Sharon, 'Studio Keeps a Lid on *O* after School Shootings', *Washington Post*,
    9 March 2001, p. C01.

White, James, 'Get Over It', *Total Film*, May 2001, p. 97.

Williams, Mary Elizabeth, 'One Shrew Thing', *Salon.com*, 1 April 1999,
    <http://www.salon.com/ent/movies/reviews/1999/04/
    01review.html?CP=SAL&DN=110>.

Woodward, Richard B., 'Tragic Kingdom', *The Village Voice*, 31 December 1996,
    <http://www.geocities.com/Athens/Parthenon/6261/Articles/village.html>.

Zacharek, Stephanie, 'Saved by the Belle', *Salon.com*, 1 November 1996,
    <http://www.salon.com/oct96/romeo961104.html>.

Index